The Emperor Has No Clothes

Teaching About Race and Racism to People Who Don't Want to Know

A volume in
Educational Leadership for Social Justice

Series Editors:
Jeffrey S. Brooks, *University of Missouri-Columbia*
Denise E. Armstrong, *Brock University*
Ira Bogotch, *Florida Atlantic University*
Sandra Harris, *Lamar University*
Whitney H. Sherman, *Virginia Commonwealth University*
George Theoharis, *Syracuse University*

Educational Leadership for Social Justice

Jeffrey S. Brooks, Denise E. Armstrong, Ira Bogotch, Sandra Harris,
Whitney H. Sherman, and George Theoharis, Series Editors

Leadership for Social Justice:
Promoting Equity and Excellence Through Inquiry and
Reflective Practice (2008)
edited by Anthony H. Normore

Bridge Leadership: Connecting Educational Leadership
and Social Justice to Improve Schools (2009)
edited by Autumn K. Tooms and Christa Boske

The Emperor Has No Clothes: Teaching About Race and Racism
to People Who Don't Want to Know (2010)
by Tema Okun

The Emperor Has No Clothes

Teaching About Race and Racism to People Who Don't Want to Know

Tema Okun
National Louis University,
Chicago, Illinois

Information Age Publishing, Inc.
Charlotte, North Carolina • www.infoagepub.com

Library of Congress Cataloging-in-Publication Data

Okun, Tema.
  The emperor has no clothes : teaching about race and racism to people who
don't want to know / Tema Okun.
      p. cm. — (Educational leadership for social justice)
  Includes bibliographical references.
  ISBN 978-1-61735-104-4 (paperback) — ISBN 978-1-61735-105-1 (hardcover) —
ISBN 978-1-61735-106-8 (e-book)
  1. Racism—Study and teaching. 2. Multicultural education. 3. United
States—Race relations—Study and teaching. 4. United States—Ethnic
relations—Study and teaching. I. Title.
  HT1506.O48 2010
  305.80071—dc22

                                                                    2010027126

Printed in the United States of America

CONTENTS

SERIES EDITOR'S PREFACE

Jeffrey S. Brooks

I am pleased to serve as series editor for this book series, *Educational Leadership for Social Justice*, with Information Age Publishing. The idea for this series grew out of the work of a committed group of leadership for scholars associated with the American Educational Research Association's (AERA) Leadership for Social Justice Special Interest Group (SIG). This group existed for many years before being officially affiliated with AERA, and has benefitted greatly from the ongoing leadership, support, and counsel of Dr. Catherine Marshall (University of North Carolina-Chapel Hill). It is also important to acknowledge the contributions of the SIG's first president, Dr. Ernestine Enomoto (University of Hawaii at Manoa), whose wisdom, stewardship, and guidance helped ease a transition into AERA's more formal organizational structures. This organizational change was at times difficult to reconcile with scholars who largely identified as nontraditional thinkers who push toward innovation rather than accept the status quo. As the second chair of the SIG, I appreciate all of Ernestine's hard work and look forward to the leadership of Dr. Gaetane Jean-Marie, University of Oklahoma, as she succeeds me in this position.

I am particularly indebted to my colleagues on the SIG's first publications committee, which I chaired from 2005-2007: Dr. Denise Armstrong, Brock University; Dr. Ira Bogotch, Florida Atlantic University; Dr. Sandra

The Emperor Has No Clothes: Teaching About Race and Racism to People Who Don't Want to Know, pp. vii–viii
Copyright © 2010 by Information Age Publishing

Harris, Lamar University; Dr. Whitney Sherman, Virginia Commonwealth University, and; Dr. George Theoharis, Syracuse University. This committee was a joy to work with and I look forward to future collaborations as we seek to provide publication opportunities for scholarship in the area of leadership for social justice.

This book by Tema Okun, the third in the series, breaks new ground in both content and presentation of research. We are excited to help provide a forum for this important voice in the ongoing conversation about equity and excellence in education, and the role(s) that leadership can assume in educational organizations.

Again, welcome to this third book in this Information Age Publishing series, *Educational Leadership for Social Justice*. You can learn more about the series at our website: http://www.infoagepub.com/series/Educational-Leadership-for-Social-Justice. I invite you to contribute your own work on equity and influence to the series. We look forward to you joining the conversation.

ACKNOWLEDGMENTS

First, I want to acknowledge the critical and unwavering support of the four people who guided me in the process of writing this book: Dr. Svi Shapiro, who skillfully shepherded me through, although I am sure at times he has wondered about taking on the job of herding this particular cat; Dr. Hanna Lyons, a friend and mentor for many years, who took meticulous care in her generous and invaluable support and feedback throughout the process; Dr. C.P. Gause who emulates the kind of teacher I hope to be with his consistent opening of doors to publishing and other opportunities; and Dr. Leila Villaverde, whose firm guidance led me to be successfully more ambitious than I thought possible with the scope of this book.

When I embarked on this endeavor, I came with knowledge and experience derived in and with a community of colleagues and friends with whom I have had the privilege to work for over 3 decades. In writing this book, I have struggled over when to use "I" and when to use "we" because everything I know and my ability to think well is the result of being in community with so many stellar people. This is not an abstract acknowledgement; much of what I write here is based on collaborative work with James Williams and the people at Grassroots Leadership, Kenneth Jones and the people at ChangeWork, Michelle Johnson and Vivette Jeffries-Logan at dRworks, and friends and colleagues I will mention specifically in a minute.

One of the things we talk about in our community is the way that privilege works to allow some people, in this case me, to take collaborative

The Emperor Has No Clothes: Teaching About Race and Racism to People Who Don't Want to Know, pp. ix–x
Copyright © 2010 by Information Age Publishing

knowledge, write it down, and then receive credit for it. This is an old and oppressive pattern. At the same time, we also know the value of having our collective knowledge documented, so that others can benefit from both our wisdom and our mistakes, something that activists and organizers seldom have time or resources to do. Therefore, I want to be clear about crediting all those who deserve credit, noting that some will be named and many others, in particular those who attended workshops or were students in my classes, are not listed by name and nonetheless contributed to whatever wisdom is here.

I would specifically like to thank all those who read drafts, giving vital feedback and providing invaluable support. I am very lucky to be part of such a loving and generous community. Any brilliance that shows up here is ours together; any ignorance or shortsightedness is mine.

Thanks then to Cecelia Alvarado, Clare Bayard, Karen Booth, Bree Carlson, Cynthia Brown, Bridgette Burge, Kia Carscallen, Dan Chapman, Ingrid Chapman, Ari Clemenzi, Elyse Crystall, Marcie Fisher-Borne, Mike Fliss, Diane Goodman, Gita Gulati-Partee, Russell Herman, Claudia Horwitz, Vivette Jeffries-Logan, Michelle Johnson, Jereann King, Jim Lee, Sharon Martinas, Thérèse Murdza, Ada Norris, Ellen O'Grady, Danyelle O'Hara, Alba Onofrio, Alexis Pauline-Gumbs, Suzanne Plihcik, Zulayka Santiago, Kriti Sharma, Jeanette Stokes, Becky Thompson, Reggie Turner, and Monica Walker. Thanks also to Tom Stern, my life partner, the person who makes all things possible with his unconditional, unwavering, and loving support. And thanks always to Kenneth Jones, whose wisdom and laughter, although no longer present in a physical sense, is always and forever in my heart, my head, my bones.

EXPLANATIONS AND TERMS

Black and white: In this book, I use capitalized words to refer to Black people, Indigenous people, Latino/Hispanic people and People of Color generally while using a lower case to refer to white people, white communities, white groups. Although standard American Psychological Association (APA) style is to capitalize all terms used to designate ethnic and racial categories (Concise Rules of APA Style, 2005, p. 24), and standard Associated Press (AP) style is to capitalize none of these terms (Bennington, 2008), I am following the lead of the historically Black press (Bennington, 2008). If this seems of slight significance, I relate the following story—in the late 1980s, I was part of a team doing work in the Arkansas Delta, an area populated primarily by African American communities holding very little in the way of financial resources. One of my responsibilities was to write a report of our findings at the end of the project. At the direction of my boss, I followed the stylistic choice of the Black press. Within days of the report's publication, which offered an overview of extensive challenges in the region including entrenched racism, a reporter from the Arkansas mainstream press gave me a call. The only question he had, and he became quite hostile when my response did not satisfy him, was why I chose to capitalize "Black" and leave "white" lowercase. He was infuriated at my spelling, unmoved by the on-the-ground circumstances reflecting historically deep power imbalances of white supremacy.

The Emperor Has No Clothes: Teaching About Race and Racism to People Who Don't Want to Know, pp. xi–xv
Copyright © 2010 by Information Age Publishing

capitalization: Two scholars in this book do not capitalize their names—bell hooks and jona olsson. Whenever their names are used to start a sentence, I do capitalize in accordance both with APA style and to make it easier for the reader. In every other case, I respect the authors' spelling of their own names.

culture: I define culture in two places in this book—at the beginning of chapter 1, where I launch my discussion of white supremacy culture, and at the beginning of chapter 3, where I initiate a look at cultural shift. To briefly repeat the main thrust of the definitions as outlined in those chapters, culture is the set of values, beliefs, norms, and standards held by a group of people in order to insure the group's ability to operate. Author and social critic David Korten describes culture as "a system of customary beliefs, values, perceptions, and social relations that encodes the shared learning of a particular human group essential to its orderly social function" (2006, p. 76). Also important to note is how "culture is closely linked with power" (Inglehart, 1997, p. 26), serving to "legitimate the established social order—partly because the dominant elite try to shape it to help perpetuate their rule" (p. 26).

dominant/mainstream: The terms "dominant" and "mainstream" referencing culture refer to hegemony, the power of one group to make the rules not only for itself, but also for the people and groups that it influences and/or dominates. Dominant and mainstream culture functions to define a society's notions of "normal." Members of dominant and/or mainstream groups benefit from the privileges attached to their association with the dominant/mainstream. Training for Change (www.training-forchange.org) defines mainstream as "the center or in-group" that "sets the tone for a group or organization or society." When race is the focus, all those who are white belong to the dominant or mainstream group (although individual white people do not have the same level of power; other identity markers such as class, gender, sexuality, able-bodiness, will modify white privilege).

LGBTQQI: These initials are a shorthand way to refer to people who identify as lesbian, gay, bisexual, transgender, queer, questioning, and/or intersex. These letters are meant to designate the diversity within the community of people who identify in these ways and signify all those who are targeted in some way (and often very different ways) by heterosexism and gender conformity.

love: I talk extensively about love throughout the book. In chapter 5, I reference bell hooks (2000, p. xxix), who suggests that "we must dare to acknowledge how little we know of love in both theory and practice" even as we commit to it. Hooks wants us to think of love as an action rather than a feeling (p. 13) and cites Erich Fromm's definition of love as "the will to extend one's self for the purpose of nurturing one's own or another's spiritual growth" (p. 4). When I talk about love, I am not referring to an "anemic love" that eschews power (King, 1967); I am talking about a level of regard for ourselves and others that recognizes our common humanity and interdependence, that acknowledges our significant differences as well as our sameness. I do not pretend the "task" of love is easy while I do maintain it is imperative.

margin: This term is used to define all those who are excluded from, underserved, exploited, or oppressed by those in the dominant or mainstream group. Training for Change (www.trainingforchange.org) defines margin as the "periphery or the out-group." When race is the focus, all People of Color are in or on the margins (although individual People of Color will also situate in mainstream identities as heterosexual, upper middle-class or wealthy, male, able-bodied, etc.).

minority/People of Color: While "minority" is typically the term used by those in the dominant/mainstream culture to designate People and Communities of Color, as well as women, this is not a term that I use in this book or in life. During my years at ChangeWork, we made the decision to no longer use this word when cofounder Kenneth Jones noticed that news anchors were referring to the indigenous people of South Africa during the apartheid struggle in the 1980s as "minorities." A formal definition of minority is "the lesser part or smaller number" (Webster's New Universal Unabridged Dictionary, 1983, p. 1146); its use in referencing indigenous South Africans obviously carried a cultural significance beyond counting. Because minority implies "less than," we choose to use the term "People of Color" as an organizing device to indicate, as Kenneth used to say, "all those who catch hell from racism." While few individuals tend to identify specifically as People of Color, preferring usually to name themselves based on a specific racial or ethnic identity (Black, African American, Cherokee, Occaneechi Band of the Sapponi Nation, Chinese, Taiwanese, Filipino, Chicano/Chicana, etc.), the term is useful to designate all those placed on the margins when referring to race and racism.

privilege: In her classic essay, Peggy McIntosh defines white privilege as "an invisible package of unearned assets ... an invisible weightless knapsack of special provisions, maps, passports, codebooks, visas, clothes, tools and blank checks" that white people, for the most part unconsciously, carry with us every day (2003, p. 165). Privilege works this way for every oppressive construct, so that heterosexuals carry "straight" privilege, men carry male privilege, wealthy and middle-class people carry class privilege, and so on. In this book, I talk about privileged resistance, which is a term I use to designate the ways in which those of us holding privilege resist or deny that we benefit from the unearned assets that come with being a member of the dominant group.

racism: I define racism, as do many in the field, as race prejudice plus social and institutional power, a system of advantage based on race, a system of oppression based on race, a white supremacy system (Okun & Jones, 2000; Tatum, 1997). The key to this definition is that racism is more than personal prejudice; to qualify as racism, thoughts, behaviors, or acts must be systemically supported by institutional and cultural power. I make a distinction between the race hatred held by a young Latino boy towards his white teacher, which is prejudice, as opposed to the racial antagonism held by the white teacher toward the Latino boy, which is racism. The teacher's prejudice, when enacted, is supported by the policies and procedures of the school system, resulting in the disproportionately high push-out rates of young Latino boys (and other boys of color from our schools) (Institute of Education Sciences, 2009).

social justice: Social justice is defined in multiple ways, as any quick search of the internet and/or the literature will reveal. In this book, I pull from the Earth Charter (The Earth Charter Initiative, 2000) to characterize my meaning, in part because it involved "the most inclusive and participatory process ever associated with the creation of an international declaration." The Charter calls for peoples and communities to "join together to bring forth a sustainable global society founded on respect for nature, universal human rights, economic justice, and a culture of peace." I also pull from Indigenous activist Leonard Peltier (1999, p. 199), who writes that "our work will be unfinished until not one human being is hungry or battered, not a single person is forced to die in war, not one innocent languishes imprisoned, and no one is persecuted for his or her beliefs." When I speak of social justice in this book, I am speaking of a world where we are invited to bring our whole selves into community with each other and the earth, to live and act respectfully and sustainably, to care enough to insure that every person has a safe home, nutritious food to eat, good health, a vibrant and meaningful education, and the skills and desire to live into and through our mutual joy and inevitable conflicts peacefully and with mutual consideration one for the other.

student writing: I quote frequently from the reflections of my students. I offer their words exactly as they wrote them; I do not correct their spelling or grammar.

white supremacy: I draw from the definition of Chicana antiracist activist Elizabeth Martínez (2004, p. 1) who defines white supremacy as the

historically based, institutionally perpetuated system of exploitation and oppression of continents, nations, and peoples of color by white peoples and nations of the European continent, for the purpose of maintaining and defending a system of wealth, power, and privilege.

Martínez notes that she prefers the term white supremacy to racism because it highlights the power relationship inherent in racism.

wholeness: Chicana feminist Gloria Anzaldúa describes a spiritual path to wholeness as one where "you struggle each day to know the world you live in, to come to grips with the problems of life. Motivated by the need to understand, you crave to be what and who you are" (2002, p. 540). In her profound essay *Now let us shift … the path of conocimiento … inner work, public acts* (2002), Anzaldúa offers seven stages or "stations" that "open the senses and enlarge the breadth and depth of consciousness, causing internal shifts and external changes" (p. 545).

Educator and writer Parker Palmer, in a book written after his experience with devastating depression, reflects that "our deepest calling is to grow into our own authentic selfhood" (2000, p. 16), an endeavor that he argues takes place in and with community. Palmer (p. 31) suggests that the great liberation movements have been fueled by "the lives of people who decide to care for their authentic selfhood" in opposition to or deviance from the systems that attempted to force them to follow false values. He states that "the people who plant the seeds of movements make a critical decision … to live "divided no more" (his quotations)" (p. 32). In other words, they "claim authentic selfhood and act it out" (p. 32), a decision that has ripple effects in the broader community.

American Buddhist Pema Chödrön talks about wholeness as a state we are in with each other and the world. She explains that "we experience ourselves as being separate from the whole. This separateness becomes like a prison," (1997, p. 97), which causes us to suffer.

I reference the concept of wholeness, then, to mark our yearning to pursue happiness within the context of mutual interdependence, loving concern, and justice.

INTRODUCTION

THE EMPEROR HAS NO CLOTHES

One of the most famous stories written by Danish writer Hans Christian Andersen (1837) is that of the Emperor of a prosperous city

> who thought so much of new clothes that he spent all his money in order to obtain them; his only ambition was to be always well dressed. He did not care for his soldiers, and the theatre did not amuse him; the only thing, in fact, he thought anything of was to drive out and show a new suit of clothes. He had a coat for every hour of the day; and as one would say of a king "He is in his cabinet," so one could say of him, "The emperor is in his dressing-room." (1837, ¶1)

In the story, the Emperor's desire for the latest style leads him to hire two men who promise to weave him a fine suit from cloth so exquisite that the material, they promise, will be "invisible to any man ... unfit for his office or unpardonably stupid" (1837, ¶2).

The Emperor, compelled by the idea that he could own a suit that would allow him to "distinguish the clever from the stupid," agrees to pay a large sum and orders the tailors to begin without delay. The two charlatans set up their looms and pretend to weave. Anxious for accounts of their progress, the monarch sends emissaries to check up on the tailors; each messenger, afraid to admit they see nothing, return with glowing

The Emperor Has No Clothes: Teaching About Race and Racism
to People Who Don't Want to Know, pp. xvii–xxx
Copyright © 2010 by Information Age Publishing

accounts. The "weaving" continues. The townspeople, abuzz with antici-pation, eagerly turn out on the day the Emperor has chosen to display his glorious raiment, only to witness him walking naked through the streets. Understanding the conditions attached to the suit, not wishing to appear unfit or stupid, they cry out their admiration. Finally a young child says aloud what is quite evident for all to see: "But he has nothing on at all." The child's father, in his turn, advises the town to "listen to the voice of an innocent child" (1837, ¶28). Each citizen whispers to the next, sharing what the child has said, admitting the truth of it.

I begin with this simple children's story because the boy is who I aspire to be and who I want my students to become, clear about the deceits we are told by the cultural elite (the "tailors," their front man the Emperor, as well as his henchmen) who weave a noxious web of lies (the race con-struct) to pad their pockets while we (the townspeople) participate in the charade that harms us all. What do we need to do to see as clearly as the young boy? My goal with this book is to explore that very question. For I believe that once we see, the possibilities are limitless.

IDENTITY MATTERS

This book is shaped by my identities as a white, Jewish, heterosexual, upper middle-class woman. I currently teach in classrooms of predomi-nantly young, white, Christian students from working class backgrounds, most assuming a collective heterosexuality. I am also informed by many years teaching in other contexts as an antiracism trainer, educator, and activist, years when I had the opportunity to work with both colleagues and communities diverse in every way. While the analysis I offer in these pages might be "universal" in terms of its applicability to people from every walk of life, the teaching strategies I explore are grounded in my experience. While any one of these strategies may prove useful to any number of people (and in fact, that is my hope), what works for a white teacher, trainer, educator, facilitator, activist is going to be different than what works for a person of color, an LGBTQQI person, or a person with any combination of margin identities.

Because I am white and speak from that identity, when I talk about white people, I use the words "we" and "our" rather than "they" and "their." This allows me to claim my experience and brings me closer to you, the reader.

WHY IDENTITY MATTERS

I have spent my life attempting to come to grips with what it means to be white in the United States of America. Born in 1952, I grew up in the Civil

Rights era in Chapel Hill, North Carolina, the child of activist parents. I went to Sunday school at a nondenominational church founded by people, my parents among them, who wanted to show support for a Presbyterian minister kicked out of his church for preaching integration. African American authors and speakers coming to the University of North Carolina-Chapel Hill campus and denied lodging at area hotels often stayed at our home. When Joanne Little was on trial for killing her white jailer in the infamous Little Washington civil rights case, my parents put up bond money and organized their friends to do the same. When the local Howard Johnson's restaurant chain refused to integrate, my parents walked me regularly through those picketing outside the restaurant, engaging me in the theater of going inside to demand answers from the manager about why so many people were congregating outside and then walking out in a staged huff of outrage.

I was raised by strong liberal parents to believe not only in the importance of race equity but also in the imperative—as white people—to do something about it. At the same time, our family politics were enacted at a safe distance—I grew up in a largely white middle-class world.

Like most white people, I grew up understanding myself as "normal" and I assumed, as those who see ourselves as normal are inclined to do, that I represented the "natural, the standard, the regular" (Webster's Dictionary, 1972, p. 1221). My first memory of race differentiation evokes an image where I am about 3 years old, standing on the front seat of our family convertible (in a time before seatbelts) as my mother drives us through town. I see an African American man walking down the street; I point at him and say to my mother, "look, Mom, a chocolate man." Grappling with her own dis-ease about race and racism, she responds with an awkward and constrained silence. This is my first awareness of racial difference—as something charged, loaded, and somehow shameful.

My first experiences working closely with People of Color and developing a radical and comprehensive understanding of the profound nature of both white supremacy and racism began in the early 1980s at the Carolina Community Project, which later morphed into an organization called Grassroots Leadership, both organizations based in Charlotte, N.C. Our mission was to support community organizing in the South; the staff was a cohort of experienced organizers and popular educators, fierce and gifted people who brought wisdom and a sense of humor to the endeavor of understanding oppression. Faced with requests for help from communities and organizations split by divisive dynamics of racism, sexism, class and other oppressive behaviors, I was fortuitously asked to work with James Williams to build a program to address these needs. Williams is an African American man, a Pentecostal minister, a loving husband and father, and a keen advocate for social justice. Funded by a generous Kellogg grant, the two of us traveled from Charlotte to Berkeley to Atlanta to New Orleans to learn from trainers and organizations offering any kind of antioppression analysis. With support from other Grassroots Leadership staff, we read and studied and discussed and planned. In 1991, we designed a 2-year long pilot program called Barriers and Bridges and invited eight social justice organizations to join us in a collective effort to understand how to meaningfully and effectively address race, class, gender issues in our organizing efforts. We led the Barrier and Bridges project through two cycles until the funding ran out.

Much of the grounding for my comprehension of how oppression works started at that time. My understanding of myself as a white person in a racist society continued to grow, as I came to more fully understand the systemic and institutional nature of racist constructs. While much of my learning came from the theory and practice of program-building, perhaps even more significant was the education I received during the long car rides with James and other staff members, hours spent in a confined space talking about the program, arguing about the validity of our different perceptions, yelling in an attempt to win our points, laughing at our own hypocrisies, telling story after story after story about our lives that helped me to see how profoundly shaped I am by my white skin, my white experience.

After the demise of the Barriers and Bridges program, I began working with Kenneth Jones, at that time the director of the Exchange Project, the training arm of the Peace Development Fund, a regional social justice foundation based in Amherst, Massachusetts. Kenneth had been developing antiracist and organizational development curriculum and leading Dismantling Racism workshops since the early 1990s. I began to learn the model he had helped to develop and eventually we began merging elements of his approach with lessons learned from the Barriers and Bridges project. Thus started a creative and life-changing partnership that lasted for almost 15 years until his premature death in 2004. I call his name here because so much of what you read in these pages, whatever wisdom you find here, is due to the love, nurture, and intellectual grounding that he offered me in our many years of work together.

In 2001, I turned to classroom teaching as a site for continuing my antiracism work. In the intervening years I have been adapting the model for the classroom, which has allowed me to sharpen my practice and deepen my understanding of what is required to see the nakedness of the Emperor.

SETTING THE CONTEXT

The purpose of this book is twofold. The first is to examine the ways in which our dominant or majority culture conditions our minds and hearts to accept as normal that which, with cultural blinders off, we would see clearly as destructive dominance. The second is to offer approaches to teaching for those who want to elucidate this conditioning in the collective endeavor of building a positive, life sustaining world.

I offer this book to name out loud the importance of teaching as one tool in a collective endeavor to make our schools and communities sites of liberation. In the spirit of Paolo Freire, Maxine Greene, Ron Chisom, Kenneth Jones, Monica Walker, and many others both famous and lesser known, I believe in the power of teachers and teaching to transform lives and our world. As such, this work is part of an effort to claim "multicultural education as part of a larger, more serious struggle for social justice, a struggle that recognizes the need to fight against systematic racism, colonization, and cultural oppression" (Au, 2009, p. 3) perpetuated by our schools, our workplaces, our places of worship, our media, our culture.

I also offer this book to add to the literature pertaining to the pedagogy of transformation. Much is written about race, racism, the history of the race construct, privilege, internalized racial identities—the content related to this topic is widely covered with great intelligence and insight. Less prevalent is a body of literature on how to teach this content. Scholars and teachers Gloria Ladson-Billings (2004) and bell hooks (1994) have written brilliantly about their approach to teaching about race and racism; Beverly Daniel Tatum (1992, 1997) references her thoughtful approach in books and articles, as does Enid Lee (Lee, 1992; Lee, Menkart, & Okazawa-Rey, 2006). Mary Ann Cowhey (2006) has written a wonderful book, *Black Ants and Buddhists*, which covers important ground about how to teach a social justice curriculum to elementary school age children. The organizations *Rethinking Schools* and *Teaching for Change* have published materials related to teaching this subject.

This book endeavors to add to this literature, to make a contribution to and intervention into the foundations of curriculum, one that focuses on how to help prospective teachers and leaders think critically and compassionately about race, particularly as they prepare to teach inside and/or lead institutions (of education, social work, etc.) that shape and are shaped by white supremacy culture. My approach is not prescriptive but rather descriptive, offering a framework for how to think about the vital task of teaching for cultural transformation.

DELIBERATE CHOICES

My focus throughout this book is on cultural dominance enacted through racism (choice one) in the United States (choice two).

I have been privileged to travel in my lifetime; I lived my third grade year in Holland, spent a year and a half of my high school years in

France, returned there for a semester in college, and since 2002 have spent every other summer in Palestine. I understand that racism is not unique to the United States. At the same time, my purpose here is to bring light to the pedagogical task of teaching about racism and I would hesitate to claim that what I know about this has application around the globe. I will not deny that it could; yet the more politic and wise route is to claim my limitations in this regard.

My choice to focus on the pedagogy of race and racism is also strategic. Ron Chisom, the brilliant founder of the People's Institute for Survival and Beyond, one of the leading antiracist training organizations in the country, explains at the beginning of every workshop that their focus on racism is to permit participants to go deep into a topic we have been taught well to either ignore or fear. He will not allow us, he explains, to engage in "escapism," which is how he refers to what happens when we raise issues about class or gender in order to avoid the intensity of coming to grips with the complexity of the race construct. One of the reasons for my focus on race and racism is this desire to go deep.

Yet this choice does not imply any lack of interest in or the critical importance of other oppressions. R.D. Laing wrote about our western culture "the condition of alienation, of being asleep, of being unconscious, of being out of one's mind, is the condition of the normal man. Society highly values its normal man [sic]" (1967, III, ¶9). The more I come to understand racism, the more I understand its inextricable link to sexism, gender and class oppression, to the discrimination and disregard we are taught to bring to all those considered less than normal in a culture highly dedicated to, as Laing so aptly notes, "its normal man [sic]."

I think (and hope) that focusing on the dynamics and pedagogy of race and racism in this country *does* offer pedagogical insight into gender, class, and other oppressive behaviors. As my friend Ada Norris (personal correspondence, August 22, 2009) points out, the "case material is race and racism but once we can think critically, that lens is transportable. Or should be.... A liberational pedagogy [teaches] us how to think differently." I touch lightly from time to time on the intersections of racism with other oppressions in the hopes of making clear the opportunities that an antiracist lens offers in terms of bridging concepts.

A CLARIFICATION

When I teach about racism, I often draw a horizontal line on the board, explaining that the line represents all white people. I then move to the right side of the line and ask students to name for me all the racist individuals and organizations they know of. They list quite a few, including those you could predict—the Ku Klux Klan, neo-Nazis, skinheads. Some students name individuals like David Duke, George Wallace, or Jesse Helms. Then I move to the left side of the line and ask them to name for me all the white individuals and organizations that have fought against racism throughout our history. Almost without exception, they cannot. I assure them that such people and organizations exist; I share stories about the white colonists who joined the Cherokee on the Trail of Tears, I mention people like John Brown and Anne Braden, I reference organizations like the Abolitionists and the Quakers (knowing that each of these references holds its own complexities).

Next I draw a large circle around the middle of the line and make the point that most white people reside in the middle, taught to see ourselves as "not racist," steeped in the individualism of our culture, ignorant of the institutional and cultural dimensions of racism. We assume our lack of racist intent means an absence of racism in the larger society. Then I note how historically, and even now, the white people on the left side of the line, the actively antiracist white people and organizations, tend to ally ourselves with People and Communities of Color, leaving the "I'm not a racist" middle to be organized by those on the right who do have a history of active recruitment.

What I share in this book is influenced both by my commitment as a white person to organize those in the white middle and my experience working with mostly white groups and classrooms. At the same time, this is not my only commitment.

Everyone in our society is confused about racism. White people *and* People of Color are confused, although typically in different ways. The students who come into my classroom have all been well taught that racism is lodged in individual behavior. Even Students of Color who have direct experience with racism struggle to understand what is happening to them, given the dominant cultural stories about a long-distant racist past evolving into a postracial "colorblind" society.

At the same time, responses to classroom content often differ based on how students racially identify. In a recent class where we covered the devastating history of the construction of race in this country, an African American student reacted by noting how the information confirmed her experience while a white student tried to disassociate herself, citing her experience with "reverse racism."

My commitment is to every student, wherever they sit in relationship to racism in the United States. I believe, based on my experience, that the analysis and strategies described here offer liberation for all of us. At the same time, some of what I discuss is specifically geared toward helping white people grapple with the implications of being white in a racist society. The chapter on privileged resistance does, by definition, focus on the ways white people resist seeing the race construct. My hope is that this focus on those in the white group, when it occurs, can prove useful to anyone teaching those who embody privilege in other ways.

ASSUMPTIONS

Five assumptions ground this book. The first, the subject of chapter 1, is that the white supremacy construct is pervasive and toxic, that all of us are damaged by it, including those of us who materially benefit (people in the white group) (Bonilla-Silva, 2006; Jensen, 2000, 2002, 2004; Korten, 2001, 2006). The second assumption is that even those who materially benefit from white supremacy sense that something is wrong, although our social conditioning makes it difficult for us to know what disturbs us. We all (or at least a good many of us) yearn to be whole (Palmer, 1993, 2000, 2004; hooks, 1994, 2000; Schaef, 1998).

My third assumption is that we have the collective ability to shift from a white supremacy construct to a healthy, life-affirming, loving culture, one that assumes a universal human dignity and serves the impulse to love (Korten, Palmer, Schaef). I am part of that community, so articulately described by Cathy Cohen in her classic essay *Punks, Bulldaggers, and Welfare Queens* (1997, p. 437), searching for "a new political direction and agenda, one that does not focus on integration into dominant structures but instead seeks to transform the basic fabric and hierarchies that allow systems of oppression to persist and operate efficiently." In this way, I might claim, with some anxiety, that this book is a practice of "queer politics," locating it, as I attempt to do, as one site of "opposition to dominant norms" in order to create a third space "where transformational political work can begin" (Cohen, p. 438).

My fourth assumption is that, because schools have historically been the site of cultural socialization (Spring, 2005), those of us who teach have a central role to play in this shift. As teachers, we can transgress our assigned role, as many have before us, and serve as leaders in the effort to help our students both to see the world and change it (Freire, 1995, 1998; Greene, 1981, 1988). My fifth and final assumption is that I have something to offer as a member of the teaching and activist communities committed to a pedagogy of liberation. What I have to offer is not the only way or the "right" way set in opposition to everyone else's "wrong" way; it is simply one way to think about a liberatory pedagogy. My hope is that what I offer here informs the larger conversation among activists and academics.

OVERVIEW

White Supremacy Culture

I begin in chapter 1 by offering an overview of the power of culture to reproduce toxic constructs of "normal" that dehumanize and oppress. I start the chapter by defining culture and talk about how it operates to establish a group's values, beliefs, norms, and standards. I offer a rationale for equating western culture with the concepts of "dominant culture" and "white supremacy culture," pulling on the work of David Korten (2001, 2006), Eduardo Bonilla-Silva (2006), Derrick Jensen (2000, 2002, 2004), Anne Wilson Schaef (1998), and others. I discuss the consequences of western, white supremacy culture on people, communities, environment, and spirit.

Using personal stories, lessons from history, and an analytical framework, I next investigate the ways in which our cultural insistence on profit at all costs (no pun intended), binary thinking, and individualism reify oppressive constructs. I chose these three because they are so fundamental to the white supremacy construct. One of the ways I know this is how regularly I have to address these assumptions in the classroom, helping students understand them as politically and culturally created.

The chapter includes a short history of capitalism, examining how our cultural story paints capitalism as inevitable and manifest destiny (both literally and figuratively). I call on historical and contemporary analysis and my own storytelling to take a hard look at the consequences of this story. Charting a similar course with individualism and binary thinking, I trace the history of these concepts, the ways in which they were and continue to be constructed as essential to both capitalism and democracy, and the consequences of these constructions.

I document the different ways these manifestations reinforce dominance and each other. I conclude the chapter by reflecting on how these manifestations reproduce themselves, in large part by building into each resistance to any effort to bring them to the light of day.

PRIVILEGED RESISTANCE

In chapter 2, I investigate the resistance of those advantaged by white supremacy to seeing or acknowledging its personal, institutional, and cultural impact. I explain how the race construct is designed to produce an aversion on the part of those who benefit from seeing our advantage, our collusion. In other words, one of the ways that our culture reproduces racism is by keeping us oblivious to our participation in its construction.

In this chapter, I offer a psychosocial history of denial, particularly as it attaches to racist white supremacy culture. I document the personal, communal, and cultural costs of denial in contemporary life, as well as how the power elite have historically manipulated fear of the other to maintain denial and defensiveness, pitting people with common interests against each other. Drawing from both practice and theory, I suggest strategies for addressing resistance in the classroom.

CULTURAL TURNING

For many years I worked with leaders and organizations seeking to proactively address racism, both internally (inside the organization) and programmatically (in the community). After several years, I came to understand the limitations of strategies aimed at changing policies and procedures; the constraints of the intense power of organizational culture to keep damaging attitudes and behaviors in place often undermines attempts at policy reforms.

The power of culture to curb structural change seems obvious to me now. A lesson from the Civil Rights movement, every movement, is the limit of hard-won legislation to bring with it the concomitant change in cultural norms and beliefs. I do believe in the importance of legal remedies to injustice and have seen their power to change the quality of lives in critical ways. I also believe that these procedural and political changes do result in attitude change. The world I live in is very different now from the one I grew up in; institutionally and culturally we have seen great strides toward race equity.

At the same time, however, we have not fundamentally shifted the cultural construction of "normal"—witness the powerful belief held by many white Americans, and not a few Americans of Color, that racism, confined to our personal attitudes, is a thing of the past. With the election of Barack Obama as the country's first African American president, the media has been awash in stories of a "postracial" America (Schorr, 2008) while at the same time the dismantling of affirmative action, the demonization of Arabs and immigrant Latinos, the devastating statistical realities of the gaps between white and other racial groups in almost every indicator of health, education, wages, wealth—these let us know that we have not fundamentally addressed the legacy of centuries of racism.

My understanding that culture is integral to the intransigence of racism led me to explore what it takes to shift culture. In this chapter, I return again to the definition of culture and look at how historical accounts of and scientific research on cultural transformation might inform our strategies to support cultural shift. The good news, as social critic David Korten points out, is that culture is a "human construct subject to intentional choice" (2006, p. 75). This, he argues, gives us the "capacity to choose our future" (p. 76). We are, as Paolo Freire (1998) so famously says, conditioned but not determined; we can be participants in shaping the culture we desire.

I pull lessons from historical shifts like those experienced during the fall of Rome and the industrial revolution. I investigate some of the research on the construction and reconstruction of dominant paradigms in the face of emerging science both historically and now. My goal with this chapter is to establish a sound context for the approaches that I plan to offer leaders, teachers, facilitators, activists, as we work together to move from a culture of profit and fear to one of shared hope and love.

TEACHING AS PROCESS

Part of my journey as an antiracist trainer and teacher involved the discovery that opening eyes, mind, and heart, both my own and others, is a process, not an event. When I first began doing antiracism work, most of the community-based efforts aimed at addressing racism were offered as one-time, short-term workshops. My colleagues at Grassroots Leadership, ChangeWork and now dRworks, understood the limitations of this approach and spent many years developing and refining a longer-term process to help people move through what we identified as critical stages in the progression from awareness of our social conditioning into a shared analysis necessary for effective action. As I brought this process into the classroom, read and studied pedagogical theory in the context of deconstructing empire, I had the opportunity to refine this process even more.

Chapter Four, then, lays out the stages of a process that support teaching about white supremacy culture. The chapter explains how students need to be taken through an iterative process of relationship-building, analysis, planning, action, and reflection. I offer this process as one way, not the only way, to teach effectively about the race construct. My hope is that describing a process, rather than a prescriptive approach, will offer teachers the flexibility to adapt the process to their specific needs.

TWO OR THREE THINGS I KNOW FOR SURE

In the mid-1990s, after a sublime experience designing my home, I decided to go to architecture school. The program required, quite wisely, that we take classes in the how and why of construction, what makes buildings stand up (or fall down). I was not a particularly good student of structures; my brain could never quite grasp the mathematics of tension and compression. But I loved the class, looked forward to going, regardless of knowing that most of the time I would leave confused. Later, reflecting on why I enjoyed the class so much, I realized that the enthusiastic professor did two important things—he exuded his love of structures in a contagious fashion and he respected us as students, regardless of our abilities. When grades were posted at the end of the semester, he gave me 11 points out of 10 for class participation because I asked so many questions; this was his attempt to reward my desire to understand even though my ability to grasp structural concepts was less than adequate. I decided to leave the program in my third year, convinced by then I had less talent than when I had arrived. But I will always remember this professor who taught me a critically important lesson about the essence of good teaching—love your subject, love your students.

I have been teaching now in one form or another for over 25 years. I am passionate about teaching, in large part because I love my subject—always true—and my students, which has taken longer. In this final chapter I borrow from the brilliant, brave, and incisive writer Dorothy Allison to discuss the things I know for sure about how to teach people to see the naked Emperor. I discuss the role of love in the classroom within the larger context of loving others as we love ourselves. I explore the relationship between loving ourselves and loving the other, the complexity of this task, and the importance of compassionate self-awareness. Using personal stories, interviews, and history, I investigate the imperative of love as a personal and collective practice in the classroom.

I discuss what is involved in leading students to question their assumptions, to support them in the task of "queering" normal. I argue that we must connect the skill of critical thinking to the equally important skill of compassion.

I talk about the important role of feelings in the deculturation process and how to acknowledge and work with feelings in the classroom. Issues of timing are discussed, both in terms of the long-term nature of undoing cultural conditioning and our responsibility to focus on those most open and willing to consider new ways of thinking.

Helping students develop the skill of holding contradictions in a binary culture is addressed, as well as the critical role of visioning. The chapter concludes with how to support students to act collectively and collaboratively, particularly given our cultural conditioning to individualism.

FINAL THOUGHTS

I have learned several things about my own desires in these years. The first is that when I was driven by righteous anger, my energy was fierce and I worked very hard. I did not particularly love myself or other white people; I was driven to "make it right" for the People of Color I loved and those I did not even know, wanting desperately to relieve or remove the devastating oppression I was witness to. I sought to be certified in my own goodness, thinking and hoping that my "white" efforts on behalf of Communities of Color would absolve me from my participation in the construction of whiteness and all of its toxic repercussions. My work, focused on "fixing" based in a belief that I actually had the power to do so, led to a severe and punishing burnout. The story of my burnout is a long one, so let me just say that I found my way through to the other side by moving, with great reluctance, from outrage to love.

I attended a talk recently given by Tibetan Buddhist teacher Bardor Talku Rinpoche who spoke about the role of outrage in motivating our work for social justice. He suggested that while outrage is necessary, we must balance our outrage with a sense of empathy. We need to relieve immediate suffering, yes, and, we must also work with those who oppress (even and particularly when those people are us), change their (our) hearts and minds.

I have learned to love myself and others enough to allow us all to be fully human, make mistakes, be irritating and wrong. I love myself and others enough to rejoice in our incredible capacity for creativity and mutual support. I love myself and others enough to realize that I am doing this for myself as much as for anyone else. And strangely, as Bardor Talku Rinpoche implied would happen, I feel my effectiveness has grown.

If I attempt to identify my self-interest, what I would say is echoed by Beverly Daniel Tatum, who explains that "those who persist in the struggle are awarded with an increasingly multiracial and multicultural existence" (1997, p. 109) as we work together in the collective effort of cultural transformation. The life I live today is rich beyond measure because I have had a chance to be in relationship with people who I never would have otherwise known. I have had a chance to see the world through multiple eyes, and as often as that has seared me to the bone, it has also saved my life.

I am more clear than I have ever been that the race construct diminishes me even while it privileges me. I am more clear than I have ever been that I am both racist and antiracist at the same time. I am more clear than I have ever been that the collective, collaborative struggle for a more just world is both never enough and its own reward. I am more clear than I have ever been that the road to justice is paved with love.

And so, in this book, I seek to teach people about the very thing we have been conditioned to believe we do not and cannot bear to know— the ways in which we are socialized into cooperating and colluding with the race construct and racism. My goal is to contribute to the endeavor of helping others do what the boy does so easily even while surrounded by a town full of people hoodwinked into lying about the Emperor's nakedness. I do this out of a belief that if we see our conditioning, we are then free to direct our energies to building a just and loving world, with all the complexities and challenges such a vision brings.

Lament for Dark Peoples

I was a red man one time,
But the white men came.
I was a black man, too,
But the white men came.

They drove me out of the forest.
They took me away from the jungles.
I lost my trees.
I lost my silver moons.

Now they've caged me
In the circus of civilization.
Now I herd with the many –
Caged in the circus of civilization.

—Langston Hughes (1924/1994, p. 39)

CHAPTER 1

THE TAILORS WEAVE

White Supremacy Culture

Something [is] wrong with a world that tells you that love is good and people are important and then forces you to deny love and to humiliate people.
I knew, though I would not for years confess it aloud, that in trying to shut
the Negro race away from us, we have shut ourselves away from so many
good, creative, honest, deeply human things in life. I began to understand
slowly at first but more clearly as the years passed, that the warped, distorted frame we have put around every Negro child from birth is around
every white child also. Each is on a different side of the frame but each is
pinioned there. And I knew that what cruelly shapes and cripples the personality of one is as cruelly shaping and crippling the personality of the
other. I began to see that though we may, as we acquire new knowledge, live
through new experiences, examine old memories, gain the strength to tear
the frame from us, yet we are stunted and warped and in our lifetime cannot
grow straight again any more than can a tree put in a steel-like twisting
frame when young, grow tall and straight when the frame is torn away at
maturity.

Lillian Smith (1949, p. 39)

Sometime in the mid 1990s, I arrived home after a particularly frustrating consultation with an organization I was working with at the time. In a
flurry of exasperation, I sat down at my computer and typed, the words

*The Emperor Has No Clothes: Teaching About Race and Racism
to People Who Don't Want to Know,* pp. 3–30
Copyright © 2010 by Information Age Publishing

flowing of their own accord into a quick and dirty listing of some of the characteristics of white supremacy culture that show up in organizational behavior. The paper I wrote in such a frenzy on that afternoon so many years ago lists 15 behaviors, all of them interconnected and mutually reinforcing—perfectionism, a sense of urgency, defensiveness and/or denial, quantity over quality, worship of the written word, the belief in one "right" way, paternalism, either/or binary thinking, power hoarding, fear of open conflict, individualism, progress defined as more, the right to profit, objectivity, and the right to comfort. The tragic relevance of the list was reinforced recently when I was cofacilitating a workshop at a national conference of progressive attorneys and law students. We asked participants to work in small groups, looking for ways in which these characteristics show up in their personal and organizational lives. Asked to report, one young student spoke for her group, sharing that the list represents all the characteristics taught by law schools as essential to success in the profession. And that's exactly the point—these characteristics are highly valued by our institutions, which is why they are so prevalent in our culture.

DEFINING CULTURE

Culture is the set of values, beliefs, norms, and standards held by a group of people in order to insure the group's ability to operate. Author and social critic David Korten describes culture as "a system of customary beliefs, values, perceptions, and social relations that encodes the shared learning of a particular human group essential to its orderly social function" (2006, p. 76).

Ronald Inglehart (1997), in his exhaustive survey of the cultural shift from modern to postmodern, explains (pp. 52-53)

> culture is not just a random collection of the values, beliefs, and skills of the people in a given society. It constitutes a survival strategy. In any society that has survived for long, the cultural system is likely to have a mutually supportive relationship with the economic and political systems.

In other words, "culture is closely linked with power" (Inglehart, 1997, p. 26) and serves to "legitimate the established social order—partly because the dominant elite try to shape it to help perpetuate their rule" (p. 26).

One of culture's most important characteristics is how embodied it tends to become in those of us living inside it. A metaphor would be the water in which fish swim; this trope communicates both the pervasiveness and invisibility of culture—if we're the fish, how many of us grasp that we swim in water?

When we do notice culture, we tend to assume its inevitability; we see it as "natural" rather than constructed. This is particularly true for those of us who have never had to navigate multiple cultures. An example is the commonly understood truism that enslaved peoples understood the white plantation families—their thinking, their habits, their values—much better than the white slave-owners understood those whom they enslaved. The survival of enslaved people depended on their knowing how to navigate white culture while slave-owners were not similarly required to intimately know or understand the culture of those they regarded as less than human and thus without cultural value.

WHITE MAKES RIGHT

I went to a talk a few years ago delivered by Nobel laureate poet Derek Walcott, who was speaking at the opening of an exhibit of artist Romare Bearden's works at the Nasher Museum on the Duke University campus. Walcott made the point that Bearden is one of America's greatest artists, something not yet recognized by most of our country's cultural gatekeepers. Described instead as a great African American artist, the arbiters of visual art do not grasp that the African American experience is quintessentially the American experience.

Hearing Walcott speak was the first time I truly took in the normative power of our white supremacy culture. The idea that an American experience can be defined as a pre-eminently white experience and that the reality or contributions of the "other," the "non-white," are appendaged to the "real" experience is devastatingly profound in its racist assumptiveness. Yet our culture reinforces this belief at every turn—in the "celebration" of Black History month, in our history books with special sections on Native culture, African American culture, Latino culture, in the ways we work to claim an essential culture that is only touched, rather than fundamentally formed by, the experience of Peoples and Communities of Color in this country.

This ability to claim a culture that is essentially white is based in a history that has conflated U.S. culture with western culture with "civilization" in ways that reinforce hierarchical ideologies of race, gender, class, sexuality. For one example, historian Edward Burns, in his exhaustive overview of the history and culture of western civilizations, while careful to denote that civilization not be a racial descriptor, defined it nonetheless as (1941, p. 34) a quality of mind, including as its essentials originality; tolerance of varying points of view; freedom from superstition; ideals of justice, peace, and humanity; and the ability to apply reason to the solution of every problem, whether physical, social, or religious. It implies mastery of self as well as mastery of environment, for the civilized man does not yield to barbarian greed or to every passion of envy and hate and desire for revenge. He does not necessarily turn the other cheek or wallow in self-abasement, but he recognizes at least that the lives and liberties of others are as precious as his own, and that others have an equal right with himself to enjoy whatever small fruit of happiness this life can be made to yield.

The irony here is Burns' emphasis on reason and mastery, which by definition excludes whole cultures of indigenous peoples whose beliefs and values incorporated mature and knowledgeable relationships to each other and the natural world. Contrast, for example, Burn's definition with that of the Grand Council Fire of American Indians, who in 1927 challenged the portrayal of indigenous peoples in U.S. textbooks with the query "What is a civilization? Its marks are a noble religion and philosophy, original arts, stirring music, rich story and legend. We had these. Then we were not savages, but a civilized race" (Loewen, 2007, p. 100).

Contemporary historian James Loewen notes how cultural arbiters associate "civilized" with "refined or enlightened" within an even larger assumption that we live along a "primitive-to-civilized continuum" (2007, p. 100) in which greater material wealth denotes higher civilization. The way we understand our history, he says, is to "observe that peoples were conquered and come up with reasons why that was right" (p. 99). These rationalizations serve to support the underlying presumption of manifest destiny where those who are superior deserve the best (and conversely those who are inferior deserve less). This positioning of "civilized" with western "progress" occurred simultaneously with the historical construction of race. As a result, white was (and continues to be) designated as civilized, superior, deserving, in opposition to those who are "savage," "barbarian," "undeserving."

Historian Robert Allen describes this as "cultural chauvinism" (1983, p. 272), pointing to how we are taught that "western culture" (his quotes) is "a unique and independent cultural heritage and development [that] somehow accounts for the greater material advancement of western Europe and North America" (pp. 272-273). As a result, we come to understand culture "as a metaphysical attribute of a people or nation" that makes invisible the exploitation, genocide, and enslavement that produced it.

Sociologist Eduardo Bonilla-Silva describes this cultural chauvinism as white supremacy, a term he suggests is a shorthand for racialized social systems that "became global and affected all societies where Europeans extended their reach;" it's an expression that encompasses "the totality of social relations and practices that reinforce white privilege" (2006, p. 9). Like Chicana scholar and activist Elizabeth Martinéz (2004), he makes the point that this racialized social system assumes the superiority and desirability of the white race and all that is attributed to it; this racist chauvinism was and continues to be presented and perceived (by those aligned with the power elite as well as many others) as natural, normal, common sense. This racialized and racist ideology is "usually associated with the "taken-for-granted" socio-political realm," influencing societal opinion, behavior, and worldview in ways that "allow a commanding control that ... benefits some people at the expense of others" (Risner, 2006, p. 290).

In other words, western culture, white supremacy culture, operates to render "people ... literally invisible to each other" in an "unequal distribution of visibility," teaching us "to identify our interests with those at the economic top" (Zandy, 2006, p. 178). An analogy would be the ladder—its highest point represents our deepest aspiration while by its very nature accommodating only a limited number. Western culture posits this ladder as a big "T" truth, human nature, an immutable reality, when it is, in fact, simply a single and very specific construct like those upon which it rests.

So while on a cultural level we are taught to equate white supremacy with groups like the Ku Klux Klan, neo-Nazi skinheads, and race fanatics, white supremacy culture conceptually incorporates a complex weave of oppression by race, class, gender, sexuality designed to serve the interests of an elite few at the expense of most. All of us are affected by this culture, this construction of the "normal man," whatever our race, gender, class, or sexuality. Most, if not all, of us collude with it in our desperate attempts to survive. As David Purpel (class discussion, November 16, 2005) explains, we do not collude because we are bad or evil, but because we're often put in positions where we have little choice. A single parent struggling to pay the rent and feed her family may have to participate in racist policies and procedures to keep a much-needed job. We also collude without knowing, because the oppressive policies and procedures have been so well justified (school testing, for example) that we act out of the assumption that we are just doing our job or even a good job.

Because one of the roles of culture is to teach us, condition us, socialize us into our understanding of what's normal, what's valuable, what to believe and what to question, as we act out of our conditioned understanding, we reinforce the cultural dynamics that keep white supremacy in place.

Throughout, then, I use the terms "western culture," "white culture," "white supremacy culture," and "dominant culture" to mean the same thing.

DIGGING DEEPER

One of my students writes in her reflection paper:

> My junior year of college, I decided I wanted to study abroad.... I submitted my Kenya application, and the journey began. As our group toured a slum in Nairobi, children chased us with beaming smiles and tattered clothing: "mzungu, mzungu, give me money." Our guide explained that we are mzungus, whites, and that whites give the children money. I did not like this at all. I wanted children to talk to me not as a white person but as a person. In the months that followed, I spent more time away from my group with Kenyans. I became increasingly aware of my skin color and how that affected what others thought about me. I had gone twenty-one years without really thinking about my race. Now that I think about it, I don't like it.

This student's story offers a shorthand illustration of the way white supremacy operates to make it possible for those of us in the white group to live with complete lack of awareness about the ways in which race has shaped our lives. I contend, without any attempt to be dramatic, that white supremacy culture is toxic, deeply harmful to both those who seemingly benefit from it and those who are exploited and oppressed by it. An underlying assumption of this book is that white supremacy culture reflects, as Anne Wilson Schaef so sharply describes, a "technocratic, materialistic, mechanistic personality" (1998, pp. 15-16) that has led to the contemporary "lack of understanding between generations, the ecological crisis, lack of intimacy, and increased conflict and dysfunction" (p. 23). Schaef suggests that "to continue to produce and distribute death-producing, mind-altering agents for economic gain is *insane*, ... to continue to pollute the earth, air, and water when our lives and the lives of generations to come hang in the balance is *insane*" (p. 170, her emphasis). She writes:

> Western culture requires a high level of disassociation from the self and our Creator (our soul) in order to tolerate what we have created. We need to remember that the culture we have created has existed for a miniscule period of time in human history, yet its destruction of the planet and the quality of human life is unprecedented. We need healing at many levels. (1998, p. 169)

Schaef spent years as a psychotherapist investigating addiction and came to understand addiction both "as a human response to a technological world" (1998, p. 16) and a response supported by white supremacy culture, which thrives on our addiction to it. We are so addicted that, like the famous Emperor, we fail to see that not only do we have no clothes, we are destroying ourselves and our world—spiritually, physically, environmentally, and psychologically.

The list of behaviors I generated in such a frenzy so many years ago is, in my view, a list of the addictive behaviors that perpetuate white supremacy culture. Because they are culturally prevalent and/or highly valued, they reinforce each other in a noxious dance of self-justification. I have observed these behaviors repeatedly in agencies, organizations, and communities. The mission or purpose of these agencies and organizations is often irrelevant; I've seen these behaviors in county health departments, environmental groups, philanthropic foundations, women's groups. Commitment to a social justice mission does not in and of itself protect a group from reproducing dominant culture behavior.

In this book, I focus on four from the list that seem most integral to the white supremacy construct. These are the right to profit, individualism, either/or thinking (the binary), and defensiveness and/or denial (privileged resistance). All of the others on the list seem to spring from these four. So, for example, perfectionism is a refined mix of individualism and either/or thinking, resulting in and promoting the idea that we can find the one right way to do anything and everything. Fear of open conflict is a function of defensiveness and denial, power hoarding is the potent mix of the right to profit and individualism, a sense of urgency comes from the short-term thinking that a profit-oriented culture produces.

In this chapter, I look closely at the right to profit, individualism, and binary thinking. Because defensiveness and denial are their own stage in white identity development (Okun, 2006) and because they manifest in our classrooms as privileged resistance, these dynamics are covered extensively in the next chapter.

THE RIGHT TO PROFIT

I had a conversation with my nephew who taught at a charter school in Chicago, a "last stop" for students who have been unable to "make it" in public school and are about to drop out. I love my nephew unreservedly and not least for his ability, throughout his young life, to put himself in and build relationships with communities of people who are very different from him. He taught at this school for 7 years; he is white and comes from a solid middle-class background; all of his students were Black and poor. He tells me that many of the young women in his classes knew that getting pregnant and having a child while they are in high school will present barriers for them as they grow into adulthood. He tells me they spoke about this and yet went ahead and had unprotected sex anyway. He asks me to give him the "liberal" explanation for this.

After vociferously denying a "liberal" identity, I tell him that what occurs to me is how the prevailing culture does the very same thing. Look at all the corporations, I say, who know they are endangering our public health and environment, yet do so anyway because it means more profit, more money in the short term. My nephew objects, pointing out how they do benefit, how they do make more money. I respond that the young women benefit too. I point out how this culture is all about sacrificing long-term sustainability for short-term gratification; this is the essential characteristic of the profit motive. The main difference, I point out, is how the corporate executive is rewarded for this behavior, while the teen living in poverty is blamed and shamed. Short-term profit at the expense of others is perfectly acceptable as long as money is being made for the right people; short-term pleasure, perhaps even a short-term sense of love and belonging, is, on the other hand, branded as completely irresponsible, particularly when enacted by those who are poor and Black or Brown. In our culture, money definitely trumps love.

In my classroom, when I ask students to fill in the phrase "money =," they all respond, almost unanimously, with the word "happiness." A few students answer with the word "power." These responses let me know that a central and unquestioned norm of white supremacy culture is the belief that more is better, particularly when we are talking about money and profit.

Western culture teaches us that the ability to profit is a right, not a privilege. Our economy is based on the idea, which many understand as an essential truth, that everything—income, consumption, house size, material goods, pleasure, joy—should continually grow. This desire for more, with no attention to the consequences, means that we do not question

> spending a trivial amount on our poor compared to that spent by every other Western industrialized nation. One fifth of [our] children live in poverty. Half of our African American children live in poverty. We are the only industrialized Western nation that does not have universal health care. (hooks, 2000, pp. 122-123)

We have lost the "will to sacrifice on behalf of another," showing that as a nation we are perfectly amenable to dispossessing "poor citizens of government-funded social services while huge sums of money fuel the ever-growing culture of violent imperialism" (hooks, 2000, p. 117) and we accept without question that "the top 20 percent of American households now earn nearly as much as the bottom 80 percent ... , a record high of inequality" (DeGraaf, Wann, & Naylor, 2005, p. 83).

Historian James Loewen traces the rise of capitalism to the economic exploitation of the Americas, initiated by Columbus, which "transformed Europe, enriching first Spain, then, through trade and piracy, other nations" (2007, p. 63). He explains how "gold and silver from America replaced land as the basis for wealth and status, increasing the power of the new merchant class that would soon dominate the world" (p. 69). He notes how this new wealth eroded Islamic power, as well as the economies of most non-European nations, including the previously thriving African trading markets, none of which could compete with the sources of gold and silver found in the Americas.

The lionization of profit as integral to the capitalist impulse traces its roots to Britain, which envisioned the colonies as a means of keeping the "English aristocracy living in the lap of luxury" (Public Broadcasting Service, n.d.). Ironically, colonial rebellion against English rule was based, in part, on the notion of frugality—"you were not a patriot unless you were consuming and wasting less" (PBS).

Capitalism evolved in the "new world," both rebelling against and taking instruction from the British and their use of the chartered corporation to "maintain control over colonial economies" (Korten, 2001, p. 62). Initially, corporations in the U.S. "were kept under watchful citizen and government control" (p. 63) lodged in the states and their power to authorize and revoke corporate charters. The Civil War brought a shift, as "industrial interests" took advantage of "the disorder and rampant political corruption to virtually buy legislation that gave them massive grants of money and land" (p. 64). In 1886, the U.S. Supreme Court gave the private corporation status as a "natural person," with subsequent court decisions citing the Bill of Rights to essentially give corporations the same protections as individuals. By the turn of the century, the courts were interpreting "the common good to mean maximum production, no matter what was produced or who it harmed" (p. 65), establishing a cultural ethos of production at all costs. The price was high, as Korten notes that in the years from 1888 to 1908, almost 100 workers were killed each day in industrial accidents (p. 65).

The corporate sector reinforced an individualistic ethos (see below for the discussion of individualism) supported by their legal duty to "try to make a profit for shareholders" (Cooper, 2004, p. 5). The aggregate of court opinions leading to this cultural sanction for a focus on profit (over and above any other responsibility) has resulted in the almost complete lack of economic incentive to consider human or environmental consequences while in pursuit of an ever-larger bottom line.

The cultural belief in "more is better" was reinforced during this same period in the late 1800s with the creation of the department store, which instituted "shopping as a leisure activity" where "stores were destinations in themselves" offering "women, who had few opportunities to escape the home, a socially-acceptable place to linger" (PBS, n.d.). As the century turned the corner, "citizens were told by government and industry leaders that consuming made them good Americans" (PBS); buying on credit came on the scene in the 1920s. Although we think of the Depression era as a time of widespread shortage, in fact "purchases of food and general merchandise did not decline" during these years—"residential use of gas and electricity jumped, and radios and refrigerators became common in American households" (PBS). The march toward "affluenza" continued relatively unabated, except for a small blip during the Arab oil embargo during the early 1970s. By the 1980s, a national magazine reported that "a flaunt-it-if-you-have-it style is rippling in concentric circles across the land," while Reagonomics was marshalling in a "massive redistribution of wealth" which resulted in "33 percent of all personal wealth in the nation in the hands of 1 percent of its households" (PBS).

Capitalism is now "a system of political economy characterized by socialized production of commodities and private appropriation of profit" (Browne, Franco, Negrón-Gonzales, & Williams, 2005, p. 27). This exclusive focus on profit has led to "an enormous misallocation of resources in almost every sphere of society. Too much of our wealth goes to maintaining the systems of domination and providing obscene luxuries for a tiny percentage of the population.... The system of domination has created its own self-legitimizing culture, and we're all conditioned to buy into it" (Cooper, 2004, p. 11). As a result,

> we're the biggest overconsumers, dependent on using more than our share of the world's resources. We also have the strongest commitment to the neoliberal economic ideology of unlimited growth and ever-increasing consumption. This is perpetuated by a national narrative that equates consumption with happiness, values money more than life, and legitimizes policies that make rich people richer by maximizing returns on financial speculation.... the real story [of our country] is one of an empire ruled by a plutocracy, a government of the rich. (Cooper, 2004, p. 11)

I note here Cooper's use of the words *narrative* and *story*; the culture uses both to reinforce values and norms that serve the most powerful in the group. So, for example, our cultural stories "about the nature of prosperity and how it is achieved serve the cause of concentrating power, not meeting actual needs" (2004, p. 11).

This culture of profit and unending growth shapes the relationships that the dominant culture has with those who are "other." Gloria Ladson-Billings, in her keynote address at the UCEA Conference (October 2007), reminded us that our history is one where women and enslaved people brought here from Africa and their descendants were until fairly recently commodities, legal property, bought and sold on the open market. This commodification of people as property by the white landowning class was a process of "othering" for the purpose of exploitation. The construction of race with white at the top served (and continues to serve) to justify the legacied accumulation of wealth for elites in the white group by using the labor of forcibly imported peoples cast as so "other" as to be less than human.

Every mainstream institution participated in this characterization, codifying and refining a system of economic slavery unlike any seen previously. Native lands were stolen, people from Mexico woke up one morning to find their border moved and their land taken, the Chinese, the Japanese, every immigrant group was exploited, cheated, and oppressed as the white group amassed wealth. This legacy continues today in our contemporary demonization of "illegal aliens," where the mainstream culture (in the guise of the media and popular opinion makers, backed up by weak politicians desperate for public approval) casts human beings as both illegal and alien while ignoring our economic dependence on their exploited labor. Ironically, many people in the white group are also exploited, cheated, and oppressed, yet history shows that attempts at class based alliances are typically trumped by carefully constructed allegiance to whiteness (Allen, 1983).

The culture of profit also functions to quickly accommodate those who resist. If we look at the history of social justice movements in this country, where organized groups of people have fought and won important and often life-saving battles, we cannot fail to note how the power elite time and again diverts these movements from agendas of equity and justice by granting limited access. Lisa Durán (2002) and King and Osayande (2007) have documented how the philanthropic community intentionally and deliberately moderated social movements in the 1960s, diverting funds to leaders advocating an assimilationist agenda. The corporate sector has responded to the gay rights movement by addressing the community's potential as consumers; much of the opening in the dominant culture towards this community has been because of its potential for profit making. A vicious cycle is put in place where historically targeted and oppressed communities receive enough access to drive the profit machine and, as a result, begin to lose a larger vision.

The culture's support for the assimilationist response is then internalized by communities that are being exploited and underserved. Toni Morrison, in her essay *On the Backs of Blacks* (1993), notes how newly arriving immigrants are conditioned early to distance themselves from the Black community, from the Black identity, in the cultural understanding that it is better and safer to align with white than Black. One theory of how our culture will handle the ever increasing Latino demographic is to assimilate the varied ethnic, cultural, and racial features of this far from homogenous group into the white group, as it has done with the Irish, the

Italian, the Jew (Brodkin, 2000; Guglielmo, 2003; Ignatiev, 1995, Roediger, 2005).

Our job as educators, then, is to help our students think critically about the imperative to profit and the ways in which that imperative reinforces white supremacy. One of the ways I do this, among many, is using an activity borrowed from another teacher, where I ask my students to choose from a range of "action projects" designed to help them reflect on their relationship to consumerism and the marketplace. Many of my students choose to count their clothes, noting where each item is made. Invariably they report astonishment at the number of clothes they own, often revealing how they have found clothing purchased but unworn, tags still attached. Researching the countries where the clothing is made, they discover the harsh working and wage conditions of an unorganized labor force of People of Color. This activity is often the first time that they have ever been asked to consider their consumption habits and the repercussions.

Encouraging our students to think critically about capitalism and the ways in which it reproduces white supremacy is never easy in a culture where we have been taught to assume that any other economic arrangement is threatening. As Korten notes, we have been socialized to understand capitalism as synonymous with private property, both posited as sacred, when both, in fact, embody "an extremist ideology that advances the concentration and rights of ownership without limit, to the exclusion of the needs and rights of the many who own virtually nothing" (2001, p. 9).

Cultural critic Derrick Jensen adds that "our financial riches come at the expense of the planet, those we enslave, our capacity to engage in relationship, and our humanity" (2002, p. 224). We reproduce this behavior as

> time and again we make this wrong choice. We have created an entire society that rewards this wrong choice, that consistently cuts off realistic possibility of making the right choice, that consistently causes us to forget that we even have a choice to make in the first place. And we do have a choice: We can see others as objects, or we can open up to them as subjects. (2002, p. 224)

We can no longer afford to make this wrong choice. To remain silent about the toxicity of contemporary capitalism and its role in reproducing white supremacy is to perpetuate the role of school as a factory designed to produce a workforce that can succeed at being "successful" while remaining ignorant of the cost to others, to ourselves. Shapiro (2006, p. 58) characterizes this "familiar purpose" of school as one which perpetuates the ideology that we should all "work hard and do well" in order to obtain the "credentials, the jobs, and the income" that makes it possible for us to "participate fully and actively in the marketplace."

What we must do instead is create classrooms, schools, an education system that promotes our abilities as critical and compassionate citizens "who take seriously [our] responsibility to make a difference in the world so that it is more just, compassionate, and humane" (Shapiro, 2006, p. 58). To do this, we have to get comfortable in the task of helping our students consider what it means to put profits before people.

A critical approach to capitalism is not an either/or endeavor, important to understand as we explore the binary later on. For example, as Shapiro argues (personal correspondence, March 19, 2009), "hope is found in [the] history of struggle and victories—Medicare, Medicaid, Social Security, unemployment benefits, ... [T]he struggles and gains of the New Deal, Great Society, the Obama election ... need to be recognized." In a similar vein, Korten argues that individual ownership does not have to translate into "unaccountable concentration" (2001, p. 9). Many individuals and groups are engaged in the endeavor of constructing alternate economic choices that do not require benefit for a few at the expense of us all.

I take heart from my students, who when invited to consider the price of profit at all costs, respond with compassion, anger and a basic impulse toward fairness. I take heart from the small, grassroots communities of people I know who are trying to live into more hopeful cultural and economic arrangements. Echoing Korten, I take heart from our ability to deconstruct what has been constructed and reconstruct something that makes more sense.

INDIVIDUALISM

I ask my students to write a response to the prompt, "when it comes to race and racism, I ..." One of my white students writes

> I just feel like because of what happened years ago that white people are still being punished and are "racism" whether they really are or not.... I feel like today people of color have just as much opportunity for things as white people do. They are still trying to use segregation as an excuse and it will one day not work anymore.

Her words reflect what many, if not most white students, come into my classroom believing—that because they have no racist intent, they are not racist, which in turn means that racism is no longer happening.

This ability to see and understand the world as a reflection of our particular experience is a manifestation of a culture that lionizes individualism. Students in my classroom, people in my workshops, are socialized to see the world through their specific dominant group lens, often unaware of the institutional and cultural manifestations of ongoing race, class, gender, and sexuality constructs that are oppressive and discriminatory to people on the margins. This obtuseness is well taught.

Not only are we obtuse, when the power of cultural conditioning is made apparent, we are often desperate to claim our freedom from it. Jean Kilbourne, producer of the *Killing Us Softly* (Kilbourne & Jhally, 2001) film series about the power of media to shape our thinking about gender, sexuality, and violence, makes a joke that at the same time we insist we are immune to advertising and proclaim our independence, we fail to notice that we are wearing the latest Gap T-shirt.

Mab Segrest, in her brilliant overview of the history of U.S. racism (1994, p. 189), describes individualism as a "psychosis of domination" based in a "failure to feel the communal bonds between humans." This psychosis required and produced the cultural rationale for the insidious genocide attached to a "drive for private ownership" coming out of a Europe emerging from feudalism. Rooted in philosophical reaction to the French Revolution and later given new meaning by the German Romantics of the mid-nineteenth century, "it was in the United States that "individualism" primarily came to celebrate capitalism and liberal democracy" (Lukes, 1971, p. 59).

In the context of the "new world," individualism was constructed as "equal individual rights, limited government, laissez-faire, natural justice and equal opportunity, and individual freedom, moral development, and dignity" (Lukes, 1971, p. 59). As a result, individualism came to be posited as integral to national values, synonymous with personal self-reliance, with individual merit irrevocably connected to (deserved) wealth.

The public school system, as a central player in the construction of cultural norms, was designed to transmit this ideology, in line with another cultural arbiter, the Protestant Church. School curriculum was designed to proliferate the Protestant belief that "a good moral education would produce a moral society" and that "poverty could be eliminated if the children of the poor were taught that they could advance in society through their own individual effort" (Spring, 2005, p. 96). Schools reflected "the existing political and economic organization of society," and taught "that any problems were the result of individual deviance or failure" (p. 83). In the early 1820s, as the high school was established, the stated purpose was to "promote the idea that achievement depends on individual responsibility" (p. 91).

By the end of the Civil War, individualism had become a cultural standard. The more humanistic individualism represented by Walt Whitman gave way to the Social Darwinists, whose pre-eminent spokesperson, Herbert Spencer, merged individualism with survival of the fittest, laying the groundwork for "an evolving ideology of private enterprise and laissez-faire, postulating absolute equality of opportunity and the equivalence of public welfare and private accumulation" (Lukes, 1971, p. 62).

Here we begin to see the intersection of the ideologies of individualism and profit. As referenced earlier, in 1886 the U.S. legal system granted private corporations the rights of individuals (*Santa Clara County v. Southern Pacific Railroad*). As a result of this ruling, "corporations came to claim the full rights enjoyed by individual citizens while being exempted from many of the responsibilities and liabilities of citizenship" (Korten, 2001, p. 66). This case helped to solidify cultural hegemony based on corporate values and priorities; in this period, free enterprise "gave way to gigantic monopolies as the dominant mode of economic organization" (R. Allen, 1974, p. 263). The law allowed "capital concentration and centralization on a scale never before seen" (p. 263). We live today with this legacy; an individual citizen or group of citizens can rarely match the literally immeasurable resources of the expanding corporate community to influence federal, state, or even local public policy.

Coupled with the cultural imperative toward profit, a corporate culture that "equates the freedom and rights of individuals with market freedom and property rights" (Korten, 2001, p. 89) creates a set of values and beliefs that encourage people to buy into or at least not question policies that benefit wealth, even when that benefit comes at their own expense. These beliefs create, as Korten so aptly puts it, a "moral justification for injustice" (p. 89). I remember years ago turning on the television to watch a popular newsman anchor a show devoted to proving the premise that greed is good. Culturally obsessed with the wealthy few, socialized to identify with them while the gap between us and those at the top reaches levels never before seen, we learn to defend the rights of individuals to profit regardless of the cost to the larger community.

Jona olsson, in her *Detour Spotting for White Anti-Racists* (1997, pp. 6-7), references the impact of the pernicious combination of "the Rugged Individual, the Level Playing Field, and the Bootstrap Theory," calling them "three of the crown jewels of U.S. social propaganda." Socialized by a culture teaching us that "America is the land of opportunity, built by rugged individuals, where anyone … can succeed if they just pull up hard enough on their bootstraps" (p. 6), individualism "is the glue that binds our interpretative field and, thus, we have a hard time understanding the centrality of larger social forces. For most Americans, individual-level explanations are the order of the day to explain class, gender, and race inequality" (Bonilla-Silva, 2006, p. 220).

Bonilla-Silva makes the point that

> regarding each person as an "individual" with "choices" [leads to the] justifi-
> cation for whites having the right ... to live in segregated neighborhoods or
> [send] their children to segregated schools ... [while ignoring] the multiple
> institutional and state-sponsored practices behind segregation and ... these
> practices' negative consequences for minorities. (2006, p. 28)

Our cultural focus on the power of the individual leads to public policy
that ignores group-based discrimination and advantage, leading to more
benefits for the dominant group, whose "unfettered, so-called individual
choices help reproduce a form of white supremacy in neighborhoods,
schools, and society in general" (p. 36).

Bonilla-Silva is talking about the power of culture to maintain the story
that racism is about the personal attitudes that we hold about each other
while ignoring the deeply systemic perpetuation of racial injustice embedded in our institutions and culture. So, for example, the media comes
alive whenever a celebrity uses a pejorative racial term while at the same
remaining silent about the steady resegregation of public schools along
race and class lines, or the epidemic of sexual violence experienced by
women and gender transgressing people, or other manifestations of multiple legacies of structural oppression.

In an individualistic culture where centuries of racism have left a toxic
legacy felt by Communities of Color across the country, we are socialized
into an ethic of "colorblindness," a twisted reconfiguration of the justice
fought for by a culturally appropriated Civil Rights movement. In this
context, individualism operates to posit the white individual as the norm
by which everyone should be measured and to which everyone should
aspire, the "everyman" whose hard work and intelligence is rewarded with
the requisite wealth. White teachers have been socialized to see ourselves
as normal, without race prejudice. As a result, we see no dissonance in
claiming our colorblindness while explaining "that a larger percentage of
African Americans and Latinos or Latinas ... are poor because of their
problematic culture" (Revilla, Wells, & Holme, 2004, p. 285).

This ethic of individualism serves as a rhetorical device to hide systemic power in other ways as well. Svi Shapiro (2006) argues that our educational focus on individual tyrants, like Hitler, distracts us from the
"need to look deeper into those who *elected* Hitler" (McCarthy, 2006, p.
44), to understand the ways in which individualism serves power. Studies
on conformity, like the famous Milgram and Asch experiments of the
1950s, show that despite our national discourse about individualism, we
are much more likely to act in concert with the dominant group than to
think for ourselves. Shapiro quotes one of his students, who has internalized that being a "good" student means "learning to conform" (2006, p.
54); Shapiro makes the point that "being successful in school has little if

anything to do with challenging and questioning accepted ideas and beliefs" (p. 54). Sarah McCarthy (2006) adds how "despite our rich literature of freedom ... unquestioning obedience is perceived to be in the best interests of the schools, churches, families, and political institutions" (p. 45).

In fact, western culture decries individuality whenever it threatens community coherence and obedience to cultural norms, supporting individualism only to the extent that it serves capitalism. So while our culture does not culturally or institutionally support the individualistic, free expression of a transgender student in our schools, we use the slogan "be all that you can be" to recruit people into the military. While we do not support the individuality of a pregnant Black or Latina teenager, preferring to see her as a statistic reflecting deviance and deficit, we follow the pregnancies of white celebrity teenagers with a cultural fascination that produces big profits for media conglomerates while leaving intact the notion of the celebrity's behavior as individually aberrant. Individualism in the context of white supremacy culture is a rhetorical tool of conditioning, designed to blame those on the margins for their poor choices, their addictions, their bad behavior when the same poor choices, addictions and bad behavior go unchallenged when committed by the powerful and wealthy.

Alfred Lubrano notices this double standard. Reflecting on his experience moving from the working class to the educated middle-class, he came to understand how "corporate norms are based on middle- and upper-class values" that reflect "learning and possessing confidence in your place in the world" (2004, pp. 77-78). He contrasts this with what he learned as the child of working-class parents where "conformity and obedience are the norm" (p. 78). He notes how the dominant culture reflects "the core value of the middle class, [which] is achievement by the individual." Similar to race privilege, Lubrano claims that the middle-class assumes its values as universal. Because the middle-class "writes our culture," Lubrano claims, it "gets to see complex depictions of itself, [while] the working class views mostly stereotypes of itself" (pp. 79-80).

Lubrano is talking about the ways in which we internalize the ideology of individualism as normal, desired, superior. Because individualism is posited as a central piece of the "American" story, it follows that a centerpiece of white identity development is learning to see ourselves first and foremost as individuals. In a range of models of white identity development (Hardiman, 1994; Helms, 1990; Okun & Jones, 2006; Tatum, 1997), the first stage in our understanding of ourselves as racial beings is that we are "normal." As we begin to grow up and encounter people who are other than white, we assume they want to be "normal" like us. Essential to being normal is assuming our individuality without questioning the ways in which we benefit as a group from white privilege while also demonizing whole groups (not seen as individuals) of people who are not like us, and therefore not "normal" but "other."

Beverly Daniel Tatum, in her landmark work *Why Do All the Black Kids Sit Together in the Cafeteria* (1997), describes this phenomenon as "aversive racism." She cites research showing that contemporary racism is no longer framed by white people holding beliefs that People of Color are "less than" or "worse," but rather our assumption that we are "better," "superior." Because white people are taught to understand racism as the equivalent of *individual* intent, we see ourselves as "nonprejudiced and racially tolerant" (p. 119) while ignoring the ways we have "been breathing the 'smog' of racial biases and stereotypes pervading the popular culture" (p. 118). This proclivity to see ourselves as better only gets stronger when we are evaluating another Person of Color who is "high-ability" or better skilled than we are.

In addition, those of us holding privilege resent being seen as part of a group. Acknowledging advantage based on belonging to the dominant group "threatens not only beliefs about society but also beliefs about one's own life accomplishments" (Tatum, 1997, p. 103).

In the same vein, individualism functions to separate white people from each other. One of the most common attitudes and behaviors of white people who have some understanding of the depth of structural racism is to adopt a self-righteousness that we then use to judge and distance ourselves from other white people, precisely because we don't want to be seen as part of the white group. As olsson (1997, p. 16) notes, we "put other white people down, trash their work or behavior, or otherwise dismiss them" in order to position ourselves as more "evolved" and better. This tendency weaves tightly with the culturally valued binary, where we learn early that we can be either good or bad, so being good is an exercise is disassociating ourselves from those who we position as bad. The consequence, which we see reflected in activist history, is that white people often abandon our own communities, leaving them vulnerable to those who *are* willing to work with and organize them, the overtly and aggressively racist right.

White people are not the only ones to internalize a pernicious individualism. African American writer and poet June Jordan writes about her own internalization of the ideal of "American illusions of autonomy, American delusions of individuality" (2002, p. 112). Reflecting on her urge toward a solitary life focused on her writing, she realizes she is emulating another, more famous artist, both eschewing family and social relationships out of a belief in themselves as "eminently respectable in the conscientiously selfish design of our days, ... virtuous and self-sacrificing" (p. 112). As she comes to realize the cost attached to giving up relationships, particularly with her son, she begins to see herself as a casualty of "beloved, national myths about you and me as gloriously rugged, independent individuals" (p. 112). She talks about how we're led to believe in our specialness, writing

> Every single American grows up believing that, in the happy ending ahead of us, we will just gleefully dust our classmates and our fellow workers and our compatriots and then, to really mix up the metaphors, we will leave them grounded, like so many ugly ducklings, while we wheel and speed and plummet and, steadily glittering, rise: 235 million Jonathan Livingston Seagulls with nary a thought for the welfare of the flock, or companionship, or a resting or a nesting environment! (Jordan, 2002, p. 113)

Jordan explains that, of course, the "flip side" of "this delusional disease, this infantile and apparently implacable trust in mass individuality" is the equally deluded belief that "every problem or crisis is exclusively our own, or, conversely, your problem—not mine" (2002, p. 113).

Jordan goes on to say that "American delusions of individuality ... disfigure our national landscape with multitudes of disconnected pained human beings who pull down the shades on prolonged and needless agony" (2002, p. 114), warning that our "mistaken self-centered perspective ... repeatedly proves to be self-defeating and even undemocratic" (p. 115). She speaks out loud that which I would guess we have all experienced in one way or another—the belief that our suffering is unique to us (perhaps this is the origin of the idea of suffering in silence). She writes that because we assume "I am inherently special and different ... no one else feels stranded," threatened, unheard. We remain silent and isolated, and "so it goes ... for each elderly American who can no longer take care of himself, and each family with teenagers addicted to drugs, and each household of the suddenly unemployed and each person married to an alcoholic" (p. 114).

The United States is in the midst of the worst economic recession since The Great Depression; we have just elected a new president who has offered as one solution a large stimulus package. As the bill passes in Congress, the media is replete with the indignation directed at families who will be "bailed out," homes saved, and, according to the conventional wisdom of the day, rewarded for their poor choices. I watch this blaming of the working poor, drawn into bad loans by money-crazed banking institutions intent on pursuing their flim-flam policies by the promise of ever greater profits. What would it take, I wonder, for our collective response to be one of compassion, of joy, that we might have found a way to help our neighbors save their homes, their lives.

My critique of individualism is not an either/or proposition where individualism is always bad and the collective always good. Queer theorist

Nikki Sullivan (2006, p. 136) points out that our ideas of community are "often represented in idealised (author's spelling) terms as an 'ecstatic sense of oneness', a sense of harmony, ... often represented in opposition to individualism or liberalism." This romantic portrayal is "not only idealistic, but problematic" (p. 137). She wants us to consider the tension inherent between "natural" community based on "things in common" and "full community" formed by an intentional and collective consciousness, to note how both can lead to "a sense of pressure to choose a single identity and thus to suppress any sense of difference that may be regarded as a potential breach of commonality" (p. 139).

Sullivan is talking about how membership in the community or collective can be challenging and problematic. Identity, Sullivan says, is ambiguous "whether or not it is natural or cultural" (2006, p. 139). Using herself as an example, she notes how claiming her lesbian identity raises problems in terms of how she is viewed or welcomed into any number of "common" or "intentional" communities. She references Zygmunt Bauman (1997, p. 145), who points to a "fundamental tension between personal freedom and belonging or community: community is tantamount to conformity, and therefore to the (at least potential) loss of individuality." In other words, to admit our differences within community, often hard to do because of communal pressure to conform, is to acknowledge our individuality, which in turn challenges community norms.

Finally, like all elements of dominance, where benefit derives from the exploitation and oppression of others, there is a cost. Parker Palmer (2004, p. 38) looks at our "cult of me" with compassion, noting that "too many people ... suffer from an empty self. They have a bottomless pit where their identity should be—an inner void they try to fill with competitive success, consumerism, sexism, racism, or anything that might give them the illusion of being better than others." He makes the point (p. 39) that "a strong community helps people develop a sense of true self, for only in community can the self exercise and fulfill its nature."

Rachel Naomi Remen, author and counselor to those with chronic and terminal illness, echoes Palmer's observation, speculating that "perhaps it is [our] striving for excessive independence that is a weakness, that makes many of us so vulnerable to isolation, cynicism, and depression" (2000, p. 197). She echoes Jordan's reflection on how individualism keeps us separated from each other. Remen states her doubt that "independence and individualism will enable us to live in the deepest and most fulfilling way" (p. 197). She wants us to aspire to service in "a relationship between equals" that helps us to discover that "life is holy" (pp. 198-199).

Our task as educators, then, is to "teach students that we all participate in larger systems, systems that, for instance, create different opportunity structures for workers, women, and minorities" (Bonilla-Silva, 2006, p.

220). The irony is that "if we do our job right, our students leave our classes understanding that ... individuals are not personally responsible for the existence of a class, gender, or racial order ..." while at the same time realizing their individual responsibility for "how their actions and behavior help perpetuate inequality ... they are the cogs that allow these systems to run" (p. 221). In the antiracism training community, we say that as white people, we are not to blame for what has happened historically *and* we are responsible for addressing the present-day consequences.

We must learn, as Bauman (1997) suggests, to navigate the tension between individualism that supports white supremacy culture and our own individuality. Jordan offers the possibility of "a tender and a powerful company of others struggling as we do" (2002, p. 114). She wants "each American one of us [to] consciously choose to become a willing and outspoken part of the people who, together, will determine our individual chances for happiness, and justice" (p. 115).

Students in my classroom have little experience, most of them, with collective and collaborative action. The ethos of a self-centered individualism is well ingrained, here in the South particularly, where the word "union" is synonymous with "terrorist" or "communist." My students might belong to an affinity group of some kind, a fraternity or sorority, a music club, a church group. They might have some experience of gathering together to provide a service. But they have no real experience with the collective possibilities that create social change.

We must help students see themselves as part of a larger endeavor, to create a sense of collective possibilities. We need to help them see the ways in which they can help each other solve problems, create solutions, agitate, and push for change. We need a new approach, one where the education system as a whole is imbued with a commitment to antiracist activism. Barring that, we need programs that acknowledge the time required to help students understand their collective power. Every education program should include classes in community organizing, specifically to help students understand the power they might wield as a collective with a common purpose.

THE BINARY

> The opposite of a correct statement is a false statement but the opposite of a profound truth may well be another profound truth.
>
> —Niels Bohr

I teach classes where we dive into the ways that oppression operates, looking at how class, race, gender, and sexually oppressive practices and beliefs are embedded in every aspect of our institutions and culture. For those who have never been exposed to the historical realities associated with the deliberate construction of white supremacy, this can be a devastating enterprise. Although I explain to my students that we are not investigating this history in order to establish who is good and who bad, often a student will desperately focus on "intent," insisting that most people do not mean to participate in these oppressive constructs. This intensity reflects a deep distress; the analysis of oppression is disrupting the student's world. She (or he) complains she can no longer watch the movies she usually enjoys because of the oppressive messages and dynamics that were not obvious to her before. She grieves how what she is learning in the classroom is changing how she sees people, threatening her relationships.

My student is not able to do for herself what she wants me to do for her—free her from blame. She is judging people in new ways, assigning them a culpability that they did not have before. He now perceives people he used to consider "good" as "bad," including, I would guess, himself.

The binary functions at the personal level to keep us entrapped in the struggle to understand ourselves in these either/or terms. Attempting to define who is good and who bad, we long to be good, which we understand as a kind of immutable perfection. Buddhist teacher Cheri Huber offers a list of qualities and characteristics taught by our culture, each paired with a list of qualities and characteristics understood as unacceptable: good/bad, right/wrong, strong/weak, kind/unkind, ... (2000, p. 40). We are socialized, she says, to believe we can only be one or the other, either/or. Wanting to be good, we cannot afford to be bad, which in turn means we cannot make mistakes. We must be perfect. Gripped in the confines of this kind of dualistic thinking, no wonder my students struggle to defend against the realities of oppression in which they have colluded and from which they have benefitted.

Anne Wilson Schaef writes that

> we resort to dualisms in order to simplify and explain a very complex world, giving us a false sense of understanding and control.... We use dualisms to simplify a very complex world and then we attempt to live there, trying to destroy anything that does not fit into our simplistic view. (1998, p. 123)

To see the world in either/or terms seems to offer security, a sense of belonging, connectedness, identity, safety from the unknown. Our desire to understand a complex world in simple terms of good and bad, right and wrong, results, for example, in such "patriotic" slogans as "love it or leave it"—where the implication is that a true patriot is one who loves his country without question. While this worldview may signal a deep and legitimate hunger for freedom from chaos and fear, it manifests on our physical and psychological landscape as hostility to thoughtfulness, complexity, "not" knowing; it requires a narrow understanding of moral choice and a dogged insistence on its own validity.

Kenji Yoshino (2000, p. 6), in his exploration of the erasure of bisexuality in modern American culture, offers three rationales for the binary. The first is based in an Aristotlean model where binaries are a simple reflection of "real oppositions in the world" such as "night/day, male/female, life/death." The second, the cognitive, is rooted in what Yoshino calls our "limited cognitive capacity as human beings [that] leads us to apprehend complex phenomena in [binary] terms." The third, the political, has to do with how the "clash of opposing sides" operates to erase and deny "intermediate ground."

Yoshino goes on to note that just because "coffee and tea are two different objects, ... we do not assume that all individuals break down into mutually exclusive sets of coffee and tea drinkers" (2000, p. 6). While he is talking about sexuality here, his argument extends—the Aristotlean "opposition" of night/day does not take into accord the varied light of sunrise and how this light differs from that of sundown, or the ways in which a day, darkened by storm, can take on the appearance of night, or how an Alaskan night sky can appear as bright as a North Carolina afternoon. Just a simple exploration of the assumed night/day binary shows how polarity is assumed, not real. We can do the same with white/black, male/female, life/death; I cannot think of a binary that does not hold intricate contradictions and complexities.

I am most interested in Yoshino's third rationale; as we start to explore socially constructed binaries, their speciousness becomes evident and so we are led to wonder what purpose they serve. Class, race, gender, sexuality are all constructed as if each can be clearly demarcated when in fact none of them can. At what point, for example, do we know "gay" from "straight"—is it the first sense of lust, the brushing of fingers, the deep longing, the first kiss, the first contact of genitals, five such contacts, ten, a hundred?

I would argue, and I am not the first, that the whole point of the binary is to erase complexities while creating a hierarchy that reinforces oppressive constructs. Queer theorist Donald Hall, referencing Jacques Derrida, points out "the binary construction of meaning—male/female, light/dark, proper/improper," to show "how these binaries are always weighted toward the first term, which is held at greater social value, but which also always needs the second term to substantiate that value" (2003, p. 62).

In other words, binaries are used to define and reify power. Paul Kivel argues that "the important distinction in the United States has always been binary—first between those who counted as Christians and those who were pagans" (2002, p. 15), then as Christianity began to spread, shifting to distinguish "European workers from African and Native-American workers," and finally to demarcate "white" and everyone else (not white).

The use of the binary to define our cultural hierarchy is made evident when we see how "moral qualities [are] attached to racial differences" (Kivel, 2002, p. 17). Kivel explains that "white" "has linguistically signified honor, purity, cleanliness, and godliness" (p. 18). This construction of language supports "a core pattern of thinking developed in elite settings in western Europe and the United States" (p. 18) based on seeing the world in either/or terms, where those terms confer value. So, for example, "white" and "western" are associated with "civilized," while "dark" is associated with "primitive, uncivilized, barbaric, savage" (p. 18). This binary weaves across class, gender, and sexuality, creating a tapestry of either/or ranking.

Inherent in western culture is the very act of defining "us" in ways that claim superiority over an opposite and increasingly threatening "them." In fact, we seem to feel that we cannot truly be "us" unless we can demonstrate our difference from and superiority to "them." Amin Maalouf, in his thoughtful book *In the Name of Identity*, notes how the West has emerged "in the course of the last few centuries ... to set physical and intellectual standards for the whole world, marginalizing all other civilizations and reducing their status to that of peripheral cultures threatened with extinction" (1996, p. 69). This "superiority" positions us to understand ourselves as right, which is the appeal of the Constantinian or western culture emphasis on binaries of right/wrong, good/bad and claims to the real truth.

So, for example, Columbus initiated the process of turning "well built" men "of quick intelligence," his early description of the Arawak people to Queen Isabella, into the later "cruel, ... stupid, ... a people warlike and numerous, whose customs and religion are very different from ours" (Loewen, 2007, p. 62) when he wanted to justify his acts of enslavement and genocide. Loewen notes how "before the 1450s, Europeans considered Africans exotic but not necessarily inferior. As more and more nations joined the slave trade, Europeans came to characterize Africans as stupid, backward, and uncivilized" (p. 143). The purpose of the binary in these situations is to reduce complex, synchronistic communities of people into simple parodies based on cultural assignment of value that then allow for continued exploitation and oppression.

This is the cultural enactment of hierarchy that defines who is "normal" and who is "other." So, to return to the "patriots" who tell us to "love it or leave it," the binary reflects the assumption that these are our only choices. We establish our national identity by demonstrating loyalty to the

American group, loyalty that can best be understood in opposition to those who are not American. This positioning of identities one against the other serves the interests of those who create the story, infusing fear of the other as the essential ingredient it is in keeping us from seeing our common humanity.

In order to insure our superiority, cultural storytellers use demeaning rhetoric to isolate those who attempt to introduce the complexities inherent in any human endeavor. Our national media is replete with pundits who, rather than address the substance of any critique, substitute mean-spirited character defamation. So, for example, Fox News intentionally labels all those attempting to enter the United States from Mexico looking for work as "terrorists." This act of othering preempts any attempt to hold a meaningful discussion about the reasons why people are coming here or the humanity of those who make the attempt. In this way, Fox News conditions their viewers, who can then be counted upon to not only repeat and reinforce the "simple" story, but to take up the mean-spirited rhetoric in order to, in their turn, squash any counter-narrative. This binary story telling spreads as the rest of us pick up this habit.

Cultures within cultures, cultures of oppressed people struggling to survive their oppression, also weave their stories in this way, so that every identity establishes itself in opposition to another. Even margin cultures, in tragic mimicry of the larger culture within which they operate, function by dividing and separating based on labeling as "other" those who they position as posing some threat to the group's unity. So, for example, the leadership of the white feminist movement of the 1960s attempted to separate themselves publicly from any hints of lesbianism; many in the gay rights community struggle to accept transgender people; the religious leaders of poor white communities often eschew homosexuality.

This process of "othering" people who, by their very existence, help to define our group (we are, they are not) has a very different impact based on the held power of the group. As Maalouf says (1996, p. 71), "reality is experienced differently by those born in dominant civilization and those born outside it." For example, western culture renders the Iraqi people specifically and Arab people generally either invisible to us or paints them as terrorist threat. This serves the purpose of othering those who, if their humanity were acknowledged, would raise questions about a foreign policy that has led to the deaths of hundreds of thousands of Iraqis, as well as the destruction of much of that country's infrastructure. At the same time widespread anti-U.S. sentiment in response to our "pre-emptive strike" (the othering of Americans) is vocally and visibly expressed, with almost no change in the daily lives of U.S. citizens (unless they are serving in Iraq or have a family member serving there).

A white person who colludes, intentionally or unintentionally, with the systemic racism of U.S. institutions and culture will perpetuate the economic and social disenfranchisement of whole communities of people. As one example, a teacher with no understanding of the white supremacy construct and conditioned by the racist culture to interpret the behavior of his Students of Color as deficient or pathological, will contribute to the escalating push-out rate of these students because he does not challenge his conditioning to experience that student as "less than." Supported by the dominant culture in her "othering" of a student she does not understand, viewing her standards as "objective," she contributes to the institutionalized cycle of the school to prison pipeline.

Meanwhile, the Student of Color who is being pushed out may respond to the teacher's inability to see him as fully human by withdrawing or acting out, behaviors that simply reinforce the teacher's assumptions. From the student's less powerful position in respect to the teacher and the school, the student may, in turn, "other" or dehumanize his teacher. In this case, the student's "othering" has no power to affect the life of the teacher, unless he acts out in an aggressive or violent way. Even then, as harmful as this may be to the teacher, the larger (white) community to which the teacher belongs is not affected.

As a result of these position and power differences, our everyday lives play out very differently. In my own experience, I have seen how Teachers of Color are held to a different standard by their white students and the administration, even when the administration has People of Color in leadership positions. I have seen how my behavior as a white person is accepted as legitimate and appropriate, when the same behavior lays Colleagues of Color bare and vulnerable.

We come back full circle to the binary's usefulness in keeping us entrapped at the personal level (individualism) in the struggle to understand ourselves as either good or bad. Huber makes another, important connection—the binary is not simply about control. We have internalized the belief that if we are good and right, then we will be loved (2000, p. 62). She notes (p. 174), "we have all the information we need to understand that other people don't experience life as we do, yet because we have been conditioned to believe that there is only one right answer, our only conclusion can be that the other is wrong." Living in an either/or world, unable to admit mistakes because to do so would be to see ourselves as a mistake, we've been taught to believe that the way we see the world is true instead of "the totality of [our] own preferences, habits, beliefs, and assumptions projected onto the world" (p. 167). Believing that our only choices are to be good and right, we develop a strong illusion of control over a chaotic world, as we strive harder and harder to manage the unmanageable.

Schaef suggests that we "jump off the dualism" (1998, p. 125). She offers a third alternative that involves "not retreating to either end of the dualism, going inside instead, to see where your feelings take you" (p. 129). Huber tells us that she has "come to the conclusion that the world of opposites actually refers not only to dualism, but to the fact that so many things are the opposite of what we've been taught to believe" (2000, p. 44). She explains, for example, "war does not result in peace. Treating a disease does not create health. Having a lot of money does not lead to happiness" (p. 44). She is making the case, as does Schaef, for developing a practice of awareness.

In our classrooms, then, we must be involved in the task of helping our students unmask and then hold the complexities inherent in our world. There are, obviously, many ways to do this. Historian James Loewen (2007) talks about the need to paint our national heroes and heroines as the complex people they are in order to help students move through the unrealistically one-dimensional portraits of people like Christopher Columbus and John Brown. When my students engage in the action project I mentioned earlier, often they write in their journals about their sense of guilt and shame around their own consumerism. I use those "confessions" to open a dialogue about the complexities that we hold, each of us, as we attempt to navigate an even more complex world.

In my last chapter, I will name this art of holding contradictions as one of the two or three things I know for sure as critical to the work of cultural transformation. Parker Palmer (2004, p. 174) describes this as learning to stand in the "tragic gap," "to hold the tension of opposites, trusting that the tension itself will pull our hearts and minds open to a third way of thinking and acting." He points out that all those known for their commitment to justice and love—his list includes the Dalai Lama, Aung San Suu Kyi, Nelson Mandela—have spent time in this gap, "torn between the world's reality and a vision of human possibility" (p. 179).

CONCLUSION

I have tried to show how three aspects of white supremacy culture—the right to profit, individualism, and the binary—work together to reinforce white supremacy. Our challenge as teachers is that we operate in schools that perpetuate and reinforce these cultural beliefs, assuming, as systems do, their essential necessity to our identity and survival as a people, a nation state, a western culture.

I have tried to show how the logical consequence of these cultural ideologies is harmful, not just to those on the bottom of the oppressive hierarchies established by western culture, but, as Lillian Smith so aptly points out at the beginning of this chapter, to all of us.

We can no longer afford to live like this.

I saw a documentary recently about the stories of the first astronauts shot into space to circle our earth (Copp & Kinsella, 2007). Each remarked on the feelings of awe they experienced seeing the earth as a singular globe slowly rotating in vast inky space. The breathtaking view led them to a spiritual understanding of our interconnectedness. I believe we are called now to learn to sit in the space that holds the tension of our specific identities and our global one, requiring an embrace of both rather than a rejection of either. Not only are we called, we are given a unique opportunity as the first generations to experience a globalization made possible by revolutionary technology allowing us to communicate with each other across national and geographic boundaries.

Our task as educators is to support our students in holding the fragile and essential contradiction of claiming our identities without using those claims to separate us from each other, or as Maalouf would say,

> everyone should be able to include in what he regards as his own identity a new ingredient, one that will assume more and more importance in the course of the new century and the new millennium: the sense of belonging to the human adventure as well as his own. (2000, pp. 163-164)

Before we can tackle the task we've set for ourselves, we must first address our tendency toward defensiveness and denial, our fear of seeing that the Emperor is actually quite naked. We have to address the most pernicious aspect of white supremacy culture—privileged resistance. White supremacy operates like the tailors in the folk tale, imbuing in our culture an aversion to seeing clearly. Whether we are the Emperor, or his messenger, or the townspeople, most of us have learned well to fear the consequences of unmasking the lies on which oppressive power depends. Understanding and addressing that fear is the subject of my next chapter.

Passover

My body feels heavy
with its longing
for liberation
from this familiar despair.

Fear pulses with each heartbeat.

Perhaps god
is visiting now
and
filling me with this pain.

Hush, she says.
You can hold this sorrow,
a prayer of sorts
as you sing your anguish
into the fearless winds.

—Tema Okun (January 2009)

CHAPTER 2

REFUSING TO SEE

Privileged Resistance

I attended high school in a small Southern college town during the period of federally mandated desegregation in the mid 1960s. Chapel Hill's approach to "integrating" its school system was to close the historically white and Black schools and transfer the students from both schools into a newly constructed building on the edge of town. This new school retained the name of the white school, Chapel Hill High, the name of the white school teams and the team mascot. The principal of the white school kept her position; Lincoln's principal was hired as the vice-principal. All of the white teachers moved into the "integrated" school, while the jobs of most of the Black teachers were terminated.

Needless to say, the Black students were unhappy, angry, and upset at this erasure of their Lincoln High school legacy and experience. They organized and staged sit-ins. White and Black students together organized a "race council," a structured time for us to meet in each others' homes and talk about what was happening.

One evening I hosted the race council at my house. We met in our basement, a sort of recreation room popular in suburban homes of that period. I have a strong memory of "talking" with a young man named Sylvester. He was shouting at me "you're racist!" I was shouting back, "no, I'm not!" "Yes, you are!" "No, I'm not!" Our "conversation" proceeded in

The Emperor Has No Clothes: Teaching About Race and Racism to People Who Don't Want to Know, pp. 33–71

this manner until a moment came when I told him I had to fetch the refreshments.

I went upstairs, where my mother was preparing the drinks and cookies. She turned to me and said, "Get a grip. You're a white girl, you grew up in a racist country, you're racist. Deal with it."

I have no memory of what happened next. I do not know if I went downstairs and admitted to Sylvester that I was, according to my mother, indeed a racist. I do know that in that instant, all the energy I had been using to deny my racism turned inward. I began to consider all the ways in which I might be racist. Thanks to this initial push from my mother, I've been considering this in one form or another ever since.

INTRODUCTION

Privileged resistance is the enactment of defensiveness and denial on the part of those sitting in positions of privilege to any acknowledgement of that privilege and the oppression that creates it. People's Institute trainer Monica Walker (2009) notes "how often people are fighting for the world as it is. The degree of resistance that we encounter is a true barometer of the degree of socialization," meaning simply that our resistance to seeing our conditioning is a reflection of that conditioning. Manifesting for the most part as defensiveness (the "no, I'm not" denials of a young white woman), privileged resistance is, in one form or another, denial based in fear. Fear is what we feel, denial is what we do, and defensiveness is how we do it.

Webster's dictionary defines denial as "a refusing to receive, believe, accept, or embrace, a rejection or refusing to acknowledge" (1972, p. 485). Milburn and Conrad define it as a "defense mechanism, an unconscious mental maneuver that cancels out or obscures painful reality" (1996, p. 1). According to Montada, denial "serves to protect against blame and punishment, self-blame and guilt feelings.... Basically, it is a strategy of defence" (2001, p. 79).

In this chapter, I explore the ways in which denial operates to preserve white supremacy. I focus on the resistance of white people, sitting in positions of unacknowledged privilege, who often do not want to consider how power and privilege operate both generally and in our lives. In the context of the workshop and the classroom, this privileged resistance shows up as everything from disengagement to disrespect for the material, the teacher, and sometimes organized campaigns to unseat both.

My attention is directed to the denials lodged in dominance or privilege; in other words I am going to look at how and why white people continue to deny the pervasive racism that is all around us, how this manifests in our classrooms, and what we can do about it. I will look at the ways our culture and institutions have promulgated denial and set the pattern for the denials that we engage in on a personal level. I will conclude with approaches that have worked for colleagues and for me in our attempts to address privileged resistance.

Like white supremacy and racism, denial happens on many levels—personal, institutional, and cultural. Denial's purpose is to encourage members of a culture to identify with the power elite and their agenda, an agenda we are socialized to believe is critical to our welfare and security, to the welfare and security of the group. The power elite disguises the ways in which their agenda harms us, the majority; they involve institutions and people in the maintenance and safeguarding of overt ignorance and a one-sided story telling about our shared history. In other words, they manufacture denial.

In the case of race and racism, we use denial to erase the fact that harm is being done to a group or a person based on race, that benefit accrues to a group or a person based on race, and that all are damaged. We deny in order to benefit, it is as simple as that.

As most social scientists now know, race is a social and political construct. Whiteness is a social and political construct as well. There is no white race; white skin is actually a biological mutation of a single DNA molecule out of a string of 1.3 billion (Wright & Stamm, 2006). The race construct was designed to safeguard the ladder referenced in chapter 1, defining whiteness as an entitlement to the top rungs, placing Black people at the bottom, with other communities of color ranged on the lower rungs in an ever-changing hierarchy (Barndt, 1991; Kivel, 2002; Okun & Jones, 2006). For example, where Arab-Americans used to be near the top, closest to white, after September 11, 2001, they fell precipitously close to the bottom, where they have remained ever since in the dominant culture association of all things Arab with "terrorist" and "terrorism."

While many participate in a denial of the existence of racism and privilege, the power of this racial construct is inescapable. Defined by the historical context in which it was created, the term "white" was developed by colonial landowners to unify indentured servants and poor European immigrants against African slaves and Indigenous and Native peoples (T. Allen, 1994; Feagin, 2000; I. F. H. López, 1996). Outnumbered by these two groups, whose servitude, labor and/or elimination was necessary for "progress" and development, the land-owning white men who controlled resources, political power, and the ability to create law began deliberately and incrementally bestowing rights and privileges on lower-class white people (with most of these rights going to white men) specifically to create a racial hierarchy that would keep groups with shared economic interests from working together, as had happened during a number of slave revolts in both Haiti and the Americas (T. Allen, 1994; Loewen, 2007; Zinn, 1980).

Robert Allen (1983), in his comprehensive look at social justice movements from abolitionism to populism to the suffrage and labor movements, notes how racism effectively split every effort by those who otherwise shared a common condition. This is the power of the race construct.

Taught by our culture that racism is simple race prejudice, most of us fail to see the potent mix of race prejudice supported by the power of institutions and culture that has privileged and continues to privilege white people at the expense of everyone else. I should note here that not all white people are privileged equally; obviously Bill Gates and Donald Trump have significantly more privilege than a single mother living in Appalachia. We are not one-dimensional human beings and our multiple identities influence where we sit in the intricate web of class, race, gender, and other constructs.

As the U.S. nation-state evolved, this construct has become more covert. So where 50 plus years ago, some areas of the country were visibly segregated as a legacy of Jim Crow racism, today institutional and cultural racism are still virulent but much less visible. Similarly, white identity has evolved from one that was publicly and enthusiastically embraced to one that is no less powerful but much less visible, even and particularly to those who hold it. The proof of this rests in the large numbers of white students who come into our classrooms convinced that because they harbor no racist intent, they cannot be racist and racism is not relevant in their lives.

George Lipsitz (1998, p. 216) explains how we manage to be individually "colorblind" while institutional and cultural racism persists. He cites the example of Franklin D. Roosevelt's New Deal, which

> contained no overt racial provisions, but the racialized categories in FHA appraisers' manuals and the denial of Wagner Act and Social Security coverage to farmworkers, domestics, teachers, librarians, and social workers made these measures systematic subsidies to white males at the expense of people of color and women.

Milburn and Conrad (1996, p. 159) point to polls showing that many white people actually believe that African Americans are "better off than whites" and only 38% of whites believe racism to be a significant problem in the United States today, in contrast to 68% of Blacks. Similarly, only 36% of whites believed that "past and present discrimination is the major reason for the economic and social ills blacks face," while 71% of Blacks believed this to be the case. The same survey found that 44% of whites believed that the average African American is "just as well off' as the average white person in terms of income." No Blacks indicated a belief in this statement. Similarly, a majority (51%) of whites believed that "the average African American is just as well off as the average white person in terms of jobs"; only 13% of Blacks agreed with this statement. A more recent poll by the Institute of Government and Public Affairs at the University of Illinois (2008) suggests that these perceptions persist; their data show "the trend is for fewer whites to acknowledge that African Americans are adversely affected by past and persistent discrimination" (Krysan & Faison, 2008, ¶4) while "African Americans are [still] more likely than whites to support race-targeted policies [and] . . . to a much greater extent likely to perceive that African Americans face substantial structural barriers in American society" (¶5).

Lipsitz claims these perceptions reflect a "paradoxical and nettling combination of racism and disavowal" (1998, p. 215) that keeps racism in place. These perceptions obviously have no basis in reality. Any number of indicators show that racism is alive and well. While the income divide income between whites and People of Color has narrowed, the "racial wealth gap still looms large" (Leondar-Wright, 2006). According to *United for a Fair Economy*, "The gap in wealth between white families and black or Hispanic families remains huge. The percentage of black or Hispanic households with zero or negative net worth (greater debt than assets) is twice as high as for white households" (Leondar-Wright, 1999). Research continues to show that African Americans are "more likely to be arrested than whites ... [and] racism among a core of police officers is pervasive in this country" (Milburn & Conrad, 1996, p. 162). In fact, one study shows that a significant number of police officers connect race with inclination towards criminal behavior (p. 162). As cultural critic Derrick Jensen notes, our country "imprisons black men nine times more frequently than it does whites and four times more than South Africa did during apartheid" (2002, p. 22) while "over 30% of this nation's African American males between the ages of 20 and 29 are under criminal supervision" (p. 22). These numbers make "clear that the judicial and penal systems have achieved the segregation of black males—into prisons—on a scale of which the KKK and their puny brethren could only dream" (p. 7). I could offer many examples, all making the point that while many white people, and even some People of Color, believe the United States offers a "level playing field" (to use popular lexicon), in fact the legacy of institutional and cultural racism is pervasive and intransigent.

How is it possible for so many people to believe that racism no longer exists while the evidence of its virulence is obvious to those who make an effort to see? As I said earlier, this is how the white supremacy race construct works—to reinforce denial both that race is constructed and that it has contemporary relevance. As one of my white students writes at the end of a semester, "I have learned that I have grown up with a very narrow view of race. Without even realizing it, I have stereotypes for different races that I hold onto and judge others by." Another white student says "I never considered myself racist but after this class I did learn that the views I had on some things were racist. I was so oblivious to the fact that racism is not just racial slurs, but it is the way we judge, think, and talk about others." They are simply expressing what is true for most of us, particularly those of us in the white group (and note how they are simply acknowledging their own attitudes, not the systemic nature of racism).

PRIVILEGED RESISTANCE

Shortly after World War II, a French reporter asked expatriate Richard Wright for his views about the "Negro problem" in America. The author replied, "There isn't any Negro problem; there is only a white problem." By inverting the reporter's question, Wright called attention to its hidden assumptions—that racial polarization comes from the existence of Blacks rather than from the behavior of whites, that Black people are a "problem" for whites rather than fellow citizens entitled to justice, and that, unless otherwise specified, "Americans" means "whites" (Lipsitz, 1998, p. 1).

Most of us in the white group, like my students above, do not understand ourselves as privileged. This denial of the ways in which we benefit by belonging to the white group is a central denial of the race construct. As Robert Terry so aptly said, "to be white in America is not to have to think about it" (Barndt, 1991, p. 51).

Ironically, or perhaps in keeping with the construct, much has been written about students, usually poor, Black and Brown, who "drop out," "act out" (as those in power would say), and refuse to cooperate with institutions well practiced in disregard and mistreatment. Federal, state, and local programs abound, all attempting to engage "at-risk" students who are perceived and labeled as "deficit," "other," "less than." Recently the literature has begun to acknowledge that these students are not just "failing," they are also resisting that which any sane person would—an institution of education aligned with a culture that has made clear in multiple ways how they are not valued (Books, 2007; Gause, 2008).

Less explored are the ways in which students who are valued by the culture also resist, particularly as classrooms become sites of analysis where they are asked to think about their positions of dominance. Also ignored are the ways in which we need to focus our attention on the dominant group as a site of change; the assumption is that we have "a Negro problem," not, as Richard Wright so aptly notes, that the actual trouble resides with the white group.

This is not a simple binary; students with margin identities can also resist an analysis of power and privilege. Because assimilation generally requires the adoption of dominant culture thinking, many if not most of us are capable of resisting the realities of race, gender, class, and other oppressive constructs. While People of Color might not assimilate dominant culture values and beliefs in the same way and to the same degree as white people (Bonilla-Silva, 2006, p. 152), they still have to "accommodate their views vis-à-vis that ideology." Also, not all students sitting in positions of privilege resist. Many actually "welcome engagement and become willing to explore the sources of systemic oppression even when this means they must consider their own accountability and complicity" (Applebaum, 2007, pp. 337-338).

And yet every teacher deals with privileged resistance of some kind and, in the worst cases, resistant students can derail a classroom altogether.

A STAGE OF DEVELOPMENT

I imagine one of the reasons people cling to their hates so stubbornly is because they sense, once hate is gone, they will be forced to deal with pain.

—James Baldwin

I remember attending a dismantling racism workshop in the Bay area; in the final hour, when we were sharing our reflections, one middle-aged white woman honestly and bravely said that it was the first time in her life she had realized that not all Black people want to be white.

During my years as a facilitator of anti-racism workshops, my fellow trainers and I developed an identity "ladder" (adapted from work done by Janet Helms, 1990 and Rita Hardiman, 1994) indicating the different stages that white people go through in our development toward anti-racist activism in a racist culture (Okun, 2006). Many educators and race theorists reference the stages that people go through as they move from socialized assumptions into a more informed understanding of the race construct. Griffin outlines stages of anger, immobilization, distancing, and conversion (1997, pp. 295-298). Tatum writes extensively about her application of racial identity development theory in the classroom in her classic text *Why All the Black Kids Are Sitting Together in the Cafeteria* (1992).

In all these white identity development theories, privileged resistance is presented as a conditioned response to "the moment when students (or indeed any of us) [are] confronted with 'seeing race' and the ways in which some racialised positions are privileged over others; when it [is] no longer possible for [us] to pretend that 'race does not matter'" (Aveling, 2002, p. 126). As such, privileged resistance is an unavoidable stage in our personal development.

In the identity ladder that dRworks developed (Okun & Jones, 2006), the stage of denial and defensiveness comes as we move from what we call the "be like me" stage, so directly articulated by the woman at the workshop. This stage reflects that of disintegration in the Hardiman model, although her model talks about denial as a response to discomfort rather than as a distinct stage in and of itself.

Asking white students to move from their grounding in "be like me" is asking them, as Diane Goodman (2007, ¶1) states, to "question their fundamental belief systems—how they see themselves and make sense of the world." As the story of cultural and institutional denial shows, we should not be surprised when students resist. We have all been well taught "to view dominant groups as normal and superior, to accept the unearned material benefits awarded to those groups, and to blame victims for their misfortune" (¶4). Our personal denials are an individualized reflection of our cultural denials.

As white people begin to notice racial difference, we assume the difference is benign as long as "they," "the other," are essentially like me or want to be like me (Okun, 2006). To the extent that People of Color do not want to "be like me," we experience them as deficient or threatening or both (to the extent that they do not want to be like me, there is something wrong with them), invisible (I do not see any difference, we are the same), or exotic (their difference is fascinating to me but otherwise insignificant or to be exploited). In this stage, we sometimes assume the role of "tour guide" to the dominant culture, trying to help People of Color better assimilate because we assume this is what they want. We are not aware of this assumption (or others like it) because we also believe that our worldview is universal (everyone thinks like we do).

We move from "be like me" to denial when something happens that forces us to see ourselves as part of a dominant group that gets benefits from systemic racism, sexism, classism or other constructs of advantage (Okun, 2006). At some point, we are forced to acknowledge the significance of racial difference, usually through the depth of an emerging relationship or by witnessing undeniable racism.

As we begin to be confronted with not just the realities of racism, but the ways in which racism privileges our lives, we often become angry because of our deep socialization into individualism (see chapter 1). We don't want to be "lumped in" with the white group. As Tatum (1997, p. 104) notes, when white men and women begin to understand that they are viewed as members of a dominant racial group not only by other whites but also by people of color, they are sometimes troubled, even angered, to learn that simply because of their group status they are viewed with suspicion by many people of color. "I'm an individual, view me as an individual!"

Once we understand that racism is systemic, we are forced to face the fact that privilege is systemic as well, and we begin to sense that perhaps we do not deserve and did not earn what we have (Kivel, 2002; Okun, 2006; olsson, 1997; Tatum, 1997). As a result, we find it even more difficult to identify as part of the white group, since to admit group privilege erases our already inflated sense of individuality. At the same time, we see ourselves as less prejudiced than other white people, presenting an interesting contradiction. We want to be seen as different from (and better than) the very white group that we do not acknowledge. Because we believe that racism is lodged in intentional individual thoughts or behaviors, and we refuse to admit such intent, we tend to take accusations of racism very personally (and react to such accusations with great defensiveness).

Tatum notes this is the point where we often "deny the validity of the information being presented or psychologically or physically withdraw from it" (1997, p. 98). In other words, we revert to the privileged resistance behaviors described above. For example, we may believe that too much attention is placed on cultural differences or that People of Color are "overly sensitive." When we do admit that racism is happening, we want to see it as an isolated incident of malevolent intent by "bad" people and refuse to admit that we might be engaged in perpetuating institutional and cultural racism ourselves.

As we move beyond our denial, we return to it again and again whenever anything happens to make us feel vulnerable and/or attacked for being white (Okun, 2006). This might happen, for example when we meet a Person of Color in a stage of rage or exclusion/immersion (reflecting a stage on their identity development ladder) who does not want to deal with us simply because we are white.

Tatum (1997) notes that how students decide to respond to a growing awareness of the power inequities built into the race construct will determine how they move to the next stage (reintegration or pseudo-independent in the Helms model, guilt and shame in the dRworks model). One price of moving on is the inevitable feelings of guilt and shame that come with acknowledging racism, privilege, and internalized white supremacy (Okun, 2006). This is an easy place for people and communities to get stuck. In fact, I argue that one of the reasons individuals and our culture as a whole are stuck in denial and defensiveness is because we fear the guilt and shame that are inevitable once we admit the pervasive toxicity of racism.

My point is that, at its best, privileged resistance is an inevitable stage of development that those of us sitting in positions of privilege must move through in our desire and efforts to be both effectively engaged and fully human. At worst, privileged resistance is a way of life. To get a better understanding of how we, as teachers and facilitators, can support the former, I offer a closer look at the elements of privileged resistance and how we might successfully address them.

ASPECTS OF DENIAL

In chapter 1, I cover the ways in which profit at all costs, individualism, and the binary serve and maintain white supremacy culture. Denial is the behavior that allows these beliefs and values to remain unchallenged. Privileged resistance arises when we are asked to abandon the denial that allows us to live in ignorance of our own privilege and the ways it shapes our lives at the expense of whole groups of people. If we want to understand the roots of resistance, it behooves us to understand a bit more about the dynamics of denial, both historically and psychosocially.

SILENCING AND SHIFTING

According to legend, when King Boabdil, the last Moorish king, received word that his capital city of Alhama was about to be lost, he burned the letter containing the news and beheaded the messenger.

—Milburn and Conrad (1996, p. 13)

When working with white people in the classroom or in a workshop setting, I am often accused of creating a problem where none previously existed. "Why" one or two people might ask, "are you raising issues of racism; we all got along fine until you started to talk about it?" Even when faced with the stories of Friends or Colleagues of Color about the impact of racism, many white people prefer to believe that the problem is not that racism is present, but that it is being discussed. The assumption is that if we don't talk about racism, then it doesn't exist. Like King Boabdil, we prefer to kill the messenger.

Cultural gatekeepers—the makers and purveyors of popular culture, the media, those who decide what is in our textbooks and what is left out—have always used denial to render invisible that which the power elite does not want us to see or know. Our history is replete with examples. Sometimes oppression is rendered invisible by actually keeping it secret; more often, though, injustice is rendered invisible through a shift in focus.

For a case in point, Howard Zinn explains in *A People's History of the United States* (1980, p. 8), that "to emphasize the heroism of Columbus and his successors as navigators and discoverers, and to deemphasize their genocide, is ... an ideological choice." Dominant culture narratives serve to reinforce a story of Columbus as a brave explorer; we celebrate one man's "discovery," offering a binary portrayal of his individual accomplishments as heroic while keeping silent about the complexities of a man who initiated the Atlantic slave trade and the extinction of a whole community of indigenous peoples (the Arawak/Tainos of Hispaniola). One of the ways we understand the power of our socialization is the level of defensiveness that arises when any attempt is made to shed Columbus in a more complex light; the mainstream response is a vociferous protest in the binary belief that if Columbus cannot be portrayed as good, then he must be bad, and to admit such a thing is intolerable to the patriotic impulse.

Educator Svi Shapiro (2006) makes a similar point in his reflections on how we teach about Hitler and the Holocaust. Shapiro notes that our tendency toward individualism keeps the focus on Hitler as the personification of evil, leaving invisible all of the Germans who participated either overtly or passively in the extermination of over 11 million people. In this way, we fail to investigate the complexities of how "normal" people like us can participate in mass murder. Nor do we examine why we "never developed toward the Germans the same kind of mercilessness we developed towards the Japanese" (Jensen, 2002, p. 196), allowing German prisoners of war to venture out of their camp in Tule Lake, California, while disenfranchising thousands of Japanese-Americans, most of them American citizens, from their property, their livelihoods, and forcing them to live in enclosed camps behind barbed wire.

James Loewen, in his revelatory book *Lies My Teacher Told Me* (2007), documents how we continue to teach history in a two-dimensional way; his analysis of the history textbooks most used in our high school classrooms shows how these books simply avoid mention of topics, like the Vietnam War, that are too disturbing to the dominant group ideology. Milburn and Conrad (1996, p. 194) contrast this with the curriculum in Germany, where students are required to study World War II.

Loewen (2007, pp. 240-249) notes that textbooks obscure Vietnam not only by devoting little space to it but also by excluding the most provocative and memorable photographic images of the war. They ignore completely the issues involved—such as why the United States fought in Vietnam—and omit mention of some of the most troubling aspects of the war, such as the My Lai massacre. Publishers of these books choose inoffensive, bland photographs, such as the troops cheering President Johnson, and fail to include images that are widely familiar to those who lived through the war years: for example, the photo showing a terrified young girl fleeing naked from a napalm attack or the picture of a Buddhist monk protesting the U.S./South Vietnamese alliance by incinerating himself on a Saigon street corner. The authors of high school texts are cautious in describing how the war originated and how the United States became involved; in fact, they simply ignore those issues altogether.

In the classroom, this kind of silencing has done its damage; students arrive deeply ignorant about racism and its role in our nation's history as well as deeply conditioned in the belief that racism is a purely individual dynamic requiring specific intent. To counter the impact of this silencing requires that we offer students a process for investigating and understanding the structural and cultural aspects of racism using relevant "course materials that make the best case for our subject matter, … that present gender, race, social class, and other dimensions of inequality as structural inequalities that relate to power differentials in society" (Higginbotham, 1996).

MARGINALIZING

Another form of silencing, one in which our students actively participate, is the marginalization of those who speak up to challenge the dominant discourse and/or the power elite, threatening their carefully crafted denial. This marginalization can be both personal and institutional.

Loewen (2007, p. 173) traces the official marginalization of the story of abolitionist John Brown, who is alternately portrayed by American history textbooks as insane or sane, reflecting "an inadvertent index of the level of white racism in our society." One 2006 textbook uses words like "fanatical" and "obsessively dedicated to the abolitionist cause," claiming Brown "hack[ed] to pieces" five men (p. 174). The language, in addition to being inaccurate (no hacking occurred) communicates the idea that "those who fought for black equality had to be wrongheaded" (p. 174). In fact, Loewen argues, John Brown knew what he was about; Brown wrote his contemporary Frederick Douglass that "the venture would make a stunning impact even if it failed" (p. 177). Brown spoke to the court before receiving his death sentence saying "had I so interfered in behalf of the rich, the powerful, it would have been all right" (p. 178).

Loewen takes the reader through a thoughtful analysis of the depiction of this man, showing us how historical inaccuracies, physical and verbal imagery were used to suggest both overtly and covertly that he was "insane" and his "actions made no sense" (p. 177), for how else to explain a white man who would take up arms and risk his life in an attempt to create a world free of slavery?

While certainly not the same as a government death sentence, a contemporary manifestation of this marginalization is the way in which white people hurl accusations of "playing the race card" or labels of "politically correct" to shut down difficult conversations about the ways in which racism is showing up in an organization or community. We need only to turn on the television to Fox News, CNN, Glenn Beck, Lou Dobbs, to see how white opinion shapers are actively engaged in playing their own race card in an orchestrated attempt to undermine the credibility of our first African American president.

I have witnessed time and again how white leaders of social justice organizations protest when racism is named, focusing organizational anger at those who raise the issue (the proverbial messenger) rather than address what is being raised (the message). In a similar vein, students or workshop participants may focus on the teacher, the facilitator, claiming we are biased, too one-sided, too "personally involved to be 'objective'" (Griffin, 1997, p. 293).

As Elizabeth Higginbotham (1996) notes, "even one vocal student can change the dynamics of a class even though the majority of students are willing or even eager to learn the new material." She makes the point that these are often students who feel extremely "secure in [their] privilege" and, as a result, assume their right "to challenge faculty and take up other students' time with his or her protests during the class." Colleague Gita Gulati-Partee (personal correspondence, August 11, 2009) notes how these students show they are "secure in their privilege and insecure about it at the same time." She says these instances show that "when privilege gets pinched, it punches back." While the form or content of the protest may differ, the purpose of the protest is to marginalize the speaker, the lesson, the point being made, to interrupt the challenge to dominant discourse.

Still another manifestation of marginalization is those students who marginalize themselves, resisting in silence, often "accentuated by such defensive posture as arms folded across the chest, caps pulled down over eyes, or focusing on non-class related reading or other activities" (Griffin, 1997, p. 294). Although not as overtly disruptive as vocal resistance, this silent version can be just as potent. I notice, for example, that this kind of resistance makes me aware that I have to be careful not to let my own fears about what the student is feeling and thinking derail me from attempts to involve her in active participation in the class.

Students also silence themselves, not as an act of resistance, but out of fear of the attack that lies in wait from classmates, friends, family when and if they speak up. I remember one day at the end of a class where all the students had left but one young white woman. She was sitting quietly, her whole body communicating distress. When I asked her to tell me what was wrong, she responded by sharing that she was enjoying the class, even though what she was learning was disturbing to her. She was distressed, she said, because she understood her relationship to racism in new ways but didn't have any idea how she was going to share her new awareness with her family. She was feeling deeply the fear of losing family and friends who could easily threaten to withdraw their love and approval if she was to insist on acknowledging racism, both personally and generally. Beverly Daniel Tatum offers stories about white students who go home for holiday breaks and "suddenly they are noticing the racist content of jokes or comments of their friends and relatives and will try to confront them, often only to find that their efforts are, at best, ignored or dismissed as a 'phase,' or, at worst, greeted with open hostility" (1992, p. 14).

I struggle with both the dynamic of the highly vocal resistant student(s) in my classrooms and workshops as well as those who silence themselves, whether from fear of isolation or as their own form of resistance. Vocal resistance can be tricky; as Higginbotham (1996) points out, "the open questioning or challenging of the premise of the course or information that is presented as facts or the truth ... should not be confused with having a difference of opinion with the teacher." Nado Aveling (2002) talks about what happens when she attempts to teach the vocally resistant student and produces her own enactment of silencing in her attempts to counter those "who became angry at what they perceive as [her] 'bending over backwards' to accommodate minority group perspectives" (p. 125). She reflects on her desire to avoid muzzling students while questioning how to maintain her "responsibility to silence individual students in the interests of students as a group" (p. 128).

We face two challenges—the first that we may mistake vocal resistance for genuine questioning and the second that we may focus on vocal resistance at the expense of other students and/or without recognizing other forms that don't require so much of our attention.

The vocally disruptive students resisting out of their own privilege are abusing the inclusive nature of the progressive classroom while assuming or even insisting on the idea that all opinions have equal value regardless of how ill informed or baseless those opinions might be. Their claims of bias would never be leveled against teachers who share their politic or a curriculum they assume is "objective" or "neutral" in its support of dominant cultural norms.

One of the ways I deal with this is to make clear early in the semester that neither teaching nor knowledge are "neutral," that my experience with the issues we are about to discuss is extremely wide and deep. I explain to my students that I am asking them to use the semester to seriously consider what I have to offer and after they leave the classroom, they can accept or reject as they wish. With this frame, I do not have to defend my "right" to present the material and analysis that I do.

We must learn to negotiate the tender line between active engagement and resistance while at the same time acknowledging the very real consequences for those who fear their own isolation from friends and family. We also have to seek out the thoughts and feelings of those who attempt to disengage, either by calling on them in class, asking for and responding to reflection papers, organizing regular paired and small group activities where they are forced to engage with other students. I give specific examples of how to do this in Chapter Four.

TRIVIALIZING

Another way to silence or marginalize is to trivialize. Paul Kivel references what he calls "minimization," describing it as how white people "play down the damage" with claims that "racism isn't a big problem anymore" and "it's not that bad" (Okun & Jones, 2006, p. 36). Jim Elder describes this as the "racism isn't the only problem" phenomenon where white people assume or insist "that racism is only a facet of a larger problem" (p. 37); in classes and workshops, for examples, many people argue that class oppression is the "real" problem and our focus should be on that. While in some cases, students make this claim from a sophisticated analysis of racism as one component of an even larger system of intersecting oppressions, most are arguing for a different focus in order to distract from the an investigation they know will make them uncomfortable.

When racism *is* acknowledged, people trivialize by portraying it as an isolated circumstance embodied by mean-spirited individuals or "crazy" fringe groups. So, for example, they characterize the Ku Klux Klan (KKK) as "buffoons," enabling the group to "acknowledge the existence of racism while pretending it is equal to unsophistication and stupidity" (Jensen, 2002, p. 36). In fact, serious scholars of the Klan knows that in their heyday, they included "sheriffs, magistrates, jurors, and legislators, … clerks and judges. In some counties … the Ku-Klux and their friends comprise[d] more than half of the influential and voting population" (p. 36).

While the KKK is not as integrated into mainstream power as it once was, our media and opinion makers do still focus on individual racist acts as aberrance while ignoring systemic evidence. For example, they discuss at length the deviance of the three young white men who tied James Byrd, a Black man, to the back of their truck and dragged him to a horrible death while remaining silent about the government sponsored involuntary and coercive sterilization of thousands of American Indian women in the 1970s or the contemporary exploitation of migrant farmworkers whose working conditions leave them with an average lifespan of 49 years (Jensen, 2002, p. 378). Our insistence on racism as individual deviance trivializes its systemic and pervasive nature.

Pat Griffin, in her reflection on facilitating social justice courses, offers a variation of this dynamic where students "focus on an identity in which they are members of the targeted group" (1997, p. 293)—for example when white women want to talk about sexism or a white person who is poor or working class wants to talk about the centrality of class—to avoid acknowledging their race privilege. People's Institute for Survival and Beyond founder Ron Chisom calls this "escapism," stating that people bring up other issues in an attempt to avoid or escape dealing with the issue of racism.

This is how a conspiracy of silence works. It does not require three men closeted in a private room making plans. People socialized to focus on individual behavior while ignoring the big picture, acting out of conditioned fear of an unsanctioned point of view, leads us to silence, marginalize, and trivialize any counter narrative, even at times our own.

Cultural critic Derrick Jensen suggests that "if the first rule of a dysfunctional system is 'Don't talk about it,' then our primary goal should be to tell the truth, to be as honest as we can manage to be" (2002, pp. 140-141). Every semester, I show my students a documentary about the My Lai massacre (Sim & Bilton, 1989) as a precursor to a discussion about the complexities attached to issues of obedience and critical thinking. The documentary offers a searingly honest and sometimes graphic portrayal of the day in 1972 when Charlie Company, under the command of Lieutenant William Calley, entered an unarmed village and slaughtered the men, women, and children living there. Most of my students respond with dismay, having never been asked to contemplate the costs of any war up close, much less the one in Vietnam. And to their great credit, many are angry, wondering why they have never been told about this incident or others like it, wondering why they do not know their own history.

Teaching history is my strategy of choice when trying to address resistance and denial based in silencing, marginalizing, and trivializing. I have found that if I teach about racism and privilege as historically constructed, it helps students understand that they are situated within a larger context, bigger and more significant than their individual attitudes. It also helps them understand how the way we see the world is shaped both by our shared history and how we have been (mis)taught that history.

I also try to make my classrooms a "safer" space for students to experience and express their fears about their own marginalization as they begin to take the ideas they are learning out into the world of their friends and family. One way I do this is to stress that an analysis is not the same as a strategy, that understanding, for example, how and why a faucet is broken is not the same as figuring out how to fix it. I learned the importance of this point when I realized that some workshop participants were communicating their newfound understanding of their own racism to friends and family without any context, receiving, not surprisingly, tremendous resistance to their pronouncements.

I am also learning to make space for students to talk about what happens when they share what they're learning in class with friends and family. Sometimes it is enough to just let people talk with each other about it; at other times we strategize a range of responses. As I talk about in later chapters, I try to be clear that a more comprehensive understanding of racism and oppression does not require that students reject, dislike, or hate those who do not share it.

RATIONALIZING ENTITLEMENT

Another way the power elite manufactures denial is to temper any responsibility for oppressive policies and practices with a rationale for what would otherwise be considered unacceptable. The rationalization essentially embedded in the white supremacy construct is a belief in our own (white) superiority.

An ideology of superiority is a binary; for one to be superior requires another to be inferior. Our country's belief in "manifest destiny," articulated in the early 1800s in the Monroe Doctrine and integral to contemporary foreign policy, is a classic example of this belief. We assume that our "higher" values based in an idealized capitalism and democracy proffer justification for the taking of land, the launching of wars, the manipulation of economies. At the same time we conveniently disregard the intense harm resulting from policies that consider whole communities of people as less evolved and therefore exploitable, expendable, and/or invisible.

Derrick Jensen, whose book *The Culture of Make Believe* (2002), is a lengthy recounting of the historic and contemporary ways in which white culture and people have rationalized race hatred, references an 1823 court decision written by U.S. Supreme Court Chief Justice John Marshall. Marshall asserted the rights of white settlers over those of the indigenous Cherokee whose treaties were being abrogated at an alarming rate. He claimed that "conquest gives a title which the Courts of the conqueror cannot deny, whatever the private and speculative opinions of the individuals may be" (2002, p. 12). In this way, the highest court of the land rationalized the superior rights of whites at the expense of an entire community of Indigenous people on the basis of entitlement. The ruling laid the groundwork for Georgia to sponsor a lottery giving white citizens title to Cherokee property.

From our position of assumed superiority, we rationalize our oppressive behavior by claiming that those on the receiving end are better off than they would have been otherwise. Historically, for example, proponents of slavery claimed that enslaved people led good lives because, like any property, they were well cared for (Milburn & Conrad, 1996). Advocates of slavery also maintained that slavery taught valuable skills like "discipline, cleanliness, and a conception of moral standards" (p. 153). These ideas are not outdated; on a recent vacation to Hawai'i, the white innkeeper informed us in all seriousness that the now elderly Japanese residents on the island had developed a good work ethic because of their experience picking coffee in the fields as young children, earning 5¢ a day. Gulati-Partee relates how she has "heard more often than you can imagine" the rationale that slavery "saved [the enslaved] from being eaten by lions in the African jungle" (personal correspondence, August 11, 2009).

Our history is replete with these stories of leaders and institutions rationalizing the unspeakable out of a sense of superiority justified in its turn by religious teaching, scientific reasoning, the courts, the political system, and, of course, the schools. One of the reasons racism is so systemically pernicious is because every institution in the country participated in its rationalization (Allen, 1974; Feagin, 2000; Kivel, 2002; Okun & Jones, 2006). This white supremacy ideology was (and continues to be) explained as a manifestation of the duty of the "civilized" western man to bring his wisdom and higher level thinking to the untamed "savage."

I teach in departments of social work and education; both institutions promulgate an underlying assumption that the goal is to integrate the deficit, inferior other into a superior whiteness. The story of the desegregation of my high school that opened this chapter is a classic example of both a widespread cultural assumption about the desirability of providing not just resources but also a higher standing to a whole community of people whose cultural capital was considered negligible if not completely deficit. One of my African American high school classmates, Walter Durham (2001), recalls entering the newly "integrated" school to see a trash bin filled with the trophies that used to stand in a case in the main hall of the historically Black Lincoln High, a visual testament to the (lack of) value attached to the Black students.

Claims of superiority are also used to justify the exploitation of the "other" for financial gain. So, for example, those who transported people from Africa in the holds of ships justified the inhumane conditions in the belief they should "maximize revenue" regardless of the consequences to their human cargo (Jensen, 2002, p. 74). The descriptions of what those men, women, and children endured are horrific—a ship built to hold 451 people would carry more than 600, leaving the "floor of their rooms ... so covered with the blood and mucus which had proceeded from them in consequence of the flux [i.e., diarrhea], that it resembled a slaughter-house" (p. 75). Those enslaved on these ships would often try to jump overboard rather than withstand such conditions, although the monetary loss this represented led the shipowners to try and prevent these suicides. Those who attempted to kill themselves by refusing to eat "had their mouths forcibly opened, or failing that, had their lips burned with hot coals" (p. 75).

Men could do this to other men, women, and children by creating a belief system that the people they were enslaving were not human. As I point out in Chapter One, these acts and the beliefs that support them occur because "people ... value money, value property, over living beings" (Jensen, 2002, p. 93). This white supremacy love of money over people remains virulently strong today.

Derrick Jensen tells the story of Lawrence Summers, currently Director of President Obama's National Economic Council, who in 1991 was the chief economist for the World Bank. Summers wrote a memo that year, later leaked to environmental activists, in which he argued that "the economic logic behind dumping a load of toxic waste in the lowest wage country is impeccable and we should face up to that.... I've always thought that under-populated countries in Africa are vastly under-polluted" (2002, p. 124).

The rationale that allows Summers to believe in the wisdom of dumping toxic wastes on already poor people and their countries not only requires an erasure or demonization of those we do not want to consider human but brings us back to our belief in our own superiority, the conviction that we, the insider group, are qualified to decide what is in the best interests of people we don't even know. Beverly Daniel Tatum (1997, pp. 118-122) describes this paradoxical twist of logic as aversive racism. She notes that contemporary racism is not so much the belief that People of Color are less than or worse but that white people are better. The consequences of this belief are that discriminatory hiring practices continue, not because of overt discrimination ("we don't hire Black people") but because the overriding assumption is that white people are more competent, even when the evidence suggests otherwise.

An end note: a Brazilian environmental secretary who responded critically both to what Summers wrote and to the World Bank for supporting it was subsequently fired, while Summers became secretary of the treasury under President Clinton and then president of Harvard University. We see how these rationales and denials interweave and intersect; the racist language and thinking of a highly placed and respected member of the power elite is unremarked as he continues in his "legitimate" leadership. At the same time, we witness the media pointing the finger at Sonia Soto-mayor, President Obama's nominee (since confirmed) for the Supreme Court, for having the "audacity" to state in a speech that "our experiences as women and People of Color affect our decisions" (Davis, 2009, p. 3A). This is how the dominant narrative operates to support the racist entitle-ment of a white member of the power elite while calling to question a rather obvious truth offered by a Woman of Color.

BLAMING THE VICTIM

Early in 2006, a young man, Muslim, recent public university graduate, deliberately drove his SUV into a public area of the university with the stated intent to kill students and "avenge the deaths of Muslims around the world" (Associated Press, 2006).

What's both fascinating and disturbing about this incident (beyond the act itself) is the public reaction—one set of students called on the univer-sity to brand this young man a terrorist; another invoked the need for patience and tolerance. The focus of the dialogue, as framed by the media, was not curiosity about what might lead the man to this act. The focus was on whether or not he should be tagged with the "terrorist" label. Here is an example of the power of culture makers to reduce a com-plex situation to a false binary.

Jackson Katz, an activist and scholar on the construction of masculinity, notes how the story changes when the perpetrators are white men. He points to the string of school shootings in the last 2 decades, all commit-ted by young, white boys (Ericsson & Talreja, 2002). He notes how the media chooses to characterize these incidents as "kids killing kids." As a result, the race and gender of these young men goes unremarked, no allu-sions to terrorism are made.

As members of the dominant culture, the privileged race and gender of these young white male killers remain unexamined; they avoid any demonizing generalizations. When People of Color transgress social norms, white supremacy culture takes the behavior of a few and attributes it to the whole, allowing the entire group to be blamed for the behaviors of an errant minority. Over and over again we see the rogue behavior of a Person of Color reflect on their racial group while countless episodes of criminal behavior by young white boys, white politicians and corporate CEOs have no similar consequences for the white group.

Morton (2004, chapter 2) argues that this habit of stereotyping, this obsession with how to label the young Muslim student, reflects a desire to make the targets extremely "other," foreign, separate so that we can characterize them as so different from us that we can respond to them however we choose while feeling morally justified and righteous about our choices.

This blaming the victim, claiming they are "inferior or dangerous" (Montada, 2001, p. 83) and thus deserving of their fate, is another form of denial. If the goal is to defend against responsibility, one way we do this is to position those for whom we might otherwise bear responsibility in ways that make it easier for us to justify our treatment of them (p. 81). Milburn and Conrad (1996, pp. 4-5) note "not surprisingly, once people come to believe that a particular group—African Americans, women, gays—are bad, they find it acceptable to take out their rage against these convenient scapegoats." Once a group has been vilified, "acting out one's rage against them becomes acceptable and logical" (p. 92).

Fear plays a role here. The irony is that while the psychological and physical harm done to People of Color by white people and the white group is historically overwhelming, the fear that white people feel toward People of Color, who have been and continue to be portrayed as dangerous and untrustworthy, is largely "manufactured and used to justify repression and exploitation" (Kivel, 2002, p. 53).

Because the U.S. has been so successful at demonizing Arabs as terrorists, we remain essentially silent about policies and practices that we would not tolerate if we were the targets. For example, the publicity surrounding torture at Abu Ghraib initially spiked attention because torture offends our general sensibilities, yet the outrage was limited in duration as we became distracted and moved onto other things, leaving the practice essentially uninterrupted. The attitude seems to be that we cannot be too concerned about torture because we do not identify with those being tortured; they remain inherently "other." We currently find ourselves engaged in a public discussion where many among the power elite are taking the position that torture can be justified in the name of safety and security ("Scaring Americans," 2008), an argument presented as credible. [An end note: the Obama administration has since rendered the policy of torture illegal.]

Milburn and Conrad offer another contemporary example by citing the popularity of Hernstein and Murray's book *The Bell Curve*, which essentially argues that disparities between white and Black people in the U.S. are genetic and as such, cannot be socially remedied (1996, p. 154). This book, published in the mid-90s, received intense media attention, making it a national bestseller. The multiple responses to the book by respected academics, contesting both the research methods and conclusions, received virtually no notice. The theory of genetically based inferiority remained essentially unchallenged in the popular culture, leaving intact the widespread assumption that People of Color are responsible for their experience of systemic discrimination.

Olsson and Johnson both point to the strategy of blaming the victim as a key tactic of denial. Olsson (1997, pp. 8-9) notes that blaming the victim successfully draws attention from the real problem, which is racism, making the people and/or institutions responsible for racism invisible. Johnson (2006) adds that by blaming the victim, those causing the problem divert attention from themselves in the process of attacking those already hurt. We saw this in the aftermath of Hurricane Katrina in New Orleans, when the poorest of the poor, majority Black, were blamed by the news media and public for not evacuating before the storm, even though their overwhelming poverty and lack of resources made it virtually impossible for them to access transportation in order to leave.

American Buddhist Pema Chödrön (1997, p. 81) says that we blame others to "protect our hearts" from whatever might be painful, so we can feel better without realizing that we do so not only at the expense of those we blame but our own. She explains that blame "keeps us from communicating genuinely with others, and we fortify it with our concepts of who's right and who's wrong." We essentially attack that which we fear in the belief that doing so makes us safe, more "solid," more "right" (as opposed to wrong, which is what links this fear to the binary that I talk about in chapter 1).

One way to address this trained tendency to blame the victim is to humanize those we position as "other." Using film, YouTube clips, first person accounts, guest speakers, and story telling, I try and make sure that my students hear the complex and rich narratives of people targeted by racist oppression. Because conditioned racist thinking depends on stereotypes where people are presented as less than human, fleshing out the complexity of oppressed people and communities goes a long way to moving people through a "blame the victim" mentality.

This has to be done with some care. As Nado Aveling (2002) points out in her reflections on teaching white students about Aboriginal people and culture in Australia, her students' enthusiasm about what they are learning does not necessarily reflect "a great shift in consciousness from a paternalistic 'wanting to help those less fortunate' than themselves—who are essentially 'the same under the skin'—to examining their own position of privilege" (p. 125). She notes how "by and large, white hegemony remained unchallenged and the tendency to romanticise Aboriginal students and their culture or to construct them as 'deficient' continued" (p. 125).

We cannot assume that humanizing those who have been traditionally othered will, as Aveling says, challenge presumptions of white supremacy. I talk later about the need to put these stories in the context of an analytical framework that includes the ways in which those in the privileged group internalize not only our humanity but also our supremacy and how that internalized supremacy creates the very stereotypes that we are unraveling.

I have found that by bringing in stories through "third parties"—guest speakers, films, articles—students who sit on the margin are both relieved of the responsibility to make themselves human and are then more willing to share their own stories. At the same time, some Students of Color find a language for their own lives; the analysis often offers the first time their experience has been "officially" validated. For example, a young African American student writes,

> I've learned about how the world pushes me and how I push back. I've learned that regardless of whether I believe it or not I internalize some messages that society sends me. I have come to realize that I am not really angered by discriminatory remarks; however I have become more passionate about the systematic causes that are behind the remarks. I have also learned that being in a subordinate group to whites helps me view other subordinate groups somewhat easier.

REVERSE RACISM

In almost every class or workshop I have at least one white person who has a story to tell about how her or his father, mother, brother, friend or she herself was denied an opportunity because of "reverse racism." This past semester, an upset student shared a story about her rejection from the state's flagship university, claiming her scores were higher than those of Students of Color who were accepted, a supposition she made based, as these stories almost always are, on purely anecdotal evidence (Bonilla-Silva, 2006; Griffin, 1997).

Because white students "do not experience systemic oppression" and because the culture shapes how we understand the world, "systemically privileged students often enter ... courses believing that systemic oppression is a relic of the past or, if it does exist, that [we] are not responsible for it" (Applebaum, 2007, p. 337). We want to believe, as we have been culturally told, "any advantage [we] enjoy is merited or 'normal' and 'natural.'" As a result, we "often resist interrogating what it means to be white since whiteness is traditionally the unmarked category that confers privilege on those who are ascribed whiteness" (p. 337).

When we are asked to investigate what it means to be white, we often respond defensively. Aveling talks about how students situated in privilege begin "to feel uncomfortable when the 'natural' order of how much time is spent on what or whom, [becomes] unbalanced" (2002, pp. 126-127). Like she, I have had students complain that the classroom perspective and material is too one-sided, particularly if they have bought into the culturally prevalent idea that white people are the new "marginalised, persecuted and silenced majority" (pp. 126-127).

Discomfited, students begin to raise the issue of "reverse discrimination," insisting the playing field is level or that People of Color get unfair advantages because of affirmative action and "quotas." Driven by the dominant narrative, they experience the taking away of an assumed privilege (admission to schools where African American and indigenous students were historically and systematically excluded) as equivalent to systemic discrimination. They follow the rhetoric of white leaders (and some People of Color, Ward Connerly most famously among them) who legitimize the idea of "reverse racism" to manipulate the dismantling of hard-fought battles aimed at insuring greater access to institutional resources by People and Communities of Color. Olsson (1997, p. 8) points out that these claims make no distinction between race prejudice and institutionalized racism.

Eduardo Bonilla-Silva explains that this "story line" of reverse discrimination, the idea that "I did not get a job, or a deserved opportunity because an unqualified 'minority' got preferential treatment" is "extremely useful to whites rhetorically and psychologically" (2006, p. 83) in spite of research that the actual number of reverse discrimination cases filed with the Equal Employment Opportunity Commission is both "quite small" and most are "dismissed as lacking any foundation" (p. 83). Pat Griffin calls this type of resistance "anecdote raised to the status of generalized fact" (1997, p. 294), where a student tells a personal story to "invalidate target group members' experience and even the oppression model" (p. 294). As in the case of my student, when white people use this story line, "precise information need not be included" because the story is "built upon a personal moral tale" tied to concepts of merit and qualifications that remain unexamined. Bonilla-Silva notes that an important characteristic of this story line is its lack of specificity, its "fuzziness" and common reference to third parties (it happened to a friend of a friend, or as in the case of my student, the evidence comes from a friend of a friend). He points out the difficulty of determining the specifics of any of these stories, which act as culturally sanctioned "defensive beliefs" (2006, p. 95).

We must understand how to "unpack" these stories (I talk about how to do this in more detail below). We need to speak to the deliberate dismantling of affirmative action based on legal claims brought by a statistically insignificant number of white people denied entry to schools or workplaces in order to redress their claims of racial bias favoring People of Color. We need to point out how the active redress of "discriminatory practices" affecting whites acts to reinforce and reinstate historic barriers to institutional and cultural access impacting communities of African Americans, Latinos, Chicanos, and other People of Color, leaving a wholesale and longstanding discrimination that remains unaddressed. We can point to the work that groups and communities have done to define and vision racial equity, like that of the Philanthropic Initiative for Racial Equity which defines a racially equitable society as one "in which the distribution of resources, opportunities, and burdens [is] not determined or predictable by race" (www.racialequity.org).

NO INTENT = NO RACISM

I recently visited a Guilford County high school where a member of the administration was sharing a history of the new school, which had been created by pulling together students from an upper middle class white community (the largest numbers) with students from a low income Black community. This administrator was a great cheerleader for the school, and spoke about how they expected to easily recruit teachers because the school had, in her words, "a nice population." My guess is she did not explicitly intend to associate white and upper middle class with "nice," or to deliberately suggest that students who do not fit this demographic are "not nice." She did intend to communicate the desirability of the school, which was implied by the higher number of white students. Her language was racially coded and my guess is everyone in the room knew exactly what she was talking about.

Author and scholar Allan Johnson (2006) makes the point that one essential ingredient of privileged resistance is the assumption that lack of intent is the same as lack of consequences (i.e., my racism can't hurt you if I didn't mean it). Paul Kivel agrees, noting that if white people use minimizing to play down harm, claiming lack of intent plays the same role. We say things like "I didn't mean it like that" or the classic "it was only a joke" (Okun & Jones, 2006, p. 36). Olsson puts the "I'm colorblind" defense (1997, p. 6) in this category, where we argue that of course we're all the same, and if racism does occur, we are not responsible because "I'm colorblind." The assumption is that if we do not intend to be racist, sexist, oppressive, then racism, sexism, and oppression is not happening.

We claim the binary position that "I'm one of the good ones," and because I am good, then I cannot be racist (or sexist). Olsson describes this as the "I marched with Dr. King" defense (1997, p. 4), where we point to all the good work we have done to "prove" that we could not possibly be racist, that we are "good." In the same vein, Jim Edler describes "the 'find the racist' game" where we "target another group member for inappropriate comments or ideas" which leaves us "feeling righteous" while we effectively "close down any opportunity for meaningful discussion" (Okun & Jones, 2006, p. 38).

One of my white students writes,

> I think that all people are the same, and that what color their skin is, or what culture they are should have no effect as to how they are being treated by others. Honestly I have never really be affected by racism therefore I cannot speak for how it feels but I'm sure it is horrible.

She reflects the reality for many white students who do not think of themselves as belonging to a white group that has a culture, much less a culture that sets the standards for everyone else. We are taught that we are "normal," without realizing that the creation of normal also requires an "abnormal" or "less than normal." Believing that we are one of the "good" ones is both a manifestation of internalized privilege and a logical consequence of a cultural binary where we are taught we can only be one of two discrete choices rather than a muddy and chaotic mixture of both.

Bonilla-Silva (2006, chapter 4) describes an archetypal story that white people tell to both defend against the association with "bad" and any notion of racism beyond the personal. He traces a "formula" that we use involving a "confession" of a racist relative or friend, a specific example of their racism (a remark made), and finally a statement of "open-mindedness" that serves to distance us from the offending, "bad" white person (I am not like them). The problem, he argues, is that this distancing claim of "color-blind racism forms an impregnable yet elastic ideological wall that barricades whites off from American's racial reality" (p. 211).

In the very act of demarcating (I am good, you are bad, I belong, you do not), we rationalize our negative attitudes and behaviors toward those who are "other" (Morton, 2004, chapter 2). The binary operates to keep us in fear; one of the reasons we want so desperately to be one of the "good" ones is our deepest fear that we are actually bad.

Cheri Huber points out "to judge what we see as good or bad derails our efforts to see *what is* (her italics)" (2000, p. 31). In our refusal to acknowledge that we are part and parcel of a powerful racist construct from which we benefit, we repress or project. As a result, we become more afraid of that which we feel we cannot bear to know. Like any addiction, the cycle is repeated and intensified in a futile attempt to reconcile our inner anxiety and dread. We never come to terms with the cost to our-selves, to our own humanity.

In fact, as Gulati-Partee points out (personal correspondence, August 11, 2009), "a lack of intentionality about power, systems of oppression and privilege, and equity will lead to the exact same outcome as inten-tional racism, exclusion, etc." One of the ways we can help students understand that intention does not erase harm is to encourage them to reflect on their own experience and the times they have been hurt, disap-pointed, treated unfairly in situations where no harm was intended. If enough trust has been built, I use dynamics in the classroom to make this point. Sometimes a comment by one student will spark feelings in another and I encourage them to take a look at how feelings and reactions emerge regardless of intent.

Making the classroom a space where feelings are welcomed provides a setting that makes it possible for us to move beyond binary thinking and grapple with the complexities of our social conditioning. Avoiding shame and blame, modeling the ways in which we, as teachers, struggle with being both good and bad, and supporting students by assuming their essential goodness while challenging their conditioned thinking are all critical elements to addressing the assumptions attached to good inten-tions.

GUILT AND SHAME

At a workshop several years ago, I met a white woman who was attending with a couple of friends, both women of color. As we progressed through the workshop, she found herself coming to grips with the ramifications of institutional and cultural racism in ways she never had before. She began to cry so heavily that she left the room. I followed her into the hall to offer comfort. When I asked why she was crying, she responded that she had never before contemplated that she might have caused her friends grief or harm; the realization was cutting her heart. I realized then that guilt and shame, as difficult as they are, also offer important indicators of our humanity, our sense of connectedness. This woman's pain, while difficult, was also redemptive, an important sign of the deep caring one for the other that our world so desperately needs. Our culture wants us to believe that guilt and shame are problematic; what if instead we considered them as natural and important indicators of our interconnectedness (thanks to my friend Noah Rubin-Blose for this insight)? Gulati-Partee concurs (per-sonal correspondence, August 11, 2009), saying,

I am troubled by the "new anti-racism" that suggests that guilt and shame are useless emotions, rather than windows into our humanity and entry points for accountability. There's yet another manifestation of privilege here—feeling entitled to only the positive emotions of the human experience (joy, peace, righteous anger) and entitled to avoid the messier or less comfortable ones. Also, guilt, shame, or any emotion have value in and of themselves—because they are natural and human—but also have the potential for spurring some behavior change or other action.

Even while redemptive, guilt is a "feeling of having done wrong" and shame (or being ashamed) is defined as feelings of embarrassment connected to having done wrong (Webster's Dictionary, 1972). Once we begin to understand the pervasiveness of racism, "many of us don't want to be white because it opens us up to charges of being racist and brings up feelings of guilt, shame, embarrassment, and hopelessness" (Kivel, 2002, p. 8). As our understanding grows and we begin to "see" white privilege, the feelings of guilt and shame become stronger. Once we recognize that what we thought was excusable no longer is, we quite naturally feel ashamed and embarrassed at our own ignorance and participation. One of the reasons we stay in denial and defensiveness is to avoid these feelings (Okun, 2006).

Gulati-Partee makes the point that "in the absence of an authentic relationship that enables accountability to People of Color, white people's guilt and shame can become pointless—that is, if there are no vehicles for change that they can fuel" (personal correspondence, August 11, 2009). Pulitzer Prize winning columnist Lewis Pitts (n.d., ¶5) argues that this unanchored white guilt, while well intentioned, is "a fundamental reason the white side of the national dialogue on race has grown increasingly intemperate in recent years." He argues that it is "human nature" that we "come to resent the thing that causes [us] guilt" (¶6), referencing our attitude toward failed diets, or work left undone. He alludes to viciously angry letters he receives from readers "so wildly out of proportion to whatever it is the writer thinks I've said or done that I have to believe I was only the triggering device, the excuse for venting long-held resentment" (¶9).

Allowing ourselves to feel the guilt and shame can usher in a stage of profound personal transformation, one in which we realize that we participate in racist institutions and a racist culture, that we both benefit from and are deeply harmed by racism, and that we perpetuate racism, even when that is not our intention. At this point we can begin to take responsibility for racism, even as we acknowledge we were not historically involved in constructing it (Okun, 2006).

White caucuses and support from other white people can be very helpful in the process of taking responsibility, because these provide "space to speak with honesty and candor rarely possible in mixed-race groups" (Tatum, 1997, p. 111).

ATTENTION AND ENGAGEMENT

I recall another workshop where a white woman who worked as one of the few women lobbyists in a northwestern state, a source of great pride to her, was strongly resisting the idea that she held any white privilege. She was quite vociferous in her objections, insisting that she had no racial advantage. At that point we were meeting in the white caucus and other white participants were attempting to help her see her race privilege. Finally someone suggested that she consider what her experience as a lobbyist might be like if she was a Black woman or Latina. She took a full minute to consider this question and then, as a metaphorical lightbulb switched on above her head, she looked at us and said "oh, now I see what you mean."

Although not a stage in identity development like guilt and shame, "resistance to class material can be a very powerful form of engagement and often marks the fact that students are being challenged in an important way" (Kandaswamy, 2007, p. 9).

One of the reasons we must avoid making assumptions about what students are capable of is how students who resist the material can become its most avid champion once they are able to move through their dissonance.

I remember, for example, a young white male student very attached to the idea that anyone can make it in this country if they just work hard. He was defending against the idea that hard work may not lead to acquisition of the "American Dream" or that blaming those who don't "make it" fails to take into account huge institutional and cultural barriers. To his credit, he voiced his opinions, vociferously defending a link between poverty and laziness. I was glad to have his voice in the classroom, for so often students hold those opinions silently for fear of disagreeing publicly with the teacher. I addressed many of his arguments, sometimes directly and just as often indirectly to insure that he was not the focus. I also encouraged other students to argue their differing views.

At one point I asked the class to do an activity designed by *United for a Fair Economy* (2006, pp. 17-18), where 10 students and 10 chairs are used to show the country's increasing discrepancy in wealth. By the end of the exercise, one student is stretched over 7 of the 10 chairs, representing the top 10% of the population that holds 70% of the wealth. The student's outstretched arm, attempting to cover four of the seven chairs, represents the 1% of the population that owns 40% of the wealth. This activity pierced the student's resistance. Once he could visually see and bodily experience the intense gap between rich and poor, he began to re-evaluate his own experience and that of his own lower middle-class family. From that point on, he did not resist any of the material in class; by the end of the semester, he was vocally supporting and even proactively offering his own attempts to disrupt cultural assumptions.

His resistance, one that required some focused attention in the classroom, marked a genuine attempt to wrestle with the material.

A more challenging form of resistance has to do with a student's need for attention, not to address concepts, but to stave off the feelings of discomfort that so frequently accompany learning about oppression. I remember several workshops where the deconstruction of racism as a system of advantage for white people resulted in participants breaking into inconsolable tears in an attempt to become the focus of comforting attention.

Olsson (1997, p. 18) talks about how one of the ways we move through our guilt and shame is by seeking "from People of Color some public or private recognition and appreciation for our anti-racism. Other times we are looking for a 'certificate of innocence' telling us we are one of the good white people." Here we return to the binary. When people use their emotions to demand attention, they want to avoid feeling anything for which they might have to take responsibility. In cases like these, I have to work hard to remember that people move through resistance in their own way and my time and efforts are best spent focused on those who seem ready to move in this moment. I am no longer hesitant to ask an attention-getting participant to "take care of himself" by leaving and returning when he feels better or giving her some one-on-one attention at a break or soliciting the help of a classmate or another workshop participant to "help" outside of the classroom or workshop venue.

A STRATEGIC APPROACH

It's difficult to get a man to understand something when
his salary depends on his not understanding it.

—Upton Sinclair (Jensen, 2002, p. 43)

Derrick Jensen points to eye movement research conducted by Lestor Luborsky establishing that people avert their eyes from photographic images, or portions of images, containing material they find offensive or objectionable. They are then unable to recall any mental pictures they find disturbing. Luborsky's research reflects our ability to "know precisely where not to look in order to have our worldview remain unthreatened and intact" (Jensen, 2002, p. 139).

We should not be surprised that our students resist seeing that which our culture would prefer hidden. How, then, to we help people move through resistance, guilt and shame, into taking responsibility? I want to reiterate here that I have an answer, not the answer. There are multiple ways to do anything well, so what I offer here is *one* way to address privileged resistance in the classroom, not *the* way.

My approach to privileged resistance assumes the critical importance of my attitude as the teacher or facilitator in a classroom or workshop. As faculty we have to attend to our own social location and its impact on the classroom. As I said in the introduction, identity matters. I agree with Elizabeth Higginbotham that "our own race, gender, social class background, and sexual identity will influence the power dynamics between us and students" (1996). The fact that I am white, older, heterosexual, makes what I am about to say easier for me than for other faculty charged with teaching this material. For instance, as Higginbotham notes, "faculty of color challenge the status quo by their mere presence in front of the class," and as such, "they might have to actively and repeatedly demonstrate their right to define the subject matter they teach." Any time our identities place us in constructed "inferior" identities, students operating from privileged ones will find us less credible, challenge us more frequently, and disregard our legitimacy.

Nonetheless I believe we have a duty to love and respect our students, even those acting out of their privileged resistance. It is tempting to position the resisting student as willful enemy. I am not sure how considering students in this way helps them or us. Most of the people I teach have never had any opportunity to see their own conditioning; I should be angry at their conditioning rather than at them. I am not talking here about the student who takes their resistance to alarming or abusive levels, which does happen and which I discuss later.

As Higginbotham says, "the classroom is one place where all faculty do have power and many students look to the faculty to use that power to establish a comfortable place to learn" (1996). Although I would not choose the word "comfortable," because the essence of effective pedagogy is to help students acknowledge and attempt to resolve the multiple discomforts that come with meaningful learning, I do believe that the classroom needs to be a "safer space" where students feel they can bring their voice, their heart, their mind without reservation.

What I want in my classroom is an environment reflected in a young white woman's comment that

> I've learned that it's ok to be myself and that my opinions matter. I think it all goes back to my fear of speaking out in class. My classmates showed me that they were an accepting group of individuals and I felt very comfortable

getting over my fear of speaking in class. I have found more self-confidence and have honestly become a more mature leader on my softball team, and it's due in large part to the great group of people that I was with in class.

I do not pretend this is easy. This last semester I had a series of difficult exchanges with an older student who I felt was being very resistant to class material, paternalistic (or maternalistic) in her responses to the other students, overly judgmental. Toward the end of the semester, in one of our e-mail exchanges, she wrote

> If I have felt "resistant" to anything in this class, it was the feeling that I was put in a box and pushed aside. I'm always "wrong" in this class and certainly haven't felt that it was an appropriate place for me to be very open.   Maybe that made me more ornery than usual. I guess we got off on the wrong foot and it's just been exacerbated all semester. My "deepening self-awareness" has taken place outside of the classroom. For you to assume that it hasn't happened is rather presumptuous. Sometimes these things are private. Is the point of the class for this growth to be stimulated or for it to occur before our classmates and teachers?

I share this to make the point that although I am writing about privileged resistance and how to address it, I do not presume that I have completely figured it out. I responded to this student's e-mail with an apology, saying quite sincerely how sorry I was that she felt I had "boxed her in." I related how as a student myself, I have been on the receiving end of the box, and how I would never wish that on a student. Our dialogue shifted as a result of her bravery at sharing her feelings with me and my willingness to express my regret; if the semester had continued, I think we might have been able to forge a more meaningful relationship, one where we could each hear the other without the defensiveness that we had been bringing to the relationship.

I also think that this response is available to me because of my identities. I have seen Colleagues of Color challenged by students in ways I have never been, making any apology or admission of vulnerability an impossibility in terms of ongoing credibility. So while I believe that love and respect for the conditioned student is a critical ingredient to effectively addressing privileged resistance, I also acknowledge that this may be a much easier imperative for me than for others.

Another way that I address resistance proactively is in the curriculum design. I use a process, developed with colleagues at ChangeWork and then dRworks, conceived to help people "see" the historical construction of race and racism in ways that acknowledge everyone's humanity and avoid, to the extent possible, blaming and shaming people. This process is described in more depth in chapter 4.

Another strategy I use is in classroom and workshop settings is to make the point that one of the reasons we have trouble talking about race is because we think it is really a discussion about who is bad and who good. I address the limits of this kind of binary thinking, which the students or workshop participants have already discussed in other contexts. I talk about how we are all complicated people and I use our classroom investigations of historical figures like Columbus to remind students how none of us are all one thing or the other. The question, I say, is not who is good and who bad, the question is what are we going to do about what we know?

I acknowledge the feelings that come up when we begin to talk about difficult topics like white privilege and internalized entitlement. Griffin (1997, p. 290) notes that "for some teachers and students the expression of feelings in a classroom is an unusual experience." She describes how students "cry while remembering painful experiences or hearing a classmate tell a painful story" (p. 290) or how students "feel frustrated by the pervasiveness of social injustice" or "deceived because they never understood oppression before" (p. 290). Griffin says that while we should not assume "that the expression of intense emotion is required for effective learning," we should be prepared for it.

I actually believe that intense emotion, particularly in the context of an intense topic like racism, *is* required for effective learning. As Anne Wilson Schaef (1998) so wisely observes, feelings trump content, meaning that we have to allow our students to feel their resistance, their defensiveness, their fear if we want them to be able to take in the intellectual analysis that is also integral to unpacking the race construct.

I offer multiple opportunities for students to express their feelings, both in and out of class. One of the ways I do this is through journals. One white student uses her journal assignment to share,

> The classroom and conversation were very tense and highly emotional at times due to various comments and assertions, and I had a strong personal reaction to this. I found myself with my heart pounding and so many things I wanted to say or ask, but did not know how. Although it was a very intense and sensitive subject, I am glad the subject of who's "fault" it is, or who is to "blame" was brought up because I would not have imagined I would have such strong feelings surrounding this. I left class completely drained and exhausted, and somewhat confused about why I felt so strongly. I talked about this with a few friends in the class and it was comforting to find that they felt similarly. Sometimes I feel like I need another debriefing class after this class to process all that happens! I am grateful for what the class brings up, and I know it is a class that is designed to bring up tough issues, and not necessarily solve them, but that can also leave us with a lot to unpack.

As teachers, we have to want to know what our students are feeling in all its texture and detail. I provide multiple opportunities for students to talk about, write about, act out what they are feeling; the more they "get into it," the better. I listen and encourage other students to listen as well. I might ask students to share their feelings with a classmate. If I want to get a sense of the feelings in the room, I will ask each student to share what is on their hearts and minds, going from one student to the next. Sometimes journal entries will prompt a one-on-one dialogue with a student who is really struggling. If I am successful, I have students write, as this white student did,

> Throughout this class I have become more and more aware of how important it is for me to not dismiss the way people feel. I have the tendency to want examples and reasons for the way someone feels and it is now easier for me to recognize that I want to hear and validate someone's feelings. Another piece of learning is that as I work for the radical acceptance of others it is important for me to continue to work towards the radical acceptance of myself.

An African American woman writes,

> I am very acquainted with the underlying anger and resentment that is produced in minority citizens in an oppressive dominant culture. I recognize the struggle within myself to remain unbiased and open. The most important thing is that regardless of whether the emotion is guilt or resentment, both of them must be addressed and then thrown away to insure change in the future and I am responsible for throwing away my part.

When students raise "intellectual" arguments to defend against the acknowledgement of contemporary racism and privilege, which inevitably happens every semester, the first thing I do is let them vent. For example, in the case of a student claiming reverse racism, I ask them to really put some thought into describing how it feels to be treated unfairly. I might ask the whole class to do the same, either through discussion or journal writing. Once they have had a chance to express how unfairness feels, I will ask them if they agree it is no fun when life is unfair. Inevitably they do. Then I ask them if life is always fair, often fair, often unfair.

My goal is to help them use their feelings as a bridge to the feelings of oppressed peoples and communities. I ask them to try and reflect on how what they are feeling informs what those on the receiving end of systemic discrimination must feel. I do all this to make sure they have an opportunity to know what they are feeling, to express it, bring it out to the light of day, so they will be able to participate in what comes next.

After feelings have been explored, we start to unpack the argument. While each unpacking is specific to the particular strategy the student is employing, I generally, with the help of others in the class, point out that the evidence for unfairness is anecdotal. I might ask the student or all of the students in the class to research the numbers related to whatever it is they are focused on (for example, the racial breakdown of who was admitted to the state's flagship university). I also point out the assumptions in their arguments; in the case where a student is talking about "reverse racism" and assumes a lack of qualifications on the part of whoever got the job, I talk about how notions of qualified are constructed. Finally, I ask them to consider all the other aspects of unfairness in the situation and why whatever anger or sense of injustice is felt so strongly when it comes to race (as opposed to preferential treatment based on class and social connections, athletic prowess, geography, etc.).

For example, in the case of the student mentioned earlier who claimed she did not get into the college of her choice because an unqualified Person of Color took her rightful place, I asked who else might have been selected unfairly (I never start with this because I want to make sure we have unpacked the assumption that the Person of Color was less qualified first). I asked why she focused her anger on unnamed People of Color when athletes, children of alumni, relatives of donors, the politically connected, were admitted over and above those who might be more qualified. Why was race the focus of her anger and distress?

In the case where a student charges that the class is "unbalanced" and too focused on the investigation of oppression (which happens even in classes named "Confronting Oppression"), I ask if they raise the same concern about balance in their other classes, where the dominant narrative is assumed. Do they, I query, demand balance in a history course if the narratives of Indigenous Peoples are not included, in an English class if the texts do not incorporate the perspectives of people and communities on the margin, in a social work class that assumes low income communities have diminished social capital? The answer, to date at least, is always no.

I make these points, raise these questions or let other students make and raise them, and give the class time to consider the arguments. I might ask students to talk in pairs. I might ask for an open discussion. I see if another student will take the resisting student on and encourage them to do so. I refer back to the films and previous class discussions we have had about how racism is the historical and systemic oppression of one group of people for the benefit of another as opposed to singular acts of discrimination. I ask them why this distinction is important.

I might introduce another analysis tool. For example, jona olsson developed an activity that asks people to identify all the institutions established for and controlled by white people. I ask my students to make a list and I write the answers in the upper left hand corner of the blackboard or on the flip chart. Then I ask for another list of all the institutions established for and controlled by People of Color. This list is inevitably much shorter and goes to the right of the first. Then I ask for a list of all the institutions established for and controlled by white people under which People of Color must live. This list, essentially the same as the first, goes up underneath the first. Finally I ask for a list of the institutions established for and controlled by People of Color under which white people must live. Usually my students cannot think of a single institution to put in this last column; sometimes they will reference a childhood experience of going to a public school that was all or majority Students of Color. In those cases, I ask questions about whether majority numbers indicate control and we explore the intersections of power, race, and class.

Then, to be honest, I let go. I have learned after long and hard experience that if I devote all of my attention to the few who are resisting the most, then I miss the opportunity to move the larger group who wants to know more. I cover in the next chapter the social and scientific theory backing up the importance of focusing on this critical "middle," in this case the students who are interested and eager to learn. Our job is not to persuade those who are too fearful to see but to offer the analysis thoughtfully and with compassion, in the great hope that one day, if not today, those who are struggling will remember what was shared and experience a critical "ah ha."

ABUSIVE RESISTANCE

Sometimes students or workshop participants extremely challenged by the material take their resistance to a verbally abusive level. They accuse the teacher or other students by using defamatory labels—"you're a Marxist," "you're teaching communism"—or they charge that we are failing to be inclusive if we counter their attempts to take over the classroom with their disruptive rhetoric. In extreme cases, they can be so aggressive as to make the teacher or other students feel physically threatened.

I offer several approaches for dealing with this level of privileged resistance, noting that in a workshop setting we have more leeway to set parameters than in a classroom subject to campus policies and procedures.

First, I want to make a distinction between being inclusive and allowing abuse. I address privileged resistance proactively, by establishing classroom guidelines where respect for ourselves and each other is high on the list. Once guidelines are established, I reference them at the earliest opportunities, so their use does not seem arbitrary when it comes to the behavior of those who are most resistant. As I explain above, I also make it very clear from the very first class, or the start of any workshop, that I am not "neutral" in my teaching and that I am not leading a "discussion" about race and racism. I explain that I have an agenda and an analysis based in literally decades of work and study, that I expect them to grapple with my agenda and analysis, to accept, reject, refute with respect. In an academic setting, I make it clear that acceptance, rejection, and refutation has to be done with a high degree of scholarship and academic rigor. Finally, I announce that one of my primary roles as a teacher is to insure that everyone's voice is heard and I let them know I will be using my power to call on people who are less outspoken and to ask those who speak a lot to step back.

When labels are used to discount another student or me, I disrupt the "discussion" to make clear that I do not allow labels. I engage the class as a whole in an investigation of the power of words like "Marxist," "communist," "racist," "illegals" (to refer to people in the U.S. without documents) so that we can appreciate how they actually reduce complexity and shut down debate. I might ask students to put some thought into what the labels mean and why I might embrace aspects of any of them.

In the case where a student or workshop participant becomes so obstreperous and out of control that they seem emotionally or physically threatening, I no longer allow them to attend. I have only done this once, in a workshop setting. In the case of the classroom, I make sure that I am familiar with whatever the campus policies are about students whose behavior begins to feel threatening so I can pursue them if necessary.

Setting limits in the classroom is a form of "tough" love. Students often test us to see if we are willing to set limits and are reassured when we do. At the same time, setting limits is something we must do with respect; we can avoid humiliating or singling out students. This is extremely difficult, particularly when one or two students are speaking up in ways that disrupt the ability and desire of other students to participate. I do ask to meet with students outside of class so I can talk with them about how their behavior is impacting other students. If a student comes to me to complain about feeling targeted or silenced by another student, I encourage them to name their options and support them in taking action on their own behalf. In these cases, I always make sure that the student who feels targeted acts in alliance with other students or me (in other words, I am clear that the student needs to act with support). In the classroom, I invoke my role as facilitator and tell the class as a whole that no one can speak for a second time until every one has spoken once.

Drawing the line on abusive behavior can be difficult for some teachers and faculty who confuse an ethic of inclusivity with the idea that we have to allow any and all behavior in our classrooms. I have seen teachers and facilitators bend over backwards to accommodate people who I feel should have been asked to leave or taken out of the classroom. Students learn from our example; allowing abusive behavior in the classroom is not something we should tolerate.

We should also remember that everything and anything that happens in the classroom or workshop is fodder for learning; if we have to ask a student to leave, we can "deconstruct" our decision with the classroom in a spirit of helping students wrestle with the often challenging implications of trying to live our values.

My point is that we should not confuse a progressive and democratic impulse toward inclusivity with allowing students to disrespect each other or us. Sometimes our role is to draw lines and say "no" to those whose sense of entitlement and discomfort attempt to hijack our classes.

CONCLUSION

This chapter on privileged resistance is my attempt to transgress the traditional "assimilationist and compensatory perspectives" (Aveling, 2002, p. 121) that assume the oppressed are the source of "the problem" and therefore the focus of "the solutions." I believe that the deconstruction of white supremacy, the transformation to a truly egalitarian, sustainable, loving culture requires both deep understanding and committed action by those who benefit from the current systems of privilege and advantage. As Richard Wright so eloquently states, we have a white problem (Lipsitz, 1998). Awareness of the white supremacy construct, white privilege, and internalized entitlement are key to meaningful cultural transformation.

If we are able to move through our privileged resistance and help students and others do the same, then what do we do next?

In his book *The Great Turning: From Empire to Earth Community*, David Korten speaks to the need for cultural transformation. He turns our assumptions about the desirability of western culture on its head. A former "member of the international development establishment" whose role was to "share the secrets of America's economic and political success so that the world's poor might become free and prosperous like Americans" (2006, p. 8), Korten came to realize that exporting western capitalist culture was essentially "disrupting the ability of villagers and their communities to control and manage their own resources to meet their needs" (p. 10). His travels around the world led him to comprehend that "the United States was the major impetus behind ... a deeply destructive and antidemocratic development model" (p. 11).

If, as Korten suggests and I believe, white supremacy culture does not serve us well, harming even those of us who ostensibly benefit, how do we change, shift, transform our current culture into "earth community" or one that supports a life-centered, democratic, sustainable way of ordering human society "that affirms the inherent worth and potential of all individuals and their right to a voice in the decisions that shape their lives" (2006, p. 38)? The answers to this question are the focus of the next chapter.

The Heart of the World

Here I am
locked in my own shadow
for more than twenty years,
and yet
I have reached my hand
through stone and steel and razor wire
and touched the heart of the world.
Mitakuye Oyasin, my Lakota brethren say.
We are all related.
We are One.

—Leonard Peltier (1999, p. 26)

CHAPTER 3

A DIFFERENT PARADE

Cultural Shift

I grew into adulthood during the Civil Rights and Vietnam antiwar movements and was privileged to witness firsthand the ways in which courageous groups of people worked collectively to prick the conscience of a
nation, shift manifestations of entrenched racism, and stop a war. I have
seen tremendous cultural and institutional change in my lifetime. Our
society accommodates and includes women, particularly white women,
more than ever before, so much so that the young women in my classroom
laugh in wonder at my stories of being forced to play half-court basketball
at my high school in the culturally widespread belief that girls could not
endure stressful physical effort. We have just elected our first African
American president; the era of formal Jim Crow is over. Several states
have passed laws legalizing gay marriage and/or same sex unions.

At the same time, the women in my classroom continue to be paid significantly less than men for the same work, they experience one of the
highest rates of sexual assault and rape on the globe, they or their sisters
live in unforgivable poverty resulting from the cultural devaluation of
both women and childrearing. Nationally we have experienced the deliberate dismantling of programs, such as affirmative action, designed to
offer some measure of race and gender equity. We are witness to devastating race and class oppression reflected in the demographics of our prison

The Emperor Has No Clothes: Teaching About Race and Racism
to People Who Don't Want to Know, pp. 75–100
Copyright © 2010 by Information Age Publishing
All rights of reproduction in any form reserved.

75

population, those "pushed out" of education and job opportunities, the poor, the chronically sick and underserved. We are currently experiencing an economic crisis unlike anything we've known, preceded by an incomprehensible wealth and wage gap, brought on by decades of corporate greed supported by the government.

In chapter 1, I define and discuss white supremacy culture, charting its manifestations and impact, particularly in regards to those of us acting from positions as teachers, leaders, and activists seeking to build a more just world. In chapter 2, I look at the ways white supremacy culture constructs privileged resistance to its own acknowledgement, as well as how we might pierce this resistance. In this chapter, I attempt to offer ideas for how we can begin to think about the challenge of shifting from a white supremacy culture based in the "technocratic, materialistic, mechanistic" (Schaef, 1998, p. 15) values of empire, to one of earth community (Korten, 2006) where we can pursue our desire to live values of authentic equity, democracy, sustainability, justice.

One reason for the limited effectiveness of social movements is the power of white supremacy culture to shape the agendas of even those who oppose it. Robert Allen, in his book *Reluctant Reformers* (1983), traces how racism has split every movement for progressive reform in this country's history, including the abolitionist, populist, women's suffrage, organized labor, communist, and student movements. My personal experience bears this out—during my years as a consultant to social justice non-profits, I found time and again that an organization's expressed desire to address racism was often insufficient in the face of cultural norms keeping oppressive assumptions and behaviors in place. Hours, days, weeks could be spent refining policies and procedures, but if the governing values and belief systems—the ones determining the collective understanding of what was acceptable, "normal," standard, necessary—did not shift, most people continued to replicate the original challenges that we had been asked to help them address.

The culture of an organization is often a reflection of the leaders' assumptions about the way to do things, too often assumed as the only way. These assumptions are influenced by dominant culture norms described in previous chapters. I hark back to the story about the young law student who shared the list of manifestations of white supremacy culture as essential to success in the profession. In the non-profit world, even in the social justice sector, "progress" is still measured by those operating out of mainstream paradigms that hold organizations to a standard of counting, reflecting the belief that more is better regardless of whether the numbers represent meaningful personal or community empowerment. My friend Edd Gulati-Partee (personal correspondence, July 10, 2009) calls this "a culture of accounting versus accountability;" his partner and organizational consultant Gita Gulati-Partee (personal correspondence, July 11, 2009) notes how "the whole notion of 'evidence-based' begs the question 'whose evidence?'" She points out the "self-referential" system rooted in white supremacy, where those in power both assume and set the standards by which everyone else is judged.

Faced with overwhelming and urgent needs, leaders often act out of limited binary thinking, believing that either this way or that is the one right way, discounting the voices of those who raise the complexity inherent in any strategy, constrained by funders who have unrealistic expectations about what can be accomplished in defined periods of time. People often more concerned with their own authority than organizational mission reflect the dominant culture's understanding of power and act unilaterally and without accountability to the people and communities they claim to serve. Even organizations with explicit racial justice missions resist attempts to address racist behaviors and practices out of a fear of losing familiar power arrangements with which they have grown comfortable.

We live in a period where those of us engaged in social justice efforts agitate about the current lack of a viable movement, despite the great range of efforts and initiatives carried on by people and communities deeply committed to a just world. We are in some way lamenting a missing form—a movement we can recognize as such based on our past experience, where mobilizations of people and resources led to hard won policy changes.

Perhaps it is time to expand our thinking.

To this end, I turn to David Korten's articulation of "earth community" outlined in his book *The Great Turning* (2006). Korten describes our current sociopolitical arrangement as one of "Empire," referring to the way in which our society is organized to benefit the few at the expense of the many, using violence in the service of an unsustainable greed for profit and power, or, as June Jordan would call it, "the Gospel of Efficiency and Maximum Profit" (2002, p. 45). Korten offers hope, as does Jordan, for he notes that empire, like the cultural constructs of race, class, and gender, is not fixed or fated, however strong. We have the ability to make a different choice. Korten argues for the possibilities of earth community; Jordan evokes the vision and yearning of Dr. Martin Luther King's "Beloved Community;" both suggest we organize ourselves around values of equity and democracy aimed at sustaining human life and our environment.

Here, then, are some ideas for how to expand our thinking about how to make this different choice.

KNOW THE UNKNOWABLE

I often show my undergraduate education majors the Jean Kilbourne documentary *Killing Us Softly* (2001), a thoughtful and devastating examination of the misogynistic portrayal of women in advertising. From an ad showing a "bloody," dismembered mannequin with the slogan "I'd kill for these shoes," to portrayals of women being raped, shot, stalked, silenced, all in the service of sales, the film traces the ways in which the mainstream media shapes our attitudes about what it means to be a woman in this society.

Although the film was made in the late 1990s, I ask my students to bring in ads from contemporary magazines to make the point that her critique is still chillingly relevant. Yet in almost every class I teach, a student raises her hand to say that she is unaffected by these ads; other students chime in to agree, some saying they see the ads as clever rather than disturbing or even thought-provoking.

As described in an earlier chapter, one defining characteristic of culture is that we take it for granted and as such "do not truly evaluate its impact on decisions, behaviors, and communication" (Keup, Walker, Astin, & Lindholm, 2001). The power of culture is precisely its ability to project a set of values without our awareness, so that we see the values as immutable (even God-given). Donaldo Macedo describes "the insidious nature of ideology," itself the product of culture, as "its ability to make itself invisible" (1998, p. xiv). Those of us living in the culture find it "hard to entertain the thought that we ... might have our own cultural peculiarities in the way we perceive the world—that our reality might be as parochial in its way as that of the Middle Ages appears to us now" (Harman, 1998, p. 18).

In this way, culture "creates a form of 'blindness' and ethnocentrism" (Morgan, 1997, p. 129), a socialization into the assumption that our "knowledge system" is the "best," which in turn leads us to assume that our values are "normal" and our perceptions "real" (Harman, 1998). In other words, we internalize and privilege our culture's experience and worldview without noticing we have done so; ergo my students sincerely say they remain unaffected precisely because the culture teaches them to understand themselves as independent individuals operating out of actualized free will.

Harman offers an example of the power of cultural conditioning to shape the way we see the world. He describes how the 1772 French Academy, in direct contradiction of the evidence—bright trails in the sky followed by the dropping of metal and stone to the ground—concluded "there are no such things as hot stones that have fallen from the sky because there are no stones in the sky to fall" (1998, p. 58). Harman explains that because the prevalent theories of the time, based on a Newtonian model, did not allow for the phenomena of meteorites, scientists instead created elaborate alternate explanations—"delusionary 'visions,' stones heated from being struck by lightening, stones borne aloft by whirlwinds or volcanic eruptions" (p. 58). The power of the Academy to frame contemporary thinking at the time was such that they discarded most of the stones (the scientific evidence) because no theory could incorporate their reality.

Activist and biologist Kriti Sharma makes the point that "the questions we ask or deem as important are so profoundly influenced by culture" (personal correspondence, July 17, 2009). She references nineteenth century immunologist Ludwik Fleck, who "when considering what scientific questions were being asked in his time" would in his turn ask "what social anxiety is finding its relief in research?" (personal correspondence, July 17, 2009).

Our culture is replete with stories of those in power "finding relief in research," constructing reality in complete contravention of the evidence. In the mid-1800s, "conventional wisdom denied that white men were impregnating the black women they owned" in spite of the many children offering physical evidence of these forced unions (Washington, 2006, p. 97). Prominent scientists focused their energies on proving that "mulattoes were too frail, feeble, and infertile to reproduce their own kind," to provide the rationale for laws prohibiting intermarriage in a (vain) attempt to stop the possibilities of "Negroes ... born white [who] would gain the capability to pass" (pp. 97-98). For a more contemporary example, Al Gore, in his movie *An Inconvenient Truth*, documents how the media has systematically distorted the overwhelming scientific consensus about catastrophic global warming under pressure from political forces that would prefer wholesale delusion about the state of the environment (Bender & Guggenheim, 2006).

Educator and theorist Henry Giroux suggests we are required to understand "how ideology works on and through individuals to secure their consent to the basic ethos and practices of the dominant culture" while at the same time understanding "how ideology creates the terrain for self-reflection and transformative action" (2001, p. 145). In the words of Paolo Freire (1998, p. 26), we should understand ourselves "to be *conditioned* but not *determined*." Korten echoes this idea, noting that because culture is a "human construct subject to intentional choice" (2006, p. 75), we have the "capacity to choose our future" (p. 76).

In fact, we can point to people and communities who have strived and continue to do just that. For one example, Maxine Greene (1988) references the French Resistance, who during WWII, came together without masks or pretenses or badges of office, [and spoke of] how they felt they had been visited for the first time in their lives by an 'apparition of freedom' … [and] had begun to create that public space between themselves where freedom could appear. (p. 15)

Greene makes the point that "although there was no guarantee that the occupation of France would end in their lifetimes, they refused to assume that conditions were unchangeable" (1988, p. 15).

In order to make choices based in a sense of possibility, Giroux argues for a pedagogy where students "critically interrogate their inner histories and experiences" so they can understand "how their own experiences are reinforced, contradicted, and suppressed" in the classroom (and I would add, in life). He is joined by a diverse group, including organizational consultants Peter Senge and his colleagues Smith, Kruschwitz, Laur, and Schley, who talk about the importance of "the ability to see the current state of things" as "crucial to creating the future" (2008, p. 51). Similarly, Cooperrider and Whitney, leaders in the contemporary and growing field of appreciative inquiry, note that "knowing stands at the center of any and virtually every attempt at change. Thus, the way we know is fateful" (n.d., p. 15). They argue the importance and necessity of what they see as a "decisive shift in western intellectual tradition" (p. 15) from the "objective" underpinnings of modernist thinking to the postmodern, "constructionist" world with "its emphasis on the communal basis of knowledge and its radical questioning of everything that is taken-for-granted as "objective" or seemingly immutable" (n.d., p. 15).

In other words, to shift culture, we require a pedagogy that helps us cultivate "a full awareness of the nature of culture," to help us see that we are all "equally abnormal" (Morgan, 1997, p. 129). We can strive to become the little boy with eyes wide open in spite of the crowds who are oohing and aahing at the Emperor's supposed finery. We are compelled to assume "the standpoint of the cultural stranger because, in becoming aware of the stranger's point of view, we can see our own in a refreshingly new perspective" (Morgan, p. 129).

I am not suggesting this is easy. Maxine Greene talks about the "camouflage spread by the establishment or the system" that "degrades all truth to meaningless triviality" in ways "not visible to people who ought to have learned to see" (1988, p. 114). She talks about the

thousands upon thousands whose basic needs have long since been met and who … focus on material satisfactions and possessions, no matter how artificial the needs now being fulfilled, no matter how much "superfluity" characterizes their lives. (pp. 114-115)

Greene references "how long it often takes for people to perceive their lives as synchronized with others in the same predicament, to realize that 'all share a common lot'" (1988, p. 115).

Educator David Purpel (class discussion, November 16, 2005), like Korten, wants us to understand that just as cultures can encourage people to be more selfish and concerned with themselves (as western culture does in this historical moment), so too can cultures nourish and encourage the impulse to love, to be kind and generous and caring. He calls encouraging the impulse to love the other as the aim of prophetic education.

Teaching about race and racism, teaching about white supremacy culture, helping students to see the power of the race construct to shape our thinking and behavior is the critical task of educators "rooted in the ethical formation both of selves and of history" (Freire, 1998, p. 23). The implications for teachers, trainers, activists is that we can learn to help people cultivate "the standpoint of the cultural stranger," challenge notions of "normal" and "abnormal," and see how culture shapes our thinking so we can "decolonize" our minds.

THE IMPERATIVE OF A POWER ANALYSIS

In my undergraduate classroom, I often assign an action project designed to help students reflect on their relationship to consumerism. Students are asked to choose from a variety of options, including counting their clothes, eating on a very limited budget, or eliminating internet technology for a limited period of time. One semester, a student decided she would attempt to live without "texting" (using her text message option on her cell phone) for three days. A day and a half into the project she gave up, admitting she simply felt too isolated from her friends. I, on the other hand, had never sent a text message in my life (and continue to resist the shift from e-mail to text, with less and less success). Scholars avidly pursue the question of how new technology shapes our thinking (Lienhard, 2000; Linturi, 2000); suffice it to say that my student is making sense of her life in very different ways than I make sense of mine.

Political scientist Ronald Inglehart notes how "mass belief systems and global change are intimately related" (1997, p. 4), finding that cultures change as a result of "intergenerational population replacement processes," when the younger generation replaces the older one, bringing their new life experiences and viewpoints. He makes the case that "economic development, cultural change, and political change go together in coherent and even, to some extent, predictable patterns." Using the shifts associated with industrialization as an example, he notes how once a group of people become exposed to a massive change (in this case

economic), a "whole syndrome of related changes, from mass mobiliza-
tion to diminishing differences in gender roles, are likely to occur" (p. 5).
    Inglehart and coresearcher Welzel point out that

> changes in the socioeconomic environment help reshape individual-level
> beliefs, attitudes, and values through their impact on the life experience of
> individuals. Cultures do not change overnight. Once they have matured,
> people tend to retain whatever worldview they have learned. Consequently,
> the impact of major changes in the environment tend to be most significant
> on those generations that spent their formative years under new conditions.
> (2005, p. 65)

In other words, because people reflect the beliefs and values of the
society's culture (cultural conditioning or socialization), cultural shifts
happen as the younger generations most affected by the changes make
sense of their firsthand experience (Inglehart & Welzel, 2005). As Gita
Gulati-Partee points out (personal correspondence, July 11, 2009), my
students, those growing up a generation or two after my own, are
"natives" to technology, while my contemporaries and I are "immigrants."
This is reflected in the story of how my student makes sense of her world
through the use of a technology with which I have extremely limited experience.
    Our attempt to make meaning is complicated, not just by changes in
the world around us, but also in how the power elite insure that, as a collective, we make sense of change in ways that serve their interests. For
example, our understanding of the world is deeply influenced by the
media. Several months ago, I was at the YMCA, where the exercise
machines face a bank of televisions. I could not keep my eyes from sliding
over to the Fox News site, where an announcer was, in a quite straightforward manner, labeling the people who risk their lives to cross the border
from Mexico as "terrorists." Activist Alba Onofrio (personal correspondence, September 11, 2008) talks about how the media functions to "substitute false experiences for real, personal experiences.... Lots of people
don't know any Mexicans, so the media helps them believe how they
should be understood." She is talking about the power of Fox News to
influence us to experience and make sense of immigrants from Central
and South America in a very xenophobic and racist way.
    All we have to do is spend an afternoon in a local movie theater watching
the previews for upcoming films to see how the industry excels at presenting
a dangerous world where "others" (from "foreign" lands, not white) are to
be feared and problems solved with ever increasing violence. We do not
make sense of our experience in a vacuum; our cultural values are strategically manipulated by corporate and capitalist interests, driven by the
desire for profit, spending billions of dollars to influence our thoughts and

behavior to accommodate that drive above all other concerns. If you are in doubt about this, take a look at DeGraff, Wann, and Naylor's exploration of the "affluenza" phenomena, where they describe in some detail the contemporary marketing approach to children, who in marketing language, must be "captured, owned, and branded" (2005, p. 57).

So while we must strive to learn, as I argue in the previous section, to see our conditioning, to see is not enough. As Giroux says (2001), we are called to thoughtfully investigate and interrogate the world in order to intentionally construct a thoughtfully better one.

An important step, Peter Senge et al. say, to creating a new reality is "knowing what kind of world we want to create" (2008, p. 55). They encourage us to cultivate a shift from what they call reaction (to a problem or a set of problems) to creating, which is the act of "bringing something you care about into reality" (p. 50). Although they are referencing the importance of visioning, which I discuss in more detail later, one challenge is how to set goals for ourselves within the confines of cultural conditioning about what is possible. For example, when I ask my students why they want to teach, they often answer by saying they want to "make a difference," "shape good citizens," "insure success" while rarely investigating the wholesale assumptions that frame their notions of difference, good, success. Without examination of the cost to people or communities, I have found that my students feel that "making a difference" means helping the "underprivileged" access the mainstream, "good" often means cooperative and unquestioning, "success" means the acquisition of money and power.

I argue that we have a responsibility to help our students understand power. Jacqueline Greenon Brooks and Eustace Thompson, in their reflections in *Social Justice in the Classroom* (2006) offer a number of case studies where teachers perpetuate the socialization of oppressive race, class and gender constructs because at best they fail to engage in an analysis of their own socialized assumptions and at worst they have internalized their assumptions as superior.

Ironically, the same dynamic occurs within the field of diversity and antiracism training, where two approaches are generally offered. The first focuses on "managing diversity," "teaching tolerance," and providing "multicultural education," stressing the need to appreciate cultural differences without talking about power. The second incorporates a concentration on the analysis of power, defining racism as race prejudice supported by social and institutional power. This approach is deliberate about the importance of taking racism beyond the realm of personal intent and placing it in the context of its historical construction by the dominant culture and institutions devoted to promulgating that culture. My colleague Kenneth Jones took the position that the first approach is actually dangerous, leaving power and privilege unchallenged at the expense of those already personally and systemically oppressed.

As teachers and facilitators, we have an obligation to be well grounded in a strong power analysis so that we can support our students as they embark on their investigations. I have witnessed too many classrooms where a lack of clarity about the relationship of cultural and institutional power to the construction and perpetuation of racism and other oppressions has allowed discussion to devolve into shouting matches about who is racist, who has racist intent or the lack thereof, leaving students and workshop participants defensive and confused.

This dynamic is not limited to the classroom. Operating from the prevailing ethos in the activist community that those in positions of privilege should follow the lead of those targeted by oppressive constructs, I have also seen many otherwise progressive organizations and communities support homophobic, sexist, or covertly racist agendas because they and/or their membership do not have the information or analytical skills to understand the ramifications of goals and strategies derived from what my mother used to call "stinkin' thinkin'" (misguided thinking based on either misinformation or misuse of the information at hand; I can see my mother now, as she sharply warned that "thinking you can both go out with your friends *and* get your homework done is some stinkin' thinkin', young lady"). While I certainly concur that oppressed people should lead their own liberation, I also acknowledge that we are all deeply affected by the power of white supremacy culture to condition our thinking and behavior. All of us, whether privileged or targeted, need to work at making good sense of our world through information gathering and the analysis of power.

This presents quite a challenge; we have to be grounded in an analysis that assures we are not duplicating oppressive dynamics in the classroom while remaining open to the ways in which our analysis can always shift and deepen. I take great hope from the progress I have seen within the social justice community. Younger activists, exposed to information and analysis much more developed than that available to me, embody a deep commitment to creating not just a movement, but one based on values of love, compassion, and open-heartedness that were not part of the left culture when I was developing as an activist in my early twenties.

To set the stage for cultural shift, then, we can work not only to see our own conditioning, we must also seek information and analysis that shed light on cultural, institutional, and personal power. We should also continue, wherever we are and in whatever context, to help people make good sense of their firsthand experience, which means giving them information and analysis tools to make sense of power, reject fear, embrace love.

THE POWER OF VISION

In her book *Bridging the Class Divide* (1996), former colleague and community organizer Linda Stout recounts a story about growing up poor in Kannapolis, NC; she tells how she dropped out of college when the tuition was raised because she was not aware she could pursue scholarships or loans. She recalls telling middle-class friends about this decision later in life, who were aghast that she had not sought out these options. She explains "back then I did not know the first thing about options. I often define poverty as a lack of options" (p. 25). Stout is talking about the impossibility of pursuing a path she could not imagine.

Peter Senge et al. invoke the biblical message that "where there is no vision the people perish," noting how "the power of genuine vision is understood in cultures around the world" (2008, p. 51). Similarly Jared Diamond, in his bestseller *Collapse*, a survey (as the title suggests) of how societies fail or succeed, notes that "public attitudes [are] essential for changes in [damaging] businesses' environmental practices" (2005, p. 485). He argues that "the public has ultimate responsibility for the behavior of even the biggest businesses" and suggests this is "empowering and hopeful, rather than disappointing" (p. 485). He says that businesses change when we, the public, "expect and require different behavior." I would simply add that our ability to expect and require different behavior requires in turn an ability to want something different from what we currently have, to imagine different possibilities.

Cooperrider and Whitney (n.d., p. 16) reference what they call "the anticipatory principle," suggesting that the "infinite human resource we have for generating constructive organizational change is our collective imagination and discourse about the future." They cite bodies of research that all point to the truth behind the Aristotlean idea that "a vivid imagination compels the whole body to obey it" (p. 17).

Freire (1998) and Greene (1988), both unapologetic about their idealism, reject cynicism and tell us to believe in and create a visioned world. They argue, in fact, that the struggle for justice *requires* a vision, or in Greene's words, we should learn to "name alternatives, imagine a better state of things" (p. 9). Greene references the French Resistance, noting how those involved "would not have felt [the Occupation of France by Nazi Germany] to be intolerable if they had no possibility of transformation in mind, if they had been unable to imagine a better state of things" (1988, p. 16). Although I might argue that we can know something is intolerable even if we cannot imagine a possibility of changing it, the promise of possibility is what makes transformative change possible. A sense of the intolerable without the sense of possibility can lead to despair and a kind of hopelessness. Viktor Frankl, writing about his experiences as a concentration camp prisoner during World War II, describes how it was this lack of possibility that led some prisoners to lose "their inner hold on their moral and spiritual selves" (1963, p. 110).

Antiracist activist and teacher working with the Catalyst Project, Clare Bayard (personal interview, April 20, 2009) echoes the importance of imagining alternatives as an important aspect of organizational and community strategy. She bemoans how so many in the U.S. antiracist community often mimic the dominant culture of "competition and scarcity" in the frequently held belief that "there are only so many "down" white antiracist activists to be had." Bayard talks about the need to imagine and then work to develop a "culture where everybody's leadership is needed and valued."

Scientist and cultural theorist Willis Harman offers a framework for understanding the power of visioning rooted in his belief that the western scientific worldview, based on a glorification of "the reliably measurable, excluding a vast realm of human concern now discounted as "subjective" or "metaphysical" (1998, p. 21), is not useful. I wrote earlier about characteristics of white supremacy culture, which include the veneration of both objectivity and the quantitative (if you can't measure it, then it doesn't count) (Okun, 2000). Harman argues that we have reached the limits of this worldview.

He frames his theories about the power of vision in the context of three metaphysical perspectives, the first (and lowest in his construction) is "matter giving rise to mind," (1998, p. 30), where we assume that the only way to "know" the world is to bring consciousness, lodged in our body/brain, to measure objective matter (outside of our bodies). The second metaphysical perspective is dualism, where we understand the world as both matter and mind; we can "know" about the world using quantitative methods *and* at the same time acknowledge the role of the mind in creating what we know. In this perspective, two different ways of knowing co-exist (and perhaps overlap). In the third metaphysical perspective, the one Harman aspires to, consciousness *is* matter. Matter "arises in some sense out of the mind … consciousness is not the end-product of material evolution; rather consciousness was here first" (p. 30).

Harman's theories echo principles of Buddhist, Hindu, and other eastern thought and philosophy. Of note is how western intellectuals and meaning-makers, bound until very recently to the rational, are beginning to take notice of both the limits of the quantitative, material world and the viability of centuries-old eastern wisdom.

Harman's theory brings us back to the idea that we can only accomplish that which we can imagine; Harman is suggesting that the act of imagining creates new realities. Davis, Sumara, and Luce-Kapler (2000) concur, arguing that "the universe is understood to change when a thought changes, because that thought is not merely in the universe or about the universe. Rather, it is a dynamic part of an ever-changing reality" (p. 64). I recall a story about a feminist therapist who used to tell her female patients that they should love themselves. After many years and quite a bit of frustration, she shifted her instructions to telling women to act as if they love themselves; the leap from self-hatred to self-love required a belief in possibility that many women could not yet imagine, so she had to begin by helping them to get to a place where they could conceptualize a different reality.

If we begin to create a changed world by imagining it, then the importance of imagining well becomes clear. David Korten notes that "real change ... depend[s] on the articulation of a compelling alternative to the existing profit-driven, corporate-planned, and corporate-managed global economy" (2006, p. 14). He references Filipino civil society leader and strategist Nicanor Perlas (p. 18) who

> helped me recognize that the power of the institutions of economic and political domination depends on their ability to perpetuate a falsified and inauthentic cultural trance based on beliefs and values at odds with reality. Break the trance, replace the values of an inauthentic culture with the values of an authentic culture grounded in a love of life rather than a love of money, and people will realign their life energy and bring forth the life-serving institutions of a new era. The key is to change the stories by which we define ourselves. It is easier said than done, but I have found it to be a powerful strategic insight.

Long-time colleague Bree Carlson (personal correspondence, September 9, 2008) agrees "there is a way in which all possibilities are around us all of the time and we are limited by what our current culture will allow us to see and believe in." She argues that sometimes culture changes when we are exposed to something we did not know was possible, that "our work is really only effective on a collective level when we are able to find some way to allow a small number of people to believe, even for a little while, that impossible things can be done."

Bayard's colleague Ari Clemenzi (personal interview, April 20, 2009) adds "because racism and all forms of oppression keep us disconnected from our feelings," our "vision should include how liberation feels," should offer some "embodiment of our success." Catalyst, the antiracism training organization where Bayard and Clemenzi work, and dRworks both attempt to create aspects of the culture we vision in our workshops. For example, we pay attention to the physical environment, insuring that our meeting spaces are full of natural light, offer comfortable seating, room to move about, access to the outdoors. We provide healthful food, including food that is culturally appropriate and meaningful to participants. We often invite participants to bring food, as sharing food is such a strong impulse in almost every culture. We ask participants to name the values that will guide conversation and learning and we work with those values as tension and conflicts arise. We make room for different ways of learning and knowing, offering opportunities for art, poetry, music, silence, movement.

Long-time antiracist trainer Monica Walker (personal interview, February 6, 2009) talks about the power of possibility as an important aspect of vision. She describes her attempt to embody an attitude towards her students that communicates "I love you because you can change, because I believe in your possibility, you are not determined, you are socialized." She notes how if we take the position that "I've been in the condition you're in," then we show not only that we know what they are going through but that change is possible. Part of our job, she explains, is to help students see that they have agency in the world.

So here we have another lesson for the cultural shift. In our teaching, we should offer possibility, giving students the opportunity to vision the world they want to encourage their engagement in shaping the world. We can and should cultivate our collective abilities to vision a positive, sustainable future, insuring that we have the information we need to vision well, even and perhaps particularly, when the vision seems less than possible.

THE MYTH OF THE MAJORITY

I have noticed, and I am sure that other teachers and trainers have too, how all it takes is one or two disruptive or disengaged students to derail a classroom of 20 or 25. One semester three of my students who were struggling with the material began to sit together in every class, informally organizing themselves to resist my teaching and the contributions of other class members. One of the three was quite outspoken, taking up a lot of space in her self-proclaimed stance as "devil's advocate" to whatever topic was the focus of our collective conversation. Together, the students were skilled at making themselves the focus of much of the classroom energy.

By the same token, I can remember cases where one person has changed the atmosphere and energy of a room in a positive way. I recall leading a white caucus, all women, for a county-based health department; participants were required to attend and most were not at all happy about that. We had just gone over the definition of racism, describing it as institutional and cultural as well as personal. I asked each woman to share her thinking and feeling after working with this broader definition. One by one, the participants made a point of noting their personal lack of racism and the irrelevance of the information to their lives. My heart began sinking lower and lower as each person, spurred on by the previous speaker, elaborated on her indifference to the material. Finally, we came to the very last woman in the circle. She began to speak slowly and carefully about her experience as a white mother of an adopted child from Korea. She shared several stories about her daughter's experiences with racism and her own pain and distress as a result. The room got very quiet and I saw some of the other women begin to nod in sympathy; after she spoke the group opened up, their defensiveness erased as they responded to the woman's powerful story.

Because our culture is rooted in the rhetoric of democracy, and because white supremacy culture values the measurable, we tend to assume that change happens as a result of "majority rule." If we reflect on our own experience and then study history, we see how, as Margaret Mead so famously said (although no source for the quote has ever been found), "never doubt that a small group of thoughtful, committed citizens can change the world. Indeed, it's the only thing that ever does." In my lifetime, I have seen huge shifts in cultural norms related to race and gender; the movements in which I have participated were not made up of demographic majorities. Relatively small groups of determined people, in many cases driven by their desire to live whole lives, can and have shifted our cultural landscape.

Margaret Wheatley, in her book *Leadership and the New Science* (2006), suggests we can see these shifts mirrored in nature, where change happens as the result of many local actions occurring simultaneously. When a "community" in one locale learns about the success of their neighbors, their own activity is strengthened. As groups network together, they suddenly and surprisingly emerge into a force both stronger than the sum of the parts and different from the local actions that gave birth to it. These forces are the result of what she calls "emergence," meaning they are birthed, they come into being.

Malcolm Gladwell, in his landmark book *The Tipping Point*, also suggests that cultural change happens this way, as a kind of epidemic, where "ideas and products and messages and behaviors spread just like viruses do" (2002, p. 7). He observes three shared characteristics of these tipping point "epidemics" (pp. 8-9). The first is unplanned "contagious" behavior where a "small number of people in [a] small number of situations ... started behaving very differently and that behavior somehow spread ... [and] a large number of people ... got "infected" [with the new behavior]; the second is the way little changes have big effects; the third is these changes happen in a hurry (as opposed to steadily and slowly). Gladwell is particularly interested in how "contagiousness ... is an unexpected property of all kinds of things, and we have to remember that if we are to recognize and diagnose epidemic change" (p. 10). He wants us to understand the geometry of epidemics, where "a virus spreads through a population, it doubles again and again" (p. 11). This explains, he argues, how monumental changes can result from seemingly insignificant events once the epidemic nature of change takes hold.

In his turn, Korten theorizes about orders of consciousness, in his case five, from "magical," the lowest to "spiritual," the highest, where each level acknowledges the increasing complexity, mystery, and oneness of the world. Like Gladwell, he argues that a numerical majority is not required. He talks about the third order of consciousness as a "swing vote" because it "is pivotal to the cultural politics of the Great Turning [the term he uses to represent a shift in culture]" (2006, p. 53). He argues that people at this order of consciousness "adapt" to the prevailing culture; our challenge as change agents, then, is to appeal to their desire for "a public good that transcends narrowly defined individual interests," one that acknowledges "the interdependent nature of our relationship to one another and the planet" (p. 55). In other words, we have an opportunity to create change with these swing voters, many of whom sit in our classrooms.

We can conclude, therefore, that cultural shift does not require a massive effort encompassing every community on the globe. Both Gladwell and Korten make a strong case for a different kind of mathematics. As noted earlier, Gladwell (2002, pp. 12-13) explains that the number needed for meaningful shifts can be as low as 5%.

The theories of cultural change offered here might seem contradictory—Inglehart's theory that cultural change happens more slowly as a result of congruent economic, political, social, and generational shifts versus Gladwell's idea that cultural change happens in an unplanned, sudden, and virus-like way set next to Korten's idea of working with the "swing voters." We do not need to resolve these theories, deciding one is right and the other wrong. The point is not so much whether culture changes slowly or quickly, but that cultural shift can emerge as the result of changes in local behavior and thinking that occurs and spreads both generationally and spontaneously.

In other words, we can build movement, teach in our classrooms, engage in our activism without anxiety about the specific numbers of people we are reaching. I take a rather perverse delight in this, given our culture's obsession with quantitative measurement.

THE PERSONAL IS POLITICAL

A memory comes at me from about 20 years ago. My colleagues and I are working with communities in the Arkansas Delta. We are hosting a meeting for local residents, all African American adults; many come from families who have lived here for generations. They are participating in a community organizing training. I am one member of the training team, although I am not a lead trainer as I have little community organizing experience. I am standing at the back of the room, listening to my colleague, a long-time activist and organizer, an African American man born and raised in South Carolina in a region not that different from the Delta. He is talking to the group; I don't even remember the exact topic or what he is saying. What I do remember is this—I was not happy with his presentation. Frustrated because he was not being clear enough, I walked up to the front where he was talking, literally put my hand out, touched his shoulder, and pushed him out of the way. I then commenced to re-explain what he had been saying, certain in my bones that I could do a better job.

As white people, our internalization of our own superiority has very direct consequences as we move through the world, assuming that while we are not racist, we do know best. As I mentioned earlier, whole disciplines are based in the ideology that assimilating into whiteness is the desired goal, while whole communities and cultures, ways of being, are devalued and erased.

As I was writing this chapter, Congress was vetting Sonia Sotomayor for a position on the nation's Supreme Court, where she would sit as the first Latina woman in that position (she has since been confirmed). Republican and conservative Congressmen, as well as the mainstream media, obsessively focused for weeks on a remark Sotomayor made years earlier, misquoted and taken out of context, about how she "would hope that a wise Latina woman with the richness of her experiences would more often than not reach a better conclusion than a white male who hasn't lived that life" (2009). Syndicated columnist Rick Horowitz adroitly summed up the racist and entitled assumptiveness embedded in the cultural and personal ire directed at Sotomayor for this statement, satirizing the essence of the comments of one of her white male critics (2009):

> I am truth. I am certainty. I am facts—facts as they are, not as some wish them to be. I am objectivity personified. I am White Guy. When I see things, I see them clearly, and without distortion of any kind. I see all things, and hear all things, and I overlook nothing. I assign each thing I see, each thing I hear, the importance it deserves—neither more nor less. My judgment in these matters isn't judgment at all—it is the simple recognition of reality. Any judgment that differs from mine, to the extent that it differs from mine, does not reflect reality. I am White Guy....

We all have work to do related to the ways we internalize and act out of these kinds of culturally conditioned beliefs. In my conversations with master teachers, I hear a renewed understanding of the feminist mantra that "the personal is political," that paying attention to the personal aspect of broad-based cultural change is important. Known popularly as "walking our talk," teachers and leaders are appreciating as never before Audre Lorde's admonition that "the master's tools will never dismantle the master's house" (1984, pp. 110-113). Lorde, in her talk/essay of the same title, makes a strong argument for the ways in which the personal is the political; she calls white feminist teachers and educators, colleagues at the institution where she was teaching at the time, to task for mimicking the destructive tendencies of the dominant culture that leads them to value some (straight white women) more than others (Black feminists and lesbians).

Clare Bayard notes how cultural conditioning leads us to "act out of anger and urgency," and even though we do not intend to bring "a guilt and shame curriculum," that's often how people engage in critical inquiry (personal conversation, April 20, 2009). Bayard is describing the risk that a critical stance can become a way of life rather than a strategically applied skill. She, along with her colleagues, talks about the importance of moving away from culturally conditioned impulses based in fear of scarcity and competition toward an intentional culture of love and respect. This, they argue, requires that first we understand the ways in which culturally conditioned responses show up in our hearts, minds, and work, and second, that we prioritize healing from the damage done to us by white supremacy culture.

Ingrid Chapman, another Catalyst trainer, talks about the value of thinking about "the impacts of white supremacy on me and my family" (personal interview, April 20, 2009). She explains that "the more I have been able to unpack that, I understand the impacts on me and my family and as a result feel very deeply a commitment to the struggle that is very much about both the interests of the broader community as well as my family and self, which leads me to be able to trust myself." Chapman notes that the "first stage [of awareness] is how I can't trust myself, as I become aware of how complicit I am in racism, I can't trust my motivation." At Catalyst, they describe this as being "frozen," a stage in our development as white people "where we're hyper-aware of our own racism and afraid of doing anything that could make it worse." Chapman goes on to note that developing "clarity about my own motivation is helpful to my ability to step up and connect to other white people, have more empathy, and build stronger relationships with People of Color, because it's not about me coming to 'save' them."

In the same vein, my colleagues at dRworks and I have created a curriculum designed to support people to bring greater self-awareness to the challenging task of combating racism and other oppressions. Seeing how often well-meaning activism becomes derailed because of the ways in which our socialized attitudes and behaviors lead us to reproduce unhealthy interpersonal dynamics and power relationships, we want to support people to develop an awareness that is both critical and compassionate—of and for ourselves and each other.

Margaret Wheatley also makes the case for self-awareness. Echoing Korten's argument that we have the power to construct a different future, Wheatley argues that once we've decided we want to change our behavior, then "we need to figure out the values and agreements that we think will support these new behaviors ... [and] work together to see what it means to live into these agreements." She does not pretend that this is easy, noting that "behaviors don't change just by announcing new values" (2001). She associates behavior change with greater self-awareness, saying "we have to become far more self-reflective than normal."

Wheatley sees the development of self-awareness as a collaborative, collective endeavor, where we "help one another notice when we fall back into old behaviors" until we gradually learn how to behave in accordance with our expressed desires. Through this process, she says, "we slowly become who we said we wanted to be." Referencing Harman's belief in the power of mind, she notes that we create our own reality in relationship with each other by choosing what to notice, what to ignore. With these choices, "we co-create our world."

One challenge is how what we notice is influenced by our culture. Friend and activist Alba Onofrio worries about this, saying (personal correspondence, September 11, 2008), "I often think about how my experiences reinforce my preconceived notions, ... I notice what confirm[s] my beliefs and ignore everything else." Onofrio's observation reminds us of the importance of placing a self-awareness practice in the context of understanding (noticing) the power of white supremacy culture to influence our thinking. As Wheatley says, noticing is a choice, although it may not seem like one, just like noticing our culture is counterintuitive to our understanding of its normalcy. Wheatley goes on to say that when a system is suffering or in denial, then it "might be lacking information, it might have lost clarity about who it is, it might have troubled relationships, it might be ignoring those who have valuable insights" (2006, p. 145). The solution, she says, is to "connect it to more of itself. The primary change strategy becomes quite straightforward. In order to change, the system needs to learn more about itself from itself" (p. 145).

For example, a significant majority of my students have been taught to understand historically systemic problems like racism as located in the individual, believing that as long as one does not hold racist thoughts, then racism does not exist. Given the breadth and depth of their misinformation about the nature of racism, my task as a teacher is to help them develop awareness of both the systemic nature of racism and then to bring consciousness to our participation in and collusion with racist systems.

Understanding our interdependence in these moments is critical, particularly if we want to avoid reproducing the "guilt and shame" curriculum that Bayard described earlier, one that comes with assumptions of individual agency free from cultural influence. Students who see themselves as free agents will generally defend against the idea they participate in racism until and unless they understand how they are an integral part of a larger construct not necessarily of their own making, one they have the potential to change by joining with others. The implications are that if we want to change behavior, either our own or others, we have to understand that are affected by each other and the larger culture. Wheatley points out how our individual desire to change is prompted in large part by a collectively inspired and declared will to change. She says "the new science keeps reminding us that in this participative universe, nothing living lives alone. Everything comes into form because of relationship" (2006, p. 145).

The cultural conditioning to understand ourselves as individual is not confined to my students. Activist and small-business owner Zulayka Santiago speaks (personal correspondence, August 19, 2009) to the paradox of doing self-work toward a collective healing. She notes how "as of lately, I have become frustrated with some of my beloved hippie/new age/sustainability-focused friends that are teetering on the verge of self-absorption." Santiago is aware of the allure of this focus on the self, wondering "how often have I been on that ledge and how can I be more accountable to my community in my own self work?"

June Jordan describes her own experience with this tension, tracing her evolution in moving from a focus on self to an understanding of our interconnection. She talks about struggling with Dr. Martin Luther King's concept of "the Beloved Community"—she assumed he "meant something simple-minded like the Bad Guys Stop the Bad Stuff and the Good Guys then Forgive Them" (2002, p. 44). "It took me a long time," she says, "before I understood that "Beloved Community" means everybody is sacred. Nobody is excluded from that deliberate embrace" (p. 44). She talks about how Dr. King "insisted upon the sanctity of values and people I could neither see nor touch" and as a result, she

> began to notice Americans who were neither black nor white, nor English-speaking ... coincidental histories among these growing American diversities ... varieties of hell on earth following from the Gospel of White Supremacy. (p. 45)

Her burgeoning understanding led her to a place of hope where she saw a possibility for "becom[ing] potentially more powerful than the hatred that surrounds and seeks to divide us" (2002, p. 46). Clemenzi also stresses the importance of doing personal work within a collective endeavor, noting that "personal work is a deep piece of antiracism work [and] it's a fine line because it can so easily, in this culture, turn into self-obsession." Done in a collective context, people can work together to "figure out how to support each other as the premise, rather than a premise of competition. We need to prioritize our own healing and support each other as individuals and unpack how we bring our own trauma into the work; we need community to do this well" (personal communication, April 20, 2009).

Wheatley explains that "individual behaviors co-evolve as individuals interact with system dynamics. If we want to change individual or local behaviors, we have to tune into these system-wide influences" (2006, p. 142). She suggests we need a process where "we keep dancing between the two levels [the whole and the part], bringing the sensitivities and information gleaned from one level to help us understand the other. If we hold awareness of the whole as we study the part, and understand the part in its relationship to the whole, profound new insights become available" (p. 143).

If, as Wheatley suggests, the work of change is "to organize new local efforts, connect them to each other, and know that their values and practices can emerge as something even stronger" (2001), then, "as people realize the problems they face are shared by others in different parts of the globe, ... they instantly recognize these as systemic issues." She goes on to say that "there is no better way for people to become skilled systems thinkers than to realize their problem is not unique to them, but is affecting many others in diverse parts of the global system" (2001).

Senge et al. concur (2008), speaking to the importance of helping people see systems (analysis) and collaborate across boundaries (collective action). They offer a number of case studies to illustrate how these two approaches can lead to Korten's vision of earth community, where we "create a future truly in harmony with a flourishing world" (2008, p. 55).

Developing a practice of self-awareness in a community or collective context provides opportunities for building a transformative leadership grounded in "values and practices that are life-affirming rather than life-destroying" (Wheatley, 2001). Wheatley suggests a process where leaders are invited (by a small group of local hosts) to meet regularly to think together, develop clarity about the practices and values that work to affirm and sustain people, and to support each other's courageous acts. Each circle is a site for critical education. People become more knowledgeable about what is going on in and develop strategies to influence their world. They teach one another, relying on their experience and compassion. Over time, these local circles develop leaders with the confidence, experience, and support to affect a larger stage. In this way, she argues, the standard, along with the definition, of effective leadership is raised.

Community organizer, educator, and master quilter Jereann King (personal correspondence, September 3, 2008) describes how this is "much of what we are attempting to do in Warren County and ... eastern North Carolina, ... organizing study circles around discussions of children and their success. The leadership that is developing is phenomenal."

Both Wheatley and King are describing the potential for sites (and the classroom is one) where people gather to develop personal clarity, become more knowledgeable, deepen awareness, and strategize collectively. The fourth lesson for achieving cultural shift, then, has to do with our ability to develop our self-awareness, not as a solitary and individual task, but as a collaborative and collective one. As teachers and activists, we want to facilitate this endeavor of self-awareness, one that prepares us and supports us to act collaboratively and collectively to create a just world.

THE POWER OF ENERGY

> Don't ask what the world needs. Ask what makes you come alive, and go do it. Because what the world needs is people who have come alive.
>
> —Howard Thurman (The James Logan Courier, 2008)

In my first decades of work, I was motivated by a strong sense of duty. I felt fulfilled contributing to a larger cause, working as a development director at a social justice non-profit; my orientation to detail led me to be successful at setting up the systems essential to effective fundraising. Years passed and I grew increasingly unhappy with the actual day-to-day tasks attached to my job; I experienced severe burnout, which made me rethink how I was spending my time and energy. I realized I could serve my values by doing what I most loved to do, that I did not have to define meaningful work as a sense of duty. [I am sure there are gender dimensions to this having to do with a woman's duty versus her desire to please herself that I am not taking time to explore here.] I began to understand the power of following my energy, which is one manifestation of Wheatley's belief that "we don't have to push and pull a system, or bully it to change; we have to participate with colleagues in discovering what's important to us" (2006, p. 152).

Harman notes that while "the history of science, mathematics, art, and intellectual achievement is replete with anecdotal evidence" of deep intuitive knowing coming from "somewhere other than the usual self, ... science has had very little to say about [it], beyond admitting that most of its own conceptual advances seem to have arrived in this way" (1998, p. 66).

The western propensity to distrust anything we cannot measure means that we "have been thoroughly taught ... not to trust ourselves—not to trust that ultimately we do know what we most deeply desire, and how to resolve our inner conflicts" (p. 70).

I refer to Chapman's story above, where she talks about needing to move through her social conditioning so she could learn to trust herself in a culture that would prefer she does not. Antiracist scholar and teacher Becky Thompson (personal interview, June 11, 2009) notes that teaching about white supremacy has an intuitive quality—the work is so often a matter of faith. You try, she says, "to keep doing the work and you don't really know; it's a little like writing, carving an image in the void, you don't know where it's going to land, and you have to do it anyway." I have come to believe deeply in the importance of intuitive energy in my own life and work. Understanding the role of this energy helps me to better respond to and honor the process that each of my students is engaging in as they work to unwrap years of social conditioning; it helps me to respond to and better honor my own process.

Turning to the creative/intuitive mind requires a reconsideration of our assumption that we decide best through "objective" strategies like planning, goal-setting, logical analyses, rules of logic, which Harman notes are "all the ways we were taught in school as the right way to think" (1998, p. 71). He states that the western bias towards the concrete and measurable, the "objective," the "reductionist" (reducing all things to their parts) has severely limited our potential, suggesting that affirmation and inner imagery are potent strategies for "dissolving resistance and releasing ... creative abilities" (p. 68). He cites evidence showing that "the more one uses the creative/intuitive mind, the more faith one displays in turning to it with difficult decisions and problems, the better it seems to perform" (pp. 70-71).

Harman points out the pragmatic aspects of this "new age" thinking, relating how the business community sponsors seminars and workshops aimed at teaching people "to imagine success, create a vision, ... and hence bring about success" (1998, p. 73). He describes how some workshops teach not just affirmation, but also the skill of accessing the deeper, intuitive mind (p. 73). Finally, he notes that the business community is, in his words, "eminently practical. If this approach is used, it is because it works. It gets results" (p. 74).

Wheatley agrees, noting that groups change "not by self-reports or the words of a few people, but by noticing what's meaningful to them as they do their work, what gets attention, what topics generate the most energy, positive or negative" (2006, pp. 147-48). She talks about a unifying energy "that makes the work of change possible" (p. 149).

We change, Wheatley says, "only if we decide that the change is meaningful to who we are. Will it help us become who we want to be? Or gain us
more of what we think we need to preserve ourselves?" (2006, pp. 147-
148). These are questions that we need to ask and answer both individually and collectively.

One challenge is that we live in a culture that has lost touch with the
natural rhythms of night and day, the seasons, the environment. Western,
capitalist culture, fearful of losing time to potential profit-making, has
erased the eminently sensible afternoon siesta rest period that gave the
individual and community body a short but much needed break in the
hottest period of the day when energies are low. A culture focused on the
financial has taught us to ignore the push and pull of energies connected
to sunlight and darkness, planting and harvest, cycles of the moon, the
significance of menstruation and menopause to over half our population.
Becoming attuned to our personal and collective energy is essential political work in a culture that prefers we shut down all thoughts and feelings
that put us in touch with both the real cost of that culture to our lives and
a way of knowing that, once tapped, is not as easily socialized and controlled.

We can also learn from how movements emerge, gain strength, and
wane in energetic waves connected to the yearnings, work, and energies of
people and communities. We cannot trace exactly why, for example, the
day that Rosa Parks took her seat on the bus sparked an emerging movement when people had been taking the same kind of actions days, weeks,
and months earlier.

We cannot depend on energy alone; Parks' refusal to move to the back
of the bus happened within a context where people and communities
were organizing, in effect preparing for the moment to occur. However,
understanding the role of energy in personal and cultural shifts can help
us to honor periods of needed rest, reflection, and preparation (perhaps
without the self-recrimination that so often happens when movements are
in ebb periods) that help us make best opportunity of periods when forces
for change align and peak.

I want to note the constraints of this approach. Community activist and
organizer Bridgette Burge (personal correspondence, September 3, 2008)
points out that while honoring our energy "resonates as such simple, deep
wisdom," at the same time

> I think of my dad's girlfriend: poor, single mom helping to raise her single
> daughter's six children—both of them abuse survivors, both smart as shit
> and tough as nails, both without good healthcare or a decent place to live.
> Talking about "opening to our positive energy" with them can seem like that
> typical "Bridgette talk" since I managed to "escape" thru good grades and
> college. On the other hand, I don't want to dismiss spiritual practice and

liberatory vision as only accessible, meaningful or desired by the class privileged. It's a contradiction I'd like to talk through more. It's along the same lines as folks working 2 or more jobs with children to boot not having the opportunities to engage with movement work in ways that they might otherwise be capable of.

Santiago (personal correspondence, August 19, 2009) speaks to this tension as well, noting how "we KNOW (her capitals) that the way things are done are NOT RIGHT, NOT LIFE GIVING and yet we are too exhausted or spread thin to devote adequate amounts of time to visioning" or be open to positive energy in the face of so much drain.

I attempt to hold this contradiction by suggesting that one mark of injustice is precisely how it forbids people and communities to attend to their most creative energies, requiring them instead to work at cross purposes to their mental, emotional, physical, and spiritual health. If we are to realize a just world, then our vision must encompass the right of every person, every community, to open to and honor their inspired energies.

Our task, then, becomes to develop our awareness collectively and collaboratively and to understand that opening to our energy is one aspect of liberatory awareness and action.

CONCLUSION

As teachers and educators, I believe we can take hope from these lessons. Assuming that cultures change as the result of new generations growing into the world with new paradigms, we can support the emerging generation(s) and hone our ability to share what we know with those who come after us as we engage collectively in shaping life-affirming cultural beliefs and values.

The lessons for those who want to participate in a cultural shift seem to be, at least in part, these:

1. Do what we can to help each other cultivate "the standpoint of the cultural stranger," as we learn to challenge notions of "normal" and "abnormal." Investigate and support each other to investigate how culture shapes our thinking so we can "decolonize" our minds.

2. Continue, wherever we are and in whatever context, to help each other think critically and compassionately about our firsthand experience, which means gathering information and developing an analysis that help us make sense of power, reject fear, embrace love.

3. Cultivate our collective abilities to vision a positive, sustainable future, insuring that we have the information we need to vision well.

4. Understand we can build movement, teach in our classrooms, engage in our activism without prioritizing numbers over relationship.

5. Develop our self-awareness, and help others to develop theirs, not as a solitary and individual task, but as a collaborative and collective one. Our goal is to come into awareness in the context of community and interdependence in order to prepare and support active engagement in the world.

6. Understand that we all need and deserve the opportunity to develop our intuitive intelligence because opening to our positive energy is one aspect of liberation.

These lessons do not in any way preempt the importance of organizing and movement building; rather they inform those efforts. Neither do they stand alone, instead weaving simultaneously—we work together to develop the personal and collective self-awareness that allows us to move beyond the culturally constructed constraints of white supremacy culture, to ground ourselves in an analysis that allows us to vision boldly a just and loving world. We develop the practice of "queering normal" in an effort to avoid creating new versions of toxic constraints. We attend to our intuitive and energetic energies, realizing that we require a strong vision to keep us going in those times when we cannot see the result of our efforts, even as we keep faith in the possibility of transformation.

Cultural critic and writing teacher Derrick Jensen says, "the only real job of any teacher ... is to help students find themselves. Everything else is either a distraction, or at best, window dressing" (2004, p. 14). The next chapter is devoted to outlining the process I use, one of many, to pull on the lessons outlined here in order to do what Jensen suggests. While on the surface Jensen's summary of our essential job may seem too simple a strategy for saving the world, it may in fact be just what is needed.

A Black Girl Talks of the United States

See, they put me out of class today
because I questioned The
Establishment.
We were discussing the United States
and I said that the name "United
States" was hypocritical.
That made everyone uncomfortable,
and the teacher told me not to be
ridiculous.
"Our forefather organized a union
where everyone has liberty and justice."
I said that was bull,
since there is a KKK and an NAACP
and a Nation of Islam
and organizations for Asians, Hispanics
and Native Americans, and every other
class of people
who are citizens.
And I said that if we were really united,
we would not need these organizations
or affirmative action, or quotas,
or minority scholarships, or welfare,
because we all would be equal,
and we would all get along,
and there would be no racial, social or
economic tensions,
and we would all be classified as
Americans,

The Emperor Has No Clothes: Teaching About Race and Racism
to People Who Don't Want to Know, pp.–102 101
Copyright © 2010 by Information Age Publishing

not by our race, color, creed or ethnicity.
And the teacher asked me to be quiet,
but I kept on talking.
I talked about Slavery
and I talked about the Native
Americans
being cheated out of their land
and I talked about Indian Reservations
and I talked about the Civil War
and I talked about the Civil Rights
Movement
and I talked about Proposition 187
and I talked about Discrimination
and I talked about Hatred
and I talked about the Government
and I kept on talking.
And the teacher, well, she put me out
but that's okay
because we all know that I was right!

—Wendy Ivy Wilson, 18, North Carolina
(1999, pp. 60-61)

CHAPTER 4

ASPIRING TO SEE

An Antiracist Pedagogy

In this chapter, I describe a process collaboratively developed with Kenneth Jones during the period he and I cofounded and worked at Change-Work throughout the 1990s up until Kenneth's premature death in 2004. The process continues to be used and refined in the work I do with the group of people who emerged from ChangeWork and currently operate together in a collaborative called Dismantling Racism Works (dRworks). In this chapter I use "we" quite often; I am referencing and honoring the work of Kenneth and many others who have contributed to the ideas that you find here, including Michelle Jones and Vivette Jeffries-Logan who I work most closely with now. All those who have had a hand in developing this process, to the extent they can be identified individually, are listed in the appreciations at the beginning of this book.

In addition to the work I do at dRworks, I spend many, many hours in the classroom. Added to the collective voices of my many training partners over the years, you will hear the voices of my students, who have generously allowed their words to be shared here. These voices represent the arc of many semesters; my promise of confidentiality allows me to give you a sense of their various identities (race, class, gender, ...) without offering more specific details.

---

*The Emperor Has No Clothes: Teaching About Race and Racism
to People Who Don't Want to Know,* pp. 103–129

Finally, in chapter 3 I identified five features linked to cultural transformation. In this chapter, I describe a pedagogy that integrates these five features and I identify those integrations as they occur.

INTRODUCTION

As I note earlier, many students enter the classroom with the belief that racism is a thing of the past; they often say things like "I don't see race" and "we are all the same." As one of my students wrote toward the end of one semester,

> I have learned about issues of discrimination and discovered enraging and unfair policies of which I was previously unaware. I had never heard of institutionalized oppression and I had no knowledge of the vast number and types of people who are still discriminated against. Almost everything I read about or discussed in this class was new information to me.

Our culture taught her well, teaches us all well, to believe that racism "was triumphed over in different times, something not relevant in today's world" (Gazel, 2007, p. 535).

Unfortunately, many teachers bring this same ignorance into the classroom. In their article on the importance of preparing teachers to understand the power of race and racism, Jost, Whitfield, and Jost (2005, p. 14) point out that "the majority of white teachers hold fairly ethnocentric views of the world" and a large number of Black teachers do as well. They identify eight "slick spots" that impede the dismantling of embedded racist practices in schools and classrooms. All boil down to the different ways that teachers are unprepared to address systemic racism and racist inequity.

The kicker is that our students are right—as human beings, we are all the same. The political and cultural constructs that operate to keep us separated serve the concentration of power at the expense of us all. And yet, to believe in our sameness with a discerning understanding of the depth of our differences, constructed to lodge power in one group at the expense of another, is very different than the shallow "we are all the same" claim that erases any acknowledgement of the horrific impact of these devastating constructs on peoples' lives. Attempting to teach about race and racism with simplistic explanations for race inequity that do not incorporate a power analysis, with little or no knowledge about the history of racism institutionally and culturally, with little or no ability and willingness to sit with our own participation or collusion in racist constructs, does more harm than good.

Adams, Edkins, Lacka, Pickett, and Cheryan (2008) conducted a study showing that courses that "do not consider racism per se" and instead talk about "stereotyping and prejudice" (p. 357) not only reinforce ideologies of individualism but also "reproduce racist realities" by misleading students to "conclude that racism plays a less extensive role in American society" (p. 358) than it does. Such classes result in lower support for remedial action than no class at all. The authors conclude that "support for antiracist policy" comes when teachers "discuss racism as a systemic phenomenon embedded in American society" (p. 358). In the same vein, Jost et al. (2005) point to research linking culturally competent teachers to higher achievement in diverse classrooms.

Therefore to teach about race and racism effectively, we must become deeply immersed in our own antiracist education and practice. My discussion of an effective pedagogy about race and racism assumes three things: (1) a strong analysis incorporating a thorough understanding of the historical and systemic nature of cultural and institutional racism, (2) comfort with the concepts of privilege and internalization, and (3) comprehension of the ways in which oppressive constructs of race, class, gender, sexuality, and "disability," intersect to reinforce white supremacy. If a facilitator or teacher does not yet have an analysis that incorporates these understandings, the first order of business is to embark on a learning process that will provide them.

TEACHING AS PROCESS AND PRODUCT

How do we help students move through a process that starts with the shallow assumption of sameness and reveals the depth of historical and systemic oppression designed to divide us in the service of power? And how do we do this in ways that speak to what we know about all that is required of us if we are serious about the task of cultural transformation?

When I think back on my own learning process, I can identify specific "aha" moments, each representing weeks, months, years of self-reflection and exposure to information that came together in a single flash of knowing. To this day I can stand in front of a group at a workshop, or in a classroom, and feel my body resound with the "oh, that's why I say that" understanding that lets me know I truly understand what I am talking about.

My colleague Kenneth Jones always introduced our dismantling workshops by explaining to participants that we were going to take them through a process. Kenneth was referring to the ways in which the process of teaching and learning moves us through layers of understanding that prepare us to achieve these "aha" moments of embodied knowing.

The process of unpacking a comprehensive understanding of white supremacy requires that we address levels of physical, emotional, and intellectual misinformation and conditioning. Our task as teachers, as activists, as humans, articulated in the last chapter, is to help each other cultivate "the standpoint of the cultural stranger," to challenge notions of "normal" and "abnormal," and to embrace instead the possibilities in our difference. Kenneth and I came to understand that we could do this best by thoughtfully moving people through a process that starts with relationship-building and leads into analysis, recurrent reflection, action, and vision, reinforcing and weaving these aspects in and through the process.

So despite the "longstanding controversy on the relative importance of process as compared with product" (Eisner, 2002, p. 139), we take the unequivocal position that we must incorporate both. The product we wish to deliver—a holistic understanding of racism, white supremacy, and the possibility of acting to address them—is dependent on the process that we use to help people receive it. In this way, the curriculum is process-driven, meaning that each step builds on the one before although each step really only makes sense as part of a whole.

Antiracist activists Ingrid Chapman and Ari Clemenzi (personal communication, May 20, 2009) reflect the significance of this dialectic. Chapman names the critical importance of relationship building across race lines because of the unique ways in which that kind of one-on-one contact helps us to know, see, and understand each other. Clemenzi adds that the process of relationship building is enhanced by the equally important political education and analysis that puts what we are learning from our relationships into a larger historical context. Process and product offer a back and forth dialectic, the two entwining in and through each other to reinforce and support meaningful learning.

Consistent with Freire's (1995) critique of the "banking method" of teaching, where students are considered "empty vessels" into which teachers pour knowledge, my assumption is that "genuine learning takes place when students interact with teachers, other learners, and the material" (Gazel, 2007, p. 544) in a learning *process*. While the importance of learning as a process is fundamental, the one I am about to describe is certainly not the only one. My goal with this chapter is to be descriptive rather than prescriptive.

As I note earlier, while more and more material is available to help us understand the construction, history, and dynamics associated with white supremacy (the product), fewer resources are available explaining how to teach about this construction, history, dynamics (the process). This is partly because much of the innovative, creative, and effective teaching about race and racism is happening in and among activist communities, where documentation is often sacrificed to tight budgets and overwhelming workloads. Another reason is the general indifference, if not antipathy, to teaching methods in the academy, with the exception of specific professors and small islands of concern in education departments.

My hope is to add to the resources available and make the case for an informed and thoughtful pedagogy. The approach described here draws from education theory, as well as the writing and reflection on the effective pedagogy of race and racism that is available.

THE PROCESS: AN OVERVIEW

To describe the process that I developed with Kenneth Jones and have adapted for use with my colleagues at dRworks and in my classroom, I begin with education theorist Eisner (2002), who contrasts a spiderweb to staircase models of curriculum development. Eisner characterizes the first as more progressive (offering opportunities for the learners to shape their own education) and the latter as more conservative (stressing the mastery of a body of knowledge). We attempt to avoid the false either/or dynamic and use both to great effect.

The process begins with personal reflection and relationship-building, moves into analysis and application, and ends with visioning. These are not concrete stages; elements of each occur and reoccur throughout the process, as do recurrent reflection and evaluation. Like Eisner (2002) and Walker and Soltis (1997), we believe in a "rhythm of education" that encompasses "the stage of romance, the stage of precision, and the stage of generalization" (Eisner, 2002, p. 142). Our process mimics this rhythm, where we ask people to reflect on their own experience (romance), derive an understanding of the world from that experience (romance leading to precision), understand the limits of that experience in understanding the world (precision), and seek out the wisdom of others in order to make better sense of the world and our place in it (precision leading to generalization).

We "set the stage" in our workshops and I do this in the classroom by grounding the curriculum in people's life experiences, in the rich storytelling and life sharing that begins to shape the development of a learning community (romance). We believe that "one should begin an engagement with any subject in a romantic way, feeling excitement in its presence, being aroused by its attractiveness, and enjoying its company" (Walker and Soltis, 1997, p. 44). We are hoping for students to feel the elation of learning expressed by this young student:

> After this first class, I felt very excited and less nervous ... When I walked in on the first day of class and saw the projection screen with a music video playing on it I knew from that day on I would love this class and the energy

about it. I am very excited about this course and feel like I will come out of this class knowing a lot more than I came in with …

By starting with personal reflection and relationship-building we set the stage for the often challenging and emotional discussions that come with taking apart the oppressive constructs of white supremacy. Giving students time and space to tell their own stories sets a tone where they are then more eager to participate.

Storytelling is done in the context of understanding and deconstructing racism. For example, I often ask people to do a paired listening exercise in which they share something about their class and ethnic background. I often follow this with an activity that gives people an opportunity to talk about the range of identities they hold in the world. I might have my students write a "Where I'm From" poem based on the activity in *Beyond Heroes and Holidays* (Lee, Menkart, & Okazawa-Rey, 2006), followed by a small group activity where they work with their individual poems to create a group poem.

One young African American student writes:

I am from...
Seven layer cookies and sweet potato pie
Competitive tree climbing with my brother
Freezing walks after snow football
Hypocritical views on homosexuality and divorce
noodles koolaid and heated blankets
Grieving for months days even years over my little brother....
RIP ETHAN
a line of preachers that never approved of my lifestyle choice
Oldies an saturday morning yard sales with my grandma.

Four white students put their poems together to create this one:

We are from long journeys over seas
    the end of a dusty dirt road
    the skies that fall in automotive accidents.
We are from kicks of dirt and dirty feet
    hand-me-downs, already broken in
    the lost and found, now mine.
We are from generations of teachers
    our side of the room and learning to dive
    challenges we've overcome.
We are from dreams that still lie in our sleep
    the bird at the window that chirps a beat
    the morning before the sun.
You know us, we are.

As I note in the previous chapter, cultural transformation requires that we reject fear and embrace love; therefore we must create a learning environment in which the focus is on building an analysis within a context of loving relationship. All of these activities, interwoven like the strands of Eisner's spiderweb, are designed to help people reflect on their own lives, learn more about the other people in the room, and prompt discussions of how our backgrounds influence the way we experience and see the world. The goal, critical to cultural transformation, is to create an environment in which we help each other think critically and compassionately about our firsthand experience, gather information that helps us put that experience in a larger context, and develop an analysis of power.

For example, I sometimes use an activity where people cross the room in silence as different identities are called aloud—first the more "obvious" ones (race, age, to some extent gender) and then those that we often have more choice about revealing (income and/or wealth level, education, sexuality, etc.). This helps people reflect on the feelings they hold about their identities, the power of those identities, and the control or lack of control they/we all have over assigned identities. I acknowledge the risks that people take in sharing who they are, appreciate the honor of being trusted with this information, acknowledge our mutual complexity as we grapple with the power of labels that try to reduce us to one-dimensional cardboard stereotypes. As a class, we then grapple with the question of "why?"—why do such labels exist, who do they serve, and what are our choices in terms of how we respond to them?

This "setting the stage" with reflection and relationship building is followed in our curriculum by the "precision" of "getting to know the subject better and studying it in detail" (Walker & Soltis, 1997, p. 44). Davis, Sumara, and Luce-Kapler state that a key to effective teaching "is to provide learners with the means of associating ideas with the events of their lives, … about helping them to notice what they haven't noticed" (2000, p. 26). Henry Giroux adds "students must be given the opportunity to learn how to use and interpret their own experiences in a manner that reveals how the latter have been shaped and influenced by the dominant culture" (1999, p. 19).

Accordingly, in this analysis phase—Eisner's staircase—we offer historical and analytical grounding, sharing information that requires the learners to place their personal experiences into a larger social and political context. I have found that pairing history with analysis frees us from attachments to our own personal stories as the only way to see the world. As Giroux notes (1999), this is critical because of how we tend to generalize based on our own experience without understanding how our thinking is culturally conditioned.

For example, many of my students, even those from low-income backgrounds, tend to believe that people can "make it" economically if they just work hard. They blame poverty on the poor, and if they are or have been poor themselves, tend to see their families as exceptions. Many do not make the obvious link between poverty and school achievement. An older, experienced teacher, a student in my class, admits that she is beginning to "better understand some of the issues about today's school system that I need to consider, … such as how poverty affects a child's ability." She lives in a culture that has allowed her to teach for over a decade without ever being asked or told to make these vital connections.

Because so many students believe that racism is about individual attitudes, white students believe that if they don't have racist intent, they are not racist and do not participate in racism. They say things like, "I think that all people are the same, and that what color their skin is, or what culture they are should have no effect as to how they are being treated by others." Students of color also often associate racism with individual behavior directed at them, without seeing the larger systemic nature of the race construct. One young Black woman writes "Some people have not been able to let go of the past and for that things like racism continue to haunt this world of ours." Most students tend to think that "serious" racism is no longer operative. Our job in a workshop or classroom, then, is to give students the information they need to make better sense of the world.

As I say above, one effective way of doing this is to bring history into the classroom. For example, I share a history of the race construct to cut through the idea that racism is lodged only in the individual and to give students an understanding that the ideas we are talking about—racism, privilege, internalized racial inferiority and superiority—are the result of cultural beliefs and institutional practices deliberately constructed over time to privilege one group of people at the expense of others. I show films, assign readings, and draw from the wealth of resources available on the internet from organizations like *Rethinking Schools* (www.rethinking-schools.org), *United for a Fair Economy* (www.faireconomy.org), the PBS website *Race: The Power of an Illusion* (www.pbs.org/race/000_general/000_00-Home), and many, many more.

The curriculum is designed to move from a historical and analytical grounding in the institutional and cultural aspects of oppression to application and action. The goal is to help people generalize from their learning in the understanding that "as more and more of the parts of the subject are mastered, the stage is set for achieving a perspective on the whole and generalization becomes possible" (Walker & Soltis, 1997, p. 44). We evaluate our success, like Jeanne Gazel in her reflections on the pedagogy of multiracial discourses, as "how well the students own the work, internalize the principles, reflect on their roles, share … their learning … and commit to a different way of being as they confront racial issues" (2007, p. 545). We feel successful when students reflect, as does one young student who writes

> I have learned that I need to question the information given to me and make sure that is correct, you cannot believe everything you hear in life. For too many years I was mislead, given biased information, and accepted it as the truth. That must change.

Like Giroux (1999), we want to develop both both critical theorizing (reasoning) and taking action (practice) in the world, to encourage reflection and action. In the end, we want our students to engage in the world as activists, in the broadest sense of that word, whether as a teacher, a parent, a friend, a sibling, a community member. We are looking for students to become, as this student has,

> more motivated and action-oriented than I did before this semester. The more I am exposed to individuals who believe they are effective in community organizing and think their cause is not only worthwhile, but also achievable, the more I am personally encouraged to take action. Always the cynic, I have rarely participated in community organizing, supported non-profit agencies, or taken the initiative to volunteer. This apathy was partially due to laziness, but mostly due to the fact that I didn't believe that one person volunteering for one social cause was actually going to make a difference. Now I find myself frequently talking about social and political issues with my family. Since my church is socially active, I asked if I could get involved in any projects this summer. I was surprised to find myself captivated by the "revolution of love" conversation that has been discussed over the past few weeks in class. Although I can't point to one particular course reading, event, or assignment that served as a turning point, I have definitely noticed a change … this semester.

RELATIONSHIP-BUILDING

The first step in this iterative process is relationship building. I spend the first two classes of every semester, the first morning of any two-day workshop, helping people get to know each other. I cannot emphasize enough the importance of this stage. As I say earlier, building relationships sets the stage for the difficult conversations that are sure to follow.

Feminist and antiracist educator Becky Thompson (2009) makes the point that we need to investigate our own role as teachers in creating resistance in our students. She talks about how we often "castigate" students, particularly white students, out of a sense of righteousness about our analysis. She makes a case for tenderness, for developing contemplative practices that help students "feel their way through to the information." Starting a semester or a workshop with relationship building activities is my way of creating a container, a space, where students know they can bring their questions, their ignorance, their curiosity, their range of feelings without having to fear they will be shamed and blamed.

Activities that build relationship also encourage students to begin talking early in the process. Activities like those I have described above and discuss in more detail below not only give people a chance to get to know one another more deeply, they also offer an opportunity for people to speak their own stories and hear their classmates' voices contributing to the classroom learning. Giving people opportunities to share early literally sets the stage for engagement throughout the semester or workshop; in my experience, structuring the class so that students do not speak until much later makes it harder to get them to engage.

One simple way to get people talking, an imperative in any classroom, is to make sure that students know each other's names. I have found this makes a big difference in their ability to build relationships with each other. Students remark time and again how much they appreciate this small act of knowing, noting how this is often the only class where they recognize and acknowledge each other outside of class, making time to stop and talk and check in. They say things like

> I had a chance to meet new people … and I was very excited how we had a chance to introduce ourselves to each other.… We can go many semesters … and not even know the persons name sitting across the room from us. I think … it bring us together like a little family unit.

And another student, who says, "when I started [school], I knew like 2 other people and now I have a ton of friends and when I see everyone on campus I love to speak to them." Thompson (2009) often starts her classes with an activity, based on an Indigenous practice, in which people introduce themselves using a form of storytelling about their name. I stress the importance of names because I believe that we build a meaningful learning community when we know what we are called by those who loved us enough to name us.

The other purpose of setting the stage in this way is to introduce people to the idea that learning is both an intellectual and an emotional experience. Relationship-building activities allow us to reach heads *and* hearts (or bodies), important because of how the body has ways of knowing that our mind may have more difficulty accessing directly (Davis et al., 2000).

Finally, relationship building offers an opportunity to develop the habit of analysis that we will be using once we begin to immerse ourselves in analyzing oppression. Once students begin to unpack their own conditioning in relationship with each other, they are less likely to become defensive about the realities of institutional and cultural oppression, more likely to become angry or outraged about their socialization.

Any number of activities can help people cut through the assumptions they carry about those sitting next to them in the classroom, establish an atmosphere of trust that encourages students to take the risks necessary to honestly explore a topic as loaded as racism, and begin the practice of emotionally and intellectually disrupting normal.

One frequently used paired listening activity invites each person to spend four or five minutes answering a set of questions—what is your class and ethnic background, what is one thing that has been hard for you because of that, what is one thing that has been a strength for you because of that? The instructions include an explanation of active listening—one person listens while the other answers the questions rather than engaging in a back and forth conversation. In a workshop or classroom setting, I always model the activity by answering the questions for myself (or even better, when I am co-teaching, modeling as one of a pair). The depth of my sharing sets the risk level for what others will do. After students have talked and listened in pairs, I debrief by asking everyone about their feelings and thoughts and why I might have asked them to do this particular activity. This process begins to establish a pattern I use in the analysis phase in which I ask them to engage in this kind of reflection and consider the "why" of things.

So, even in this relationship building phase, we develop and hone analytical skills. For example, the class and ethnic background questions provide opportunities to look at why some people know their ethnic backgrounds and others do not, the cost of assimilating into whiteness for different ethnic groups, and the power of assumptions—for example, the assumption that some of us are normal and others are not and the assumption that we all experience the world in the same way, which we disrupt by noticing the widely differing responses to the activity.

I continue to provide opportunities for students to build relationships throughout the semester. I frequently set up paired conversations and small group work, making students move around the classroom and interact with those sitting across the room; by the third or fourth class, each student has had a conversation of some kind with every other student. I often ask them to debrief a film in pairs or small groups before we talk about it as a large group. I might ask them to form small groups to analyze an assigned reading or to do some quick and dirty research to then present to the class. One student writes "I feel like this class has a sense of unity because we are always working together on assignments and feeding off of others' comments. We learn a lot from each other too."

I try to move fluidly between personal experience and the larger context to help students place themselves in that context, exploring how the larger story informs their own and what it means for their choices today. I might ask students to reflect on their experience with race and racism in some way—a paired listening activity or a journal assignment or a response to a film. Then I offer some analysis to put race and racism in the larger context (discussed in detail below) and then I come back to the personal, asking the students how the new information affects their thinking and what they plan to do with it.

ANALYSIS

As I note earlier, although I talk about analysis as the next phase, the habit of analysis has already been established in the relationship-building activities, where students consistently consider "why" as we reflect together on our thoughts, feelings, and experience.

Analysis as a phase, then, is demarcated by focusing class time on helping students deepen this habit. I offer information they need to move beyond their cultural conditioning and make more informed sense of their world. The goal is to move the group to a shared definition of racism that integrates race prejudice with social and institutional power. Concepts of oppression, privilege, internalized privilege and supremacy are introduced. The implications for white people and People of Color are discussed, particularly in relation to application and action.

The analysis phase starts by setting the context for a deeper discussion of race, class, gender, and other oppression constructs. In an education class, I might start by asking students to question what education is for— do we teach, as hidden curriculum tends to do, obedience to social norms, do we define success as "making it" and "making it" as the ability to consume? In a social work class, we might deconstruct the notion of the "helping" profession by asking who is helping whom and to what end? This allows us to develop our analytical skills—we learn to ask "why," discover and disrupt unseen assumptions, and question what we have been taught is "normal." One student, asked to reflect on her most significant learning in the class, writes, "the greatest thing I have learned is to ask why. Why am I taught this way? Why do we allow poverty to remain in our country? Why are people racist?" The goals are to develop analytic habits and to offer a conceptual framework that we can use later when we broach the topic of race.

In a classroom setting, as I prepare to delve into race, class, gender, and sexuality issues, I start with class oppression. My experience is that many students can speak fairly easily about class, in part because even those students who grew up with few financial resources do not tend to see themselves as "poor," but rather as the exception to the condescending and blaming stereotypes about poor people which they themselves often carry. I think the investigation of class is also easier because of our dominant cultural stories, contradictory as they are, that we are a "classless" society and that those who reach the elite levels do so as a result of hard work. Our socialization about class does not seem to carry the emotional rage and defensiveness attached to race, at least not until we begin to delve more deeply. This greater openness allows me to use class oppression to introduce the framework of oppression as more than personal, as institutional and cultural.

My initial goal when talking about class is to debunk the idea that people are poor because they don't work hard, that, as one student writes, "throughout childhood and early adulthood, I was often told if you work hard enough you can do or be anything you desire. I believed what I heard." We look at the ways that institutions exclude, underserve, exploit, and oppress based on class. We investigate how cultural oppression can be defined as the ways the dominant culture reinforces beliefs, values, norms, and standards that attach superiority to wealth and inferiority to poverty. For example, we might investigate how the culture rewards the corporate executive who, to take a recent example, uses government subsidies to avoid bankruptcy and continues receiving an unimaginably large paycheck while a poor single mother who has to depend on "welfare" to feed her children is portrayed as lazy and irresponsible.

Students often easily grasp the concept of privilege when we're talking about class; sometimes they open the door to the conversation when they talk about "underprivileged" children. I assign reading that offers firsthand accounts of these concepts in addition to the theoretical, where the authors talk about their personal experiences with self-hate and entitlement. One student, after reading an assigned article by a journalist who talks about "straddling" his roots in the working class and his middle class education and profession, writes,

> I can already detect the beginning of a rift between my family and myself. I am sure this rift will not be life altering or tear apart our relationship or even negatively affect the bond in any way, there will simply be a difference. I believe that I will continue to have a divergence of ideals from what my parents instilled in me, and I will probably not understand why my Mother believes and acts as she does as she will wonder where on earth my values came from.

A student reflection like this one helps us start to talk about the cost of assimilation, which I can then refer to when we begin to talk about race and issues like "acting white" in school.

Once students have a grasp of these concepts, I move into a discussion of race by asking the question "who is poor"? We talk about and do some research on the relationship between poverty and race. I often show a section of the video from the PBS series *Race: The Power of an Illusion* (Adelman & Smith, 2003) that tells the history of how the "Fair" Housing Act was created by the government to build suburbs and wealth for white families while simultaneously shutting out Black families and communities from home ownership. The film spells out how this policy, later adopted by the banking industry, led to a literal devaluation of the Black community. At the end of the semester, when I ask students to reflect on their learning, this story is often cited as helping them to understand institutional racism. As one older African American student reflects "I have experienced some racism in my life, but I was not aware of the redlining system."

Somewhere in this discussion, sometimes at the beginning, other times in the middle, whenever I start to see defensiveness and apprehension about concepts of white privilege and racism come up, I make the point that one of the reasons we have trouble talking about race is because we think it is really a discussion about who is good and who is bad (see my earlier discussion about this in Chapter One when I talk about the power of the binary). I raise the issue of binary thinking. I talk about how we are all complicated people. The question, I say, is not who is good and who is bad, the question is what are we going to do about what we know? I am hoping students will be able to acknowledge, as this young white woman does, that "I realize I have my own biases and prejudices and I must acknowledge them and work through them … to be truly antiracist, I must actively combat racism daily." Another young white woman writes,

> I have learned that I was a lot less open-minded than I thought. I never considered myself racist but after this class I did learn that the views I had on some things were racist. I have changed who I am and how I talk to people. I am a lot more respective to other's opinions and views.

This is the level of self-awareness I am looking for in the classroom.

Then we define racism by drawing on the definitions used in the antiracist activist community—race prejudice + social and institutional power, a system of oppression based on race, a system of advantage based on race, a white supremacy system (Okun & Jones, 2000). I break the definition down into its various terms—prejudice, social and institutional power, system, advantage, oppression, white supremacy, ending always with race. I form small groups and ask each small group to take a term and define it. Each group presents its definition and we talk about it until people have a thorough understanding of what the term means.

When we get to the term "race," I spend quite a bit of time talking about how race is constructed. I take them to the website of *Race: The Power of an Illusion* (www.pbs.org/race/000_General/000_00-Home) and we use the interactive tools offered there to explore this idea. Then, using a PowerPoint version of a timeline created at dRworks, I show the historical construction of the concepts of race, white, and white privilege. As I note earlier, history moves racism out of the realm of personal opinion and offers concrete evidence of its institutional and cultural manifestations. After we have explored the history, I ask them to name the institutions that participated in constructing race; at this point students inevitably understand that every institution has played and continues to play a role in the construction of a hierarchical idea of race with white at the top. Students also come to understand the ways in which prevailing cultural beliefs were and are promulgated by institutions to justify this construction.

Although I am offering a detailed description of the ways in which I offer an analysis, I do not mean to imply this is the only or even the best way to do this. My point is that we have a responsibility to provide an analysis and that this analysis should be grounded in a framework that helps students understand racism as institutional and cultural (as well as personal). I've seen this done in various ways. I recently returned from a conference where a session on transgender oppression offered a different and equally useful framework of "The Four I's"—ideological, institutional, interpersonal, and internalized (Dewey, Costello, & Garcia, 2009). Regardless of the specifics, I suggest that the framework needs to include the ways in which every act of oppression garners privilege and the ways in which oppression and privilege are internalized.

The strategies for providing a grounding framework are limitless. As mentioned earlier, I use film, articles, music, and storytelling. I always ask my students to engage the analysis, doing their own research and storytelling. In a workshop setting where time is limited, we might ask participants to select an institution and conduct a contemporary analysis from their own experience, looking to see if they can find examples of the ways in which the school system or the institution of social work excludes, underserves, exploits, and oppresses people and Communities of Color. In the classroom setting, I often assign the task of coming up with a contemporary example of institutional or cultural racism.

I might show the short film *A Girl Like Me* created by Kiri Davis (2006), a young African American high school student who informally recreated Kenneth and Mamie Clark's "doll test" used as evidence in the landmark *Brown v. Board of Education* case (Library of Congress, 2004). Davis filmed her recreation of the test to show the continued power of race to produce internalized messages of inferiority in young Black children. I also bring in guest speakers to offer an embodied perspective of racism and internalized inferiority that I, as a white teacher, cannot offer.

Sometimes I ask students to facilitate a class on internalized oppression and entitlement after giving them guidance on resources they might use. I am always impressed with the resources they find on their own; one student working on internalized oppression found YouTube clips of Michelle Obama and Malcolm X both talking, in their own ways, about this concept; her teaching of the class was much more effective than anything I might have done.

To illustrate the concept of internalized superiority I read from or refer to Beverly Daniel Tatum's discussion of "aversive" racism (her term), in which she cites research describing how contemporary racism is not so much the belief by those of us who are white that People of Color are worse but the internalized belief that we are better (1997). One young white woman writes,

> Ughh. I feel as though I am learning so much about myself and the world in general.... I've never experienced so much self-evaluation and guilt before. I'm realizing I'm more normal than abnormal and I don't like that. It's sad that I am just now realizing that, but am glad I am realizing it.... I can't wait to see what else I learn. Learn about myself and others. Learn about this world and the future students I'm going to have.

And I tell stories, lots of stories, including the one about the "integration" of my high school, which gives us an opportunity to deconstruct the racist assumptions and the consequences framing that event.

FEELINGS AND SELF-AWARENESS

The goal of this process, in keeping with what we know is required for cultural transformation, is to develop our self-awareness (as teachers) and to help others (students) develop theirs. As I note in the previous chapter, this is not a solitary and individual task, but rather a collaborative and collective one, in which the awareness we develop together (teachers and students) is not only about ourselves but also about our larger community, our interdependence. Because one of our responsibilities as teachers is to encourage students to open to their positive energy as one aspect of awareness, we must develop great skill in knowing our own energies and when we are vulnerable to our own cultural conditioning that reinforces, for example, classist, racist and sexist assumptions about who is smart and who not, fear of the "other," the student who does not act in accordance with our own understanding of how students should act, the desire to meet our own needs without regard to the needs of our students.

As teachers, developing awareness means we must make room for feeling as well as thinking. Kenneth Jones used to joke that if we could dismantle racism by how well we think (how intelligent we are), then we would expect to find less racism in communities where presumably intelligent people hang out (like Harvard). This always got a laugh and provided an opportunity to talk about the cultural/race implications of a word like "intelligence."

Emotion is an important ingredient of any educational process. Kincheloe and Steinberg argue that "emotions are ... powerful knowing processes that ground cognition" (1993, p. 312). Understanding the role of emotion in learning is critical because white supremacy culture wants us to believe in objectivity, a kind of learning that assumes logic can be separated from emotion. The emotional, posited as "an inferior form of human consciousness" (p. 312), has always been associated with the irrational feminine; its expression is usually considered "unprofessional" and "inappropriate" in the classroom.

In fact, our feelings have everything to do with the perpetuation of racism or the dismantling of it. Even when we understand something intellectually, feelings of defensiveness or shame continue to operate; these feelings often dominate our intellectual "logical" choices. As feminist theorist Anne Wilson Schaef points out (1998), feelings trump intellect. In other words, whenever feelings are unresolved or unacknowledged, they determine the outcome of an interaction, regardless of what is agreed upon intellectually. To realize this is true, one only has to consider the long-term ramifications of a meeting where people officially agree on a decision to which they are not emotionally committed. One of the goals of any transformative curriculum, then, is to invite and respect feelings, as one way to model how greater understanding of those feelings can enhance self-awareness and effective communication with others.

The process is designed to help students build self-awareness through reflection on their feelings as well as their thoughts. This is why I frequently ask students to reflect on what they are feeling, thinking, learning about themselves as well as the topic. One students writes that it has been hard for her to "reevalute my beliefs. I think it's hard for anyone really to realize that your opinion is wrong." Another realizes "I am often very shy around those that I do not know well so it has been a great challenge in opening up to those around me. The first day of class was EXTREMLY hard ... this is something I really struggle with and hope that I can do better at in time [as] the ability to do so will be essential as I collaborate with my future colleagues." Another notices that she is "probably not assertive enough when working in a group."

Aligned with the importance of helping people develop a practice of self-awareness by noticing their feelings and thoughts is the importance of acknowledging the necessary tension that occurs when any group of people is honestly grappling with an issue as complex and evocative as racism. Rather than assuming we can move through a workshop or class without any tension, I tell people to expect and welcome it as a point of learning. Tension indicates that something important is being touched and this tension provides opportunities for incredible insight if we can remain open to it.

Jerry Levine, in his article *Impassioned Teaching and Critical Thinking* (2003), makes this point when he says that

> Passion in the classroom means that students will take sides, express moral positions, argue, feel strongly, and express those feelings. It does not mean that they will abandon reason. It is the mixing of feeling and reasoning that gives true integrated meaning to our knowing. (p. 52)

Some of my most combative students, as I mention in the chapter on privileged resistance, are some of the most engaged, wrestling to make sense of material that, as one student writes, "no other class has ever taught me." Students also appreciate the opportunity to actively interact with one another; one writes that what she "perceived to be 'the way' which was my way was not always the best way. Hearing [other students'] perception of the issue opened my eyes to a new solution and a new way I have never thought about before." Another says

> I liked listening to other points of view, particularly those with which I could not identify. Recently, I've been observing that I ask myself why someone would believe something that is the opposite from what I believe. I make it a game to see if I can convince myself of the other perspective's validity. I would not have started doing that if I had not seen how well some of my fellow classmates could argue against things that I firmly believe are true.

Some students may be excited by the analysis, finding language and a validation for their experience that they have never had before. Many students will be interested, intrigued, and perhaps even angry about encountering new information, wondering why they are only just now being exposed to it. Many students will be deeply unsettled as the implications of the analysis begin to manifest, particularly as they attempt to share their new learning with their friends and family. One student writes,

> The most difficult thing for me in this class was reconciling my previous beliefs with new information. Nearly every class I went home wondering what I should believe and why I should believe it. I discussed most of the topics covered in class with my parents, friends, and classmates. Although

this sometimes helped to ease the cognitive dissonance, there are still some social issues that I have no strongly formed opinion about.

Another of my young white women students relates how "learning about these topics" has changed her

positions on topics to the point where people did not understand. My boyfriend and I got in an actual argument one night because I had taken some ideas from class and shifted my position and he could not understand where I was coming from because he was exactly where I was when I first walked into this class. It was very frustrating because he felt as though I had changed as a person.

In the chapter on privileged resistance, I talk about the fear of loss that comes with an acknowledgement of the institutional and cultural realities of oppression and privilege. Providing students some avenue to express their experience, their fears, their grappling is critical to any chance they will have to continue on a path of critical and conscious thinking about the world.

Dennis Sumara (Davis et al., 2000, p. 184) encourages his students to journal, to write without stopping as a means of helping them access their unconscious thoughts. I have also found journaling to be a useful tool in almost every teaching/learning environment. Depending on the energy in the room (if there is a need to center or deepen it), the level of risk people have been willing to take (if a sense of group intimacy has been established), I may ask people to voluntarily share some of what they have written as a way of continuing to build relationships. I may ask each person in the class to share while the rest of us listen, without responding; depending on what people say, I may ask them to journal again, to give space for them to reflect on what they have heard. I may ask them to share what they have written with another person.

Whatever the technique, the idea is to provide an opportunity for people to engage in individual and personal reflection, to have the time and space to express what they are thinking and feeling. As I discuss in the chapter on privileged resistance, we cannot expect our students to embrace a new understanding of the world if we don't give them the opportunity to acknowledge how it feels to leave their old concepts behind.

Like Maxine Greene (1981), I conceive of "human beings as always in pursuit of themselves, always futuring, always struggling to create themselves in the changing situations of their diverse lives" (p. 387). A specific method is not my point; my point is our responsibility to make space for our students to reflect on their feelings about the material as well as the material itself. In this way, we respect the need, identified in the previous chapter, to help students develop a self-awareness that will serve them well as they begin to engage in the world in new ways.

DIVERSE METHODS

The idea of learning as a process is based on the belief that participants bring a range of life experience, a diversity of ways they have interpreted that experience, and a multiplicity of ways in which they feel comfortable learning, all within the context of a dominant culture that has taught them to over or under value themselves and their own wisdom based on their particular situation. As teachers we need to figure out ways to tap the wide range of experience and wisdom present in the room if we are to offer a successful learning experience to both the individuals and the collective.

The case for the use of diverse methods is, in popular parlance, a "nobrainer." Howard Gardner's well-known work on multiple intelligences is relevant here. Gardner (2004) has identified eight intelligences: linguistic, logical-mathematical, musical, spatial, bodily-kinesthetic, interpersonal, intrapersonal, and naturalist. He is considering adding "a ninth or existential intelligence—one that captures the human proclivity to raise and ponder fundamental questions about existence, life, death, finitude." Given that we can be "intelligent" in multiple ways, Eisner makes the point that when we acknowledge the "aptitude differences among students with respect to the knowledge and performance systems they use best," then "the grounds for using diverse modes of presentation and response become even stronger" (2002, p. 148). Levine notes a responsibility to "develop classroom opportunities which give students a relevant curricular experience on which to reflect" (2003, p. 54).

As a result, any effective antiracist curriculum will incorporate a range of methods, including physical movement, solitary reflection, writing, drawing, lecture/lecturette, discussion, film, periods of silence, song, sharing of life experiences in pairs, in small and large groups.

APPLICATION

Another critical goal of any effective process is to help "students to reinterpret their own lives and uncover new talents as a result of their encounter with ... knowledge" (Kincheloe & Steinberg, 1993, p. 301). We encourage critical and compassionate thinking about the world in order to understand our place in it and then take action to improve it. Giroux refers to the importance of replacing "the myth of the autonomous individual with the problem of what one has to do to struggle to become a self-determining social agent acting on, rather than responding to, the world in which we live" (1999, p. 15). The goal is to support people in taking informed action in the belief that "collectives of persons are capable of actions and understandings that transcend the capabilities of individuals on their own" (Davis et al., 2000, p. 68). Levine talks about building a "committed community of learners" and describes it as an inevitable process resulting from increased engagement, risk-taking, and the freedom to "expose [our] authentic inner-selves more fully to each other" (2003, p. 56). Our challenge is to help people know themselves within this larger context and support them to take thoughtful action in the world.

One dilemma is that our students rarely regard themselves as change agents in any collective sense (or even in any individual sense) while at the same time they do believe in the imperative to take action. Both are the result of cultural conditioning that tells us to be a team player (don't rock the boat) while lionizing individual heroes who "save the day" for the rest of us. For example, I often encounter students early in this process who are anxious to get to what we're going to do about the analysis we are developing. In other words, they become impatient with the talking and want to get to action.

D. G. Smith talks about our addiction to action, noting that western culture "privileges" action and activism without taking responsibility for "the negative consequences Western activism has inflicted on the world" (1999, p. 470). He goes on to say that "the most profound disease in Western pedagogy is activism, or action for its own sake" (p. 470). In class, I make the point that we (meaning those of us living and working in this western culture) often want to move from awareness of a problem to doing something about it without taking the time and care to analyze, vision, and plan first. The result is that we often feel good about doing something but end up doing a pretty poor job of actually addressing the problem. The process I am describing, therefore, is structured to support people in taking a breath so they can slow down enough to actually allow themselves time to really grasp the problem (in this case racism), to feel it, taste it, breathe it, grapple with it collectively before trying to "fix" it.

On the other end of the spectrum, sometimes people want to over-analyze a problem in an attempt to insure that any action they take will be perfect. In this case, I work with students to move them beyond talk and into action, helping them to see that understanding a problem thoroughly does not constitute action or insure perfection. I may deconstruct the concept of perfection itself. I make the point that sometimes we have to act without being completely certain about all aspects of our strategy. Distinguishing the fine line between an imperative to act unwisely and moving toward informed action is challenging, and one of the reasons to help students develop a practice of reflection is to help them negotiate this tender tension.

Because of dominant culture emphasis on individualism and individual hero as savior, people often only conceive of action as individual. As a result, they often place themselves at risk when they do act, either by stepping out in ways that make it easy for those in power to target or marginalize them, or by stepping out in ways that put those they are trying to help at risk. Therefore, another important goal is to work with our students to help them understand the power of collective and collaborative action, historically and in their own lives.

Regardless of these challenges, the process is oriented towards praxis—the purpose of the analysis is to lead people towards thoughtful action, to "peel away the layers of meaning that give shape to our everyday lives, ... to serve as a guide to action designed to alter those life forces that embody the power of an oppressive reality" (Giroux, 1999, p. 11). Over the course of the process, the semester, the workshop, the hope is that participants will make the "transition from critical thought to reflective intervention in the world" (p. 11).

One way I encourage praxis is by assigning "action projects" in the classroom. Attempting to be sensitive to the dynamic of sending students out into the community to "help" in ways that often cause more stress than benefit to those being "helped," I structure these projects so that students can incorporate them into their everyday lives. For example, one student decided to adopt a "lovingkindness practice," where she attempted to bring loving attention to whoever and whatever was before her in the moment. As a result, she had a transformative experience in the elementary classroom where she was student teaching. She brought the practice to one very withdrawn and non-expressive student, a young boy who had essentially been written off by the lead teacher. She sat with this student in a quiet manner that communicated no expectations, asking questions, allowing silence, listening, and in this way began to draw him out. A relationship was formed that she had previously assumed impossible. This young woman began to see herself as "capable of being a powerful and effective teacher" who "discovered that we are all connected in a strong and meaningful way ... the hardest thing [is] not to be scared that I won't make a difference."

While not a collective practice per se, she brought this experience to our classroom, where we could all learn from what she had tried, and in that way she influenced our understanding of how to apply a lovingkindness practice in our daily lives. Students do these action projects with others, so that while they might perform the action project as an individual, they have to plan, reflect, and present their learning with their group.

I always ask students, as we move through the analysis, to connect the analysis to teaching, to social work, to their activism—what, I ask, are they going to do with what they are learning? For example, one of my assignments in my education classes each semester is a Columbus curriculum. I start the class by asking them to tell me what they know about Columbus. I usually have a few students who bring strong historical knowledge, but for the most part all students can do is identify the date 1492 and recite the mythological "discovery" story. I then show a cartoon film (Mel-o-Toons, 1996) that essentially tells the stereotyped version of Columbus' voyages to the "new world" and check in with students to see if the animated movie represents their understanding of what happened. Then I show them a more complete history, including the facts that Columbus never actually landed in what is now known as the U.S., that he led a genocidal campaign against the indigenous Arawak/Tainos people, and that he initiated the slave trade.

Next I ask students to develop their own Columbus lesson plan for whatever age group and in whatever subject they plan to teach. I make a variety of resources available, including James Loewen's *Lies My Teacher Told Me* (2007), Mary Cowhey's *Black Ants and Buddhists* (2006), Bill Bigelow's *A People's History for the Classroom* (2008) that is an adaptation of Howard Zinn's classic *People's History* book, and Bigelow's collaborative effort with Bob Peterson, *Rethinking Columbus* (1998). I offer a host of websites where they can find solid and thoughtful information about Columbus, the history of his voyages, and the short and long-term impact of first contact.

This assignment turns out to be rich in multiple ways. For one, it stimulates discussion and thought about how soon children can begin to engage in critical thinking. Many of my students assume that young children cannot handle challenging or complex information; this gives us an opportunity to examine their assumption that young children are not already dealing with challenging and complex experiences related to racism, abuse, violence, or poverty. Cowhey's book (2006), in which she presents her approach to teaching a social justice curriculum to first and second graders, helps me address this concern.

Second, the Columbus assignment lets me know how well students are doing in terms of their own critical thinking. The ways in which they approach the assignment reflect lesser or greater degrees of skill in working with a critical lens and give me a basis from which to push or support students in their development as critical thinkers. Finally, it gives them the experience of preparing for their "real-world" responsibility of teaching their own students to think critically. I am always amazed at how many students who have already participated in curriculum development classes are really challenged by this assignment because the focus is on using history to develop critical thinking skills (as opposed to teaching specific content or "to the test"). I am also astonished by what students come up with. A music major, for example, developed a very creative and engaging lesson focused on ballad writing that incorporated the complex Columbus story.

My hope is that this assignment gives my students a direct experience of application that they will remember when called upon to develop curriculum for their classrooms in the future. In some cases, students actually get the opportunity to try their lesson plans in the classes where they are student teaching; they then share their experience with the rest of the class, which is always very energizing.

Another approach to application is to invite people into the classroom who are applying the concepts we are learning in their life and work. For example, I often ask a local high school teacher to come and share his experiences teaching a social justice curriculum. This teacher is young, much closer in age to my students than I am, white, male, and he takes them through a critical lesson about education using lyrics from a Dead Prez song, a passage from Frederick Douglass' autobiography, a Power-Point presentation using images to show a short history of education. He asks them to offer their opinions about the purpose of schooling. In this way he demonstrates how he teaches, what he teaches, and engages them in the energy and possibility of critical and engaged classroom teaching.

In my social work class, every semester I (or we, since I often co-teach this class with Michelle Johnson), invite six or seven community activists to come and talk to the class and share what they know about working effectively across race, class, gender, sexuality, and other identity lines. This class is always intensely powerful, as students spend the first half listening to these experienced people offer their deep wisdom about what they have learned as a result of years of community-based activism. The second half of the class is designed to allow students and activists to meet in small groups, so that students get a chance to ask questions and engage in discussion more directly. Students always reference this class as one of their favorites in their end of semester evaluations.

In these ways students get to see an embodied representation of application, to imagine themselves acting in similar ways in the world. This is critical because so often, during the course of the semester, students agonize about how they are going to use the information, skills, and new self-awareness they are acquiring. Hearing from and talking with people who are using the information offers an up-close look at the possibilities. One student writes,

> Hearing all of our speakers during their visit to class was an amazing reminder of how much good work is happening in our communities and

how I can get involved on various levels.... I can make choices about how to be involved. Get out there—even if it is uncomfortable at first. Bottom line of advice [to myself]: get involved.

In workshops, we try to build in application from the very beginning, asking participants to come in organizational or community groups, knowing that the action phase of the process will be both easier and more effective if a group can work together as a "change team" rather than asking one individual to interpret the learning and meaning of the workshop to their organization or community. As teachers, we can make real-world connections, encouraging students to identify communities, organizations, and ongoing efforts with which they can become involved so they can take what they are learning in the classroom to those efforts and bring what they are learning in the world back to the classroom.

It is beyond the scope of this chapter to discuss all the different ways in which we can engage our students in the application/action phase of this process. Much can and has been written about the possibilities and liabilities of student activism in the community (particularly when students are coming from a service mindset without awareness of power and privilege) (Billig & Eyler, 2003; Kahne & Westheimer, 1996). And conversely, much can and has been written about the importance of student engagement and the power of that engagement when students become politicized and come to understand their power as change agents (Berger, Boudin, and Farrow, 2005; Cowhey, 2006; N. López, 2008; The Hoot, 2009).

My point here is to note the importance of application and action as a phase in the pedagogical process of teaching about race and racism. Learning and action are interdependent, each feeding on and enhancing the other.

VISION

In my early years as a trainer and consultant to social justice organizations, I often asked leaders and activists to participate in an visioning activity early in the process, believing that a strong vision could and should anchor the mission and work of the organization. As I note in the previous chapter, teaching for cultural transformation requires a cultivation of our collective abilities to vision a positive, sustainable future while grounded in the information and analytical skills to vision well. I have now shifted to asking students and workshop participants to vision towards the end of our time together. I have found our visions are much stronger and more meaningful when we have spent time developing a strong analysis about our world.

Activist, artist, and scholar Jim Lee (personal correspondence, October 13, 2009) notes that effective visioning requires a degree of modeling. He notes that "the mere act of being where one is not supposed to be, doing what one is not supposed to do, saying what one is not supposed to say, thinking what one is not supposed to think, are all potentially revolutionary acts." While Lee does not assume that "the mere performance of the act" is a guarantee of change, "under the right circumstances these acts of defiance can ignite more acts and lead to … action."

I include historical examples of both visioning and modeling in the classroom to insure that students understand their potential to influence their world. Along with sharing the history of the race construct, I also share the history of movement-building (largely unknown by my students). My goal is to demonstrate that people and communities have always banded together to effect social change; whenever possible I make sure to include the role that students have played in movement building so they can see people like themselves taking action and making change.

I have found that working with people to develop a vision of the world they want to inhabit, particularly when grounded in an understanding of the vision and action of previous generations, is incredibly powerful for everyone involved. At a recent workshop, a participant opened the visioning session with a dance she had created to communicate her desire for a wider embrace of diversity and complexity. Others then read poems or small pieces from longer prose, a seductive and inspiring litany of possibility that had almost all of us in tears.

One participant offered the following:

> I envision a world
> where compassionate creativity flows
> where righteous anger knows no bounds
> where boundaries sound a bell of safety
> and ease
> not captivity
> and harmful march.
>
> where an arm is stretched by muscular love
> and difference is a dance of ritual celebration
> in a round
> in circles
> in circles
> that overlap
> and uncover each other
> gently
> and re-cover a child
> asleep.

where listening
is communication
and silence spills into
a carried space
of peace.
—Rebekah Resnick, May 2009

The session closed with another dancer circling the room, kneeling one by one in front of each of us, looking us in the eyes and calling out our shared commitment. In these moments, I understand the force of our shared vision and the imperative to bring that energy into being.

CONCLUSION

As I said at the beginning of this chapter, I describe my process to highlight the importance of taking people through a cycle of relationship-building, analysis, application, and vision, where ongoing reflection enhances both individual and collective awareness of our relationship and response to oppressive constructs. I do not mean to imply that this is the only process, the one "right" way. I do mean to state that learning is a process and that learning about difficult topics, like racism, does require moving people through a process that starts with relationship-building, offers a strong and grounded power analysis, and supports people to take action towards a larger and more hopeful vision.

After many years of training and teaching, revising and refining this process in both workshops and the classroom, I have come to know some things for sure about effective pedagogy in relationship to race and racism. This knowing is the focus of my next and final chapter.

Red Brocade

The Arabs used to say,
When a stranger appears at your door,
feed him for three days
before asking who he is,
where he's come from,
where he's headed.
That way, he'll have strength
enough to answer.
Or, by then you'll be
such good friends
you don't care.

Let's go back to that.
Rice? Pine nuts?
Here, take the red brocade pillow.
My child will serve water
to your horse.

No, I was not busy when you came!
I was not preparing to be busy.
That's the armor everyone put on
to pretend they had a purpose
in the world.

I refuse to be claimed.
Your plate is waiting.
We will snip fresh mint
into your tea.

—Naomi Shihab Nye (2002, pp. 40-41)

CHAPTER 5

REFLECTIONS ON THE PARADE

What I Know for Sure

In this chapter, I take my cue from Dorothy Allison, the extraordinary poet and writer, who in her memoir, *Two or Three Things I Know For Sure*, tells about what she has learned from her experience growing up poor, female, lesbian, as she did in Greenville, South Carolina. She describes a place that smelled like

> cut wet grass, split green apples, baby shit and beer bottles, cheap makeup and motor oil. Everything was ripe, everything was rotting. Hound dogs butted my calves. People shouted in the distance; crickets boomed in my ears. That country was beautiful, I swear to you, the most beautiful place I've ever been. Beautiful and terrible. It is the country of my dreams the country of my nightmares: a pure pink and blue sky, red dirt, white clay, and all that endless green—willows and dogwood and firs going on for miles. Two or three things I know for sure, and one of them is the way you can both hate and love something you are not sure you understand." (1995, pp. 6-7)

Allison weaves stories of her family with a perception both heartbreaking and precise. She punctuates her story with what she has come to know for sure from years of living through the challenges presented and reflected by a family attempting, in its turn, to navigate a society offering at best disregard and at worst a kind of hatred.

The Emperor Has No Clothes: Teaching About Race and Racism to People Who Don't Want to Know, pp. 133–165

I deeply appreciate Allison's ability to identify what she knows after many years of living. My life has in no way been as straight up hard; I was raised with the "grace" of class, education, and heterosexual privilege that offered more choices, more respect, more acceptance. At the same time, I have found that "unlearning" my social conditioning, particularly that attached to my privilege, has not been easy, as I have worked for many years to sort out the truth I was taught from what I really believe.

So with great respect and attribution to Allison, who gives me courage to claim what I have come to know, here are two or three things I know for sure about teaching for liberation, things I've learned by doing (practice) and things I've learned by study, reading, and reflection (theory).

LOVE

Two or three things I know for sure and
one of them is just how important love is.

When I think back to my first years as a trainer, I shudder with dismay. In those early days, when we broke into caucuses (where white people and People of Color meet in separate groups to explore the different impacts of racism on each), I was quite clueless about my role as the facilitator. I understood the rationale for caucusing, but was focused on being the "right" kind of white person, one of the "good ones." So for several years I led the caucus from a position of confusion, preferring to distance myself from other white people in my attempt to be "better" in the stand-alone category of "not like other white people."

In my next phase, I understood more clearly my task to help those in the white group understand the impact of white privilege and internalized white superiority on our individual and collective behavior. My attitude, however, was lodged in high righteousness. I took the pose of "I've got my act together, what about you?" At this point I felt other white people had to prove their "goodness." It is a credit to all those who attended these workshops that they managed to move forward in spite of this tactless and offensive stance.

Finally, after many years, I began to understand how much I was learning about myself from these sessions, how much better I was able to see my own challenges and weaknesses and approach them with mercy rather than harsh judgment, how much my capacity to love myself and others was increasing. I came to understand my affinity with others in the white group and to love the people in the white caucus, as I saw how we were all struggling with the deep racist conditioning that infiltrates the bodies and souls of white people in a racist system. I realized that (for the most part) at some level we all want to be whole, we all want to be good, we are all doing the best we can with the information and tools that we have. This is the point at which I became an effective antiracist trainer and facilitator.

Derrick Jensen speaks to this, noting that

> the people in my classes, including me, did not need to be controlled, managed, or even taught. What we needed was to be encouraged, accepted, and loved just for who we are. We needed not to be governed by a set of rules that would tell us what we needed to learn and what we needed to express, but to be given time in a supportive space to explore who we were and what we wanted, with the assistance of others who had our best interests at heart. I believe that is true not only for my students, but for all of us, human and nonhuman alike. All we want, whether we are honeybees, salmon, trash-collecting ants, ponderosa pines, coyotes, human beings, or stars, is to love and be loved, to be accepted, cherished, and celebrated simply for being who we are. Is that so very difficult? (2000, pp. 336-337)

In my experience, the answer to Jensen's question is "yes indeed." For one of the functions of white supremacy culture is to divide us each from the other, with the constant construction of ever more refined differentiations to keep us suspicious and afraid of those we consider "other" (Allen, 1974; Jensen, 2002; olsson, 1997).

What do I mean when I talk about love? I agree with bell hooks (2000, p. xxix) that "we must dare to acknowledge how little we know of love in both theory and practice" even as we commit to it. I believe, as she does, that "we yearn to end the lovelessness that is so pervasive in our society" (p. xxix). Hooks advises us to think of love as an action rather than a feeling (p. 13); she references Erich Fromm's definition of love as "the will to extend one's self for the purpose of nurturing one's own or another's spiritual growth" (p. 4).

This imperative to both be and teach love reflects a universal instruction and therefore deserves our educational attention. One of Judaism's best known stories is that of Rabbi Hillel, who when asked for a summary of the Jewish religion, said: "That which is despicable to you, do not do to your fellow, this is the whole Torah, and the rest is commentary, go and learn it" (The American-Israeli Cooperative Enterprise, 2008). Endorsed as a concept in one form or another by every major religion, known to many as the golden rule, invoked also by Jesus and Confucius to summarize their essential teachings, this is an idea that has influence among people and religions of many and diverse cultures. Such cross-cultural currency suggests a moral imperative that deserves attention in our classrooms.

As a Jew, what I love about Hillel's commandment is how he tells us what *not* to do (so very Jewish of him) and, with all due respect to Jensen, how extremely difficult such a simple instruction is, particularly as I try to apply it to my daily life.

For one thing, the commandment to love the stranger as ourselves is also a commandment to love ourselves well. Learning to love ourselves becomes a radical act within the context of a capitalist (economically driven) culture constructed in hierarchies of race, gender, and class, a culture that more than anything values the ability to make a profit, regardless of the human, psychological, social, or cultural price. We so often confuse love with consuming in a search for individual happiness without regard for the costs of our behavior to ourselves, to the larger community.

Those of us who consume in the belief that material wealth is the goal experience an estrangement and detachment that actually erodes self-love and self-awareness (DeGraaf et. al., 2005; Palmer, 2004; Schaef, 1998). Those of us who profit, literally and psychologically, from this culture do not, at core, really thrive; an underlying sense of insecurity based in some level of understanding that our gain is at the expense of others leaves us uneasy, fearful. We engage in the continued construction of illusory systems of control (from sophisticated weaponry to gated communities to dehumanizing ideologies) that do not actually safeguard our happiness and, in fact, leave us feeling even more uneasy, more fearful (Low, 2004; hooks, 2000).

When I speak of love in the classroom, I am talking about extending Fromm's notion of regard, one that assumes our common humanity, a shared desire for a meaningful life, and the sense that we are deeply interconnected, our fates tied together. To do this well, we must also develop a deep regard for ourselves.

African American master teacher and long-time antiracist trainer Monica Walker (personal communication, February 6, 2009) talks about how she grew up to see white people as superior, our behavior as something she needed to emulate. Although her universal respect was unmerited, she says, "I revered [white people] more than myself." She could not have been the teacher she is now at 20 years of age "because there was no one I scorned more than myself." She makes a connection between her ability to love herself and her ability to love those she teaches. We cannot give the love we do not possess or have, she says, which means that we have to do what is necessary to embody the love so needed in the classroom.

Walker explains that teaching must be a gift that we want to give and we have to love the people we want to give it to. In her view, the ability to love is essential to effective teaching. Every potent teacher she knows offers deep concern and love to their students, although Svi Shapiro (personal correspondence, August 10, 2009) notes this "must not be confused with sentimentality [or] ... our Hallmark card view of love." The learning gaps in our schools, Walker claims, exist because teachers do not love all their students. Our job, she explains is "teaching people to renew, restore loving," and "we can't restore what we don't know how to do." Bad teachers, she believes, are those who are not clear about loving the people they teach, which means they have work to do in terms of loving themselves.

Our culture has constructed education as a competitive event, where the underlying assumption is that only a limited few can be smart and, as a result, valued. But learning is not a commodity and love is not something to hold in reserve, as school systems hold the highest grades for those most "deserving." Love cuts through the idea of education as a material object and begins to build toward the assumption that we can all learn, grow, and be in meaningful relationship with each other and the world.

Ari Clemenzi, a trainer with the Catalyst Project, talks about the need to "figure out how to support each other as the premise." Clemenzi is talking about the importance of mutual support within the context of the white community, where, as I said earlier, our culturally conditioned tendency is to compete to be one of the "good" ones. Rather than vie with each other out of a misplaced idea that only some of us can succeed, Clemenzi notes, we need to create a culture of love and respect, "to prioritize our own healing and support each other as individuals and unpack how we bring our own trauma into the work; we need to heal." Like Walker, Clemenzi is talking about the critical link between our personal and collective work. Clemenzi cautions that this is a fine balance; we can so easily, in this individualistic culture, turn personal work into an obsession with our own "healing" outside of any larger context.

Developing our capacity to love both ourselves and our students is what makes it possible for us and them to change. "We ought to be disappointed," Walker says, "when students are not engaged or moved by our teaching." She explains that "it matters" whether our students like us or not because "like" leads to respect. In turn, "if I want someone to like me, then I'll work for them" as a teacher. She calls it "the like factor," that if students like us, then they will want to work for us and we for them. At the same time, Shapiro warns that this too is a fine line, for "we all want to be liked but it can get in the way of the difficult work that confronts and makes students uncomfortable" (personal correspondence, August 10, 2009). As I note below, this is one of those contradictions that we must learn to hold.

I have mentioned already the need to be unabashed in our regard for our students; as I said, I constantly tell my students that I think they are fabulous. I do this understanding that students can be, like any of us, smug, ignorant, lazy, manipulative.... What I try to communicate is my belief that we are all essentially good, all essentially trying to do the best we can as we engage in the task of becoming aware of and then struggling with our social conditioning. This belief in our essential goodness does not mean I am "easy" or that I demand less from my students nor does it mean that I always please them; it simply means that I choose to appeal to positive potential rather than taking a punitive or reductionist approach.

In Chapter Four, I talk about the importance of relationship and community building and give examples of how to accomplish this in our classrooms. I also extend love in the ways I respond to students' journals and papers, offering positive and supportive comments along with pointed critique, sharing my own experiences and doubts. I pose questions and use papers to create a dialogue with each student. When material is particularly challenging and when I see students really struggling, I often ask them to journal about what they are thinking and feeling. I affirm whatever struggle they are experiencing (to the extent they express it) and appreciate whatever effort they are making to work through difficult concepts.

I am not a Pollyanna. I think of Dr. Martin Luther King's instruction that love without power is sentimental and anemic, while power without love is abusive (1967). I push students to think harder, deeper, to go beyond conditioned shallow thinking. If a student offers a viewpoint with which I disagree, I appreciate the argument and make one of my own. If their points are not well argued, I point out some of the underlying assumptions and ask them to address these. I push, often quite hard, and yet I never imply, or at least try to never imply, that they are stupid. In other words, I work to avoid feeling or showing contempt for my students, even when I consider their thinking shallow, inadequate, or wrong.

And I always recognize our common humanity. When students share difficult stories from their own lives, if I am moved to tears, then I cry without trying to hide it (and without drawing attention to it either). If students appear angry, I encourage them to express it. I support students in their feelings as well as their thoughts. I facilitate exercises to get them more familiar with identifying their feelings and how feelings might influence thoughts. I express my own frustration when I feel it, although I try to never direct it at a student. I often praise the class as a whole—"this last group of essays was really excellent and here's why"—as well as push them as a group—"you all really need to work on making your essays more thoughtful and here's what I mean by that...." I use humor, tell stories from my own life, expose my own vulnerabilities, my own strengths. For example, when we talk about dominant culture standards of beauty, none of which I exhibit, I make a point about how ludicrous these standards are because "obviously they don't describe someone like me and I think I'm beautiful." This always gets a gentle laugh. I try to exhibit love, be love, feel love, offer love at every opportunity.

I do not mean to suggest that loving our students is easy; I understand that I am a white woman currently teaching in an environment where most of my students are white. My "success" with these students has much to do with the fact that they see me as credible and without an agenda, at least when it comes to race and class (which is ironic, since I do have an agenda and tell them so in the very first class). I have been firsthand witness to how Black and Indigenous colleagues, covering the same material and even following the same syllabus and lesson plans, have been received critically and negatively by white students and even some Students of Color who respond to them and what they are teaching with suspicion and disrespect.

Troy Richardson and Sofia Villenas, in the 2000 spring issue of *Educational Theory* (p. 255), write about their experiences as "racialized indigenous teacher educators who again are confronting white privilege in [their] often 'well-meaning' and 'colorblind' pre-service teachers." At the beginning of the semester, they ask themselves a predictable litany of questions having to do with how many accommodations they will have to make, whose language they will be using, and, ultimately, how much of their soul they will have to sell. They describe how students read about the lives and experiences of "others" from their white middle-class perspectives and how "often, as the 'only' professors of color, [they] provide a window to the exotic and are voyeuristically consumed and digested through Eurocentric worldviews" (p. 269). They note how multicultural education is often designed in white institutions for white people and how they find their "energies … are being siphoned off to accommodate white folks and not our own communities" (p. 269).

For Walker, too, training and teaching white people presented a "serious paradox—how do I care about people who don't care about me?" She came to understand "the depth of their [white peoples'] need to understand race and racism as both different and the same as my own. I tap into their humanity and connect it to mine."

As a white middle-class teacher of predominantly white working class and middle-class students, I do not have to confront these challenges. I do have to disrupt our tendencies to see ourselves as "normal," to insure that we do not exoticize or voyeuristically consume those people and communities who are posited as "deficit" precisely because they are not like us. While this requires diligence on my part, I do not have to worry about being challenged based on students' racist projections onto me and my credibility as their teacher.

We live in a culture where racism, all oppressions, operate to keep us separated from each other and ourselves. I readily admit that loving our students, loving ourselves, is a different task depending on who we are in the world in relationship to our students. As I said in the introduction, I assume our common humanity, not from a shallow "we're all the same" perspective, but grounded in a understanding of our profound differences based in the myriad ways we have experienced and been experienced on by the constructs of race, class, gender, language, power. And yet one of the things I know for sure is that we must figure out how to do this important work of loving, both ourselves and others, whoever we are, if we are to transform the world.

The opposite of love is not hate, it is fear. Capitalism manufactures fear because fear leads to profit—the military-industrial complex could not exist in a culture of love. In the face of a culture that encourages us to fear each other and, in many cases, to fear ourselves, we must, as June Jordan says, insist on "[our] own truth and [our] own love, especially when that truth and that love will carry [us] across the borders of [our] own tribe" into a "tenable family of men and women as large and as invincible as infinite, infinitely varied, life" (2002, p. 195).

If we learn to truly love ourselves, as hooks advises, understanding love as an action rather than a feeling, and if we love others as we love ourselves, then we create justice. For once we love others, it becomes very difficult to be afraid of them, want to control them, kill them, exploit them, or otherwise harm them.

In Judaism, there is a story about the origin of the world, which began, so the story goes, with the Or Ein Sof, meaning light from the Holy Source. The vessel holding this light broke, shattering into an infinite number of "holy sparks"—as a result the light of God shines in everyone and everything (Remen, 2000). Our purpose is to search for and "uncover" these holy sparks, to "free the hidden holiness in everything and everyone" (p. 326). We do this "through our loving-kindness and compassion.... Every act of lovingkindness, no matter how great or small, repairs the world" (p. 326).

So the first thing I know for sure is that love is the answer, love is the question, all we need is love. Like Rabbi Hillel's commandment, knowing this is both very simple and ever so challenging.

CRITICAL AND COMPASSIONATE

Two or three things I know for sure and one of them is that we have to question everything with a critical eye and a compassionate heart.

At the end of every semester, I ask my students to reflect on their learning, to consider what they would do differently in regards to the class if they could. One white student writes

> I would admit that white privilege is real and I have benefited from this privilege. I have wanted to defend my race for so long because I never

wanted people to think that all white people have negative thoughts about people of color. My energy defending my race could have been used toward teaching those who do have negative views.

Another white student writes "I am a lot less open minded than I thought. I never considered myself racist but after this class I did learn that the views I had on some things were racist. I have changed who I am and how I talk to people. I am a lot more respectful to other's opinions and views." Still another notes

I have learned that I have more prejudices, privileges, options and ignorance than I thought I did. The discussions made me realize how much I have simply accepted because "that's the way it is." I discovered that some of my beliefs and values I hold very strongly still and other ideas I have allowed to be challenged and adjusted.

An African American student writes

I learned that I had not been taught how to think critically about social issues that affect women, race, sexual preference, culture, class, disabilities and the human race. I feel like this class has changed my life and I have learned so much about me and the world and students.

Many of my students' reflections show this sense of growing self-awareness; and some do not. I feel successful when my students indicate that they are developing the ability to think critically, to stand outside dominant culture conditioning about what is normal.

I believe, as Greene so beautifully articulates, in "the possibility of transcendence, at least the transcendence of wide-awakeness, of being able to see" (1981, p. 398) and then to act. Parker Palmer (2004) talks about this transcendence in terms of our yearning to live an undivided life, to help ourselves and others become whole. Eisner also uses the word "whole" when he describes progressive education's role in educating the "whole child," which means perceiving the child or learner as "a social and emotional creature, not only ... an academic or intellectual one" (2002, p. 71).

My years of teaching have led me to believe that we yearn for wholeness, my students and I. We have a sense that the world is awry and we are anxious. I believe our yearning for wholeness is situated in the context of our understanding, even if only on a visceral level, that we live in an unjust world while desiring a just one.

Given this yearning, as teachers we can and must, as Maxine Greene says (1981, p. 390), help people understand that

the bricklayer sees the construction job differently from the foreman, ... the superintendent of schools sees the classroom differently from the members of the third grade, that Chicanos in Los Angeles view Beverly Hills real estate differently from movie stars," (p. 390)

and that given these multiple perspectives,

almost without exception, the person with more power, more access to the public space, is thought to have the true perspective. (p. 391)

Becoming whole in the context of social justice means developing the ability to question "normal," which means using our intellect, our emotions, our intuition to understand power in its personal, institutional, and cultural manifestations. Understanding power helps us act more effectively in the world. I want students to have the skills to analyze their situation as one that is affected by power relationships in the world. I want them to develop or build on a sense of their personal power and consider how they can use that power to contribute to a collective endeavor, to the possibilities of change-making.

So, for example, part of my job with white students is to support them in questioning their assumptions about concepts like "qualified," helping them see how they are shutting themselves off from valuable knowledge and insight when they assume their normality and centricity. My job with Students of Color, LGBTQQI students, any student who lives an identity on the margin, is essentially the same. For our white supremacy culture infects us all. Even though students may have experienced racism, or sexism, or heterosexism firsthand, they are often still confused about it, tending to accept the overarching cultural messages that their experience is isolated, individual, or their own fault. Often in their effort to negotiate multiple identities, those on the margin have a strong understanding of their experience as "other" while continuing to operate out of their privileged identities with a lack of awareness.

Working with students to develop awareness of our conditioning means we can begin to see ourselves as what both Freire (1998) and Greene (1981) would describe as unfinished, able to grasp that our knowledge is constructed, inseparable from our situation, our historical context, our identities, our privileges. Greene (1981) and hooks (1994) define this as the intellectual work of being able to identify and name what is going on, how things operate, and how our interests are or are not served.

It is not enough to develop critical thinkers, however. Critical thinking can be as destructive as ignorance if not tempered with a sense of love and mercy in the timing and weight of its use. For example, I started to notice how often the analysis that we offer in the dismantling racism workshops would be used, not to engender greater understanding and cooperation, but as one more tool for blaming and judging others. I began to realize that I, and many of my colleagues and friends, had come to see critical thinking as a way of life rather than a skill to be strategically applied when appropriate and set aside when not. I gradually came to understand, as author and therapist Rachel Naomi Remen says, that "we serve life best when we water it and befriend it" (2000, p. 247), even as we critically investigate it. So I make sure that critical thinking in my classroom is coupled with a commensurate development of compassion.

One way to do this is to place the task of questioning or "queering" normal within a broader context of love. Parker Palmer talks about reframing education as a spiritual endeavor, where we seek knowledge "that originates not in curiosity or control but in compassion or love" (1993, p. 8). He explains that the purpose of a knowing "born of compassion" serves to "reconcile the world to itself" in a "reunification and reconstruction of broken selves and worlds" (p. 8). He implores us to redirect the "minds we have used to divide and conquer creation" to instead "raise to awareness the communal nature of reality, to overcome separateness and alienation, ... to reach out ... and renew the bonds of life" (pp. 8-9).

Situating critical inquiry in a context of love is particularly important because questioning normal is deeply unsettling, particularly for those who have never done it before. As teachers, we are asking people to interrogate their most deeply held and assumed beliefs. If we are to be successful in supporting our students to question normal, then we must, counterintuitively, prepare the ground of critical investigation with deep regard for who they are in the present moment. There is some irony in the discovery, as Anne Wilson Schaef explains so clearly, that "we have to be who we are before we can be someone different" (1998, p. 235). What I learned by slow experience is considered a basic truth of Jungian philosophy (Jung & Dell, 1933)—we cannot change that which we do not at first accept.

Because we are about to deeply unsettle our students; we have a responsibility to offer them the love and regard they need to survive what we are asking of them. Remen talks about the power of "believ[ing] in someone at a time when they cannot yet believe in themselves." At times like these, she says, "[our] belief becomes a lifeline" (2000, p. 292).

While starting with our students where they are, we then have to help our students develop both critical and compassionate thinking about others. I remember years ago attending a reading, writing, and meditation retreat, where a Buddhist monk shared a story about a pirate who raped a young woman and threw her overboard. The monk suggested that we must have great compassion for the woman and, at the same time, compassion for the pirate; we must, she said, consider the cost to the pirate of his vile act. I was outraged; I literally could not bear the idea that the pirate would or should receive an ounce of my or anyone else's compassion. And while I still struggle with this, knowing as I do many women who have experienced sexual assault and violence, I understand that hateful judgment does not offer possibility for real change. We accomplish little when we replace hierarchical, binary white supremacy thinking with a flipped version of hierarchical, binary "radical" thinking.

The act of standing outside our conditioned knowing is both a critical and compassionate one; we are not simply deconstructing what we know and how we know it. We are also seeking the ability to construct or reconstruct a way of knowing that is deeply rooted in assumptions of our common humanity, our collective possibility, our yearning for justice and for love.

TIMING

Two or three things I know for sure,
and one of them is that timing is everything.
Two or three things I know, two or three things I know for sure,
and one of them is that you can't push the river.

It took me a long time to realize that my job as a teacher/facilitator/workshop leader is not to "convert" those who are unwilling to consider any challenges to the preordained cultural stories. I used to spend valuable time focusing my time and attention on those who were loudly expressing their dissatisfaction with the agenda, the content, or the process. Finally I realized, despite the loud agitations of a few, most of the people in any group are willing to explore, ask heartfelt questions, challenge with the desire to understand rather than to oppose. I learned to handle the aggressive and outspoken challengers more directly, turning their questions over to the group in cases where that seemed useful or being quite frank that I was not going to consider a specific question or challenge until and unless we were able to attend to the process that had previously been planned.

Paul Kivel, antiracist trainer and author of *Uprooting Racism*, remarks on this phenomenon:

> In many of the workshops, I find there are a few white people—often young or adult males—who resist even acknowledging that racism exists. They are sometimes loud and vociferous, sometimes soft-spoken, but they demand lots of time and attention from the group.... I wonder if we should be paying so much attention to these people.... I have never found that getting into a long discussion with someone who is defensive is useful. It just increases their defensiveness and my frustration.... My goal is not to neutralize, overcome, persuade, convince, overwhelm, or seduce them if they

are resistant. This decision has increased my effectiveness as a facilitator because it means I don't get locked into a passionate debate with participants as often, and I no longer try to meet their every defense with an effective response. I can listen to them and move on to working with other participants and, more importantly, with the group itself.... (2002, p. 110-111)

Anne Wilson Schaef states that while most people come to [her] workshops to learn,

there are always a few who pay money to: 1) prove that they already know how to do this work … ; 2) reframe it in terms of their own biases; 3) fight with it and attack; 4) come laden with so many assumptions, which often are premeditated resentments, that they can't let themselves experience anything that doesn't fit into their assumptions; 5) prove their hypotheses about this work, whatever those hypotheses are.... All of these agendas inhibit the possibility of learning. We cannot learn something new if we think we already know it. We can't learn something new if we have to reframe it into something we already know. We can't learn something new if we have to disprove it before we experience it. When our minds are closed, learning cannot take place. (p. 148)

I quote Kivel and Schaef here to make the point that, like them, I have learned to be strategic in my response, putting my time and energy into those who come with at best a desire to learn and at worst the lack of an agenda to resist. I do not mean to suggest this is an either/or choice; often one student's defensiveness becomes a teachable moment for the rest (and even, eventually for the student himself). I talk in great depth about resistance and defensiveness in a previous chapter; my point here is that we have some strategic decisions to make in the classroom.

I discuss earlier, in the chapter on cultural shift, how Korten echoes this strategic approach in his book *The Great Turning* (2006, pp. 53-56) when he argues that the actual numbers of people needed to support what he calls "earth community" is actually relatively small. In other words, we do not have to reach every student. I advocate an approach of teaching to those most open while trying not to conclude (as best I can) that those who seem antagonistic or shut down will never move from their positions. I also try not to assume that I have understood their resistance correctly, realizing that the problem might lay with me.

Antiracist educator and writer Enid Lee (1992), describing her approach to bringing an antiracist perspective to the classroom, explains that she can usually divide every group she is teaching into three: those "who change because they feel a moral imperative … and want to do the right thing," those who "are entirely pragmatic" and "change out of enlightened self-interest" and those who "change because it's legislated, because they are told they have to." She summarizes the three motivations as "it's right, it will help me, I must."

Lee (1992) goes on to say

> In my experience, those three groups can be found almost everywhere. And I think we attack accordingly. I do use the word "attack" advisedly, because we are engaged in a struggle. We are attempting to reorganize the state of the universe, certainly the state of the school, and definitely the state of the class.

Antiracist activist and founder of the Challenging White Supremacy Workshop Sharon Martinas (personal correspondence, August 14, 2009) says that her strategy takes these groups into account; Martinas teaches "primarily to the first group and sets up situations where they can teach to the middle," she "challenges respectfully those there for pragmatic reasons," and finally attempts to "set up alliances of the 'principled and the pragmatic' to nudge the ones who are there solely because of community and institutional pressure."

The strategies we use to reach our students are often deeply influenced by timing. On a recent morning walk with a friend, we talked about how long it can take us to realize the meaning of something that has been clearly explained to us many times. My friend was noticing with some amusement her frustration with a colleague who, months into a new project, finally acknowledged a central concept that had been clearly defined in writing at the beginning. I recalled in turn the number of times I am struck by a point weeks, months, even years after first hearing it, and the many times I have heard the same thing over and over only to have it make sense when I am ready to make sense of it. I reference earlier my "aha" moments, where in the middle of offering a definition or idea that I have been working with literally for years, I can "suddenly" really know what I mean in a way I had not been able to before, how I can embody what I am saying or explaining in completely new ways. Shapiro (personal communication, August 10, 2009) concurs, saying that "learning is more of a spiral motion than linear—we return to things again and again."

People come to awareness on their own timelines, if they come at all. Hooks refers to this when she talks about realizing that she needed to "surrender [her] need for immediate affirmation of successful teaching ... and accept that students may not appreciate the value of a certain standpoint or process straightaway" (1994, p. 42). Students have told me (as they have hooks), "six months or a year, even two years later, that they realize the importance of what they have learned" (1994, p. 153) in the classroom.

In addition, I am always wrong about which students will be open to the material and which will not (and I have known other teachers to say the same). I might assume that a student with progressive politics and/or a LGBTQQI student and/or a Student of Color will embrace learning about race and other constructs while a white/heterosexual student from a rural conservative area will be more closed. What I have found, in fact, is that I might easily have a harder time with someone invested in a sense of themselves as one of the "good ones" or someone very focused on one aspect of their identities than with a student who has never considered these issues before and is both troubled and excited about learning more. As Martinas points out (personal correspondence, August 14, 2009), the students who have most success are those, regardless of identity or background, who can move beyond their own experience, putting themselves in the broader context of institutional and cultural oppression.

As teachers, we have no control of how and when people come to us in their own development process. Some come when they are at the right place to take in what we have to offer and do something with it; some are more focused on other aspects of their lives.

A respect for timing is an important response to white supremacy cultural tendencies to attempt to control, often with some urgency, that which cannot be. A respect for timing requires us to rethink our understanding of time. Carl Honoré (2004), in his exploration of what he calls our "cult of speed," notes how "everything and everyone is under pressure to go faster" (p. 3). He describes the costs attached to "turbo-capitalism," where "we exist to serve the economy, rather than the other way around" (p. 5). He observes how the terms "fast" and "slow" have come to signify "ways of being," where fast is "busy, controlling, aggressive, hurried, analytical, stressed, superficial, impatient, active, quantity-over-quality" (p. 14), many of the qualities exhibited by, and even revered, by our culture.

So, for example, our schools assume that children of the same age should master the same material in the same timeline; when that does not work for many students, the response is to try and get the students to change rather than rethink our approach to learning and time.

Another way this aggressive approach to time shows up in a class or workshop is at the point when we begin to take a close look at the institutional, and cultural manifestations of empire. Once the systemic nature of the race construct starts to hit home, someone always insists on knowing what we are going to *do* about it. Their demand, often echoed by others in the room, reflects a culture addicted to action—as the Nike ad so proudly proclaims, "Just do it!"

Reiterating what I described in the previous chapter, whenever people begin to insist on action, I stop and draw a diagram on the board. The easy part, I say, is being aware of the problem, whether it is racism or the lack of rain (the Southeast is experiencing a record drought as I write this) or that my hot water heater does not work (also true in this moment). Once we know what the problem is, we inevitably want to fix it. Unfortunately, in our zeal to fix, we often make the problem worse precisely because we have not taken time to actually understand its cause, its complexity, its larger context.

For example, in our urgency to "do something" about a drought caused by uncontrolled growth coupled with the public assumption that water is not so much a natural resource as an entitlement, our leaders respond to the loudest and most well-heeled voices with solutions that rarely address the more complex underlying issues.

I contend we want to move quickly to action both from a passion for justice *and* in order to avoid the hard work of understanding a problem and our complicity in it; this is particularly true for those of us sitting in positions of privilege. We move quickly from awareness to action because we want to gain a sense of control; one way we feel in control is by identifying a right way to proceed, to "fix" things. So we argue about the "right" way to "fix" the drought without actually focusing on the causal reasons for it, which would require a communitywide acknowledgement of entitled and wasteful behaviors in the face of climate change. Our public discussion on education is about identifying the "right" approach, which supports our illusion that one size fits all, while we ignore both the larger questions about what we should be educating for and the mounting numbers of children, particularly Children of Color, who are pushed out of our schools because they don't "fit." The cultural imperative to "do" is so strong that many students insist they do not want to have to think; they just want to know the right answer so they can get the right grade (Jensen, 2004).

I do not mean to imply that urgency is never required; in fact, circumstances often demand a response that acknowledges a literally life-and-death importance. We can look at any number of instances where this is true, from the catastrophe of the aftermath of Hurricane Katrina to the news of the deportation of a student's family. As Martinas notes (personal correspondence, August 14, 2009), responding quickly in these situations is a matter of solidarity and accountability.

I am talking about the danger of urgency as a way of life. The social justice movement is very vulnerable to this tendency, either moving directly from awareness to action or acting from the belief that there is one right way to address any issue. I recall with chagrin how I used to lead workshops designed to make the point that organizing was the "right" way to address community problems. At that time, I was not able to consider that every strategy brings with it elements of significant transformation as well as pitfalls or that the "rightness" of a strategy depends in large part on how it is implemented. It took me a while to grasp that we are not engaged in a competition for the best strategy, that social change happens as a result of collaborative approaches with people and communities informed by both their experience and strong analysis. Not until years later did I catch on to the damage caused by the unintended consequences of strategies developed out of a sense of righteousness or urgency rather than a thoughtfulness that might acknowledge the limits of our own abilities to know whether or not something is actually "right."

So to address this desire to compulsively "do," I draw a diagram in the shape of a circle that "starts" with awareness of a problem, moves to information gathering and analysis, then to visioning and planning, finally to action, where it does not stop, as the final stage is evaluation and reflection, which in its turn leads to deeper awareness and understanding of the problem, starting the cycle anew. I should admit that "cycle" is itself a somewhat linear concept that assumes discrete stages, when the reality is that the stages often occur in an overlapping or even simultaneous fashion. My point in using the diagram is to try and help students get more comfortable with the idea that we will be spending a lot of time gathering information and deepening our analysis before we proceed to application and action. [The perfidiousness of the stages shows up immediately, as information gathering and analytical work are also application and action steps.]

Moving through this cycle is a process both for the group and for individuals in the group. Even as we hope to support people in moving through the process, we cannot control that. As someone who lines up her neatly rolled socks in their assigned drawer, this has not been an easy lesson for me to learn. Wheatley (2006, pp. 153-154), in her reflections on how science can inform our leadership, echoes this sentiment, noting

> the greatest challenge for me lies ... in learning generally to live in a process world. It's a completely new way to be. Life demands that I participate with things as they unfold, to expect to be surprised, to honor the mystery of it, and to see what emerges. These were difficult lessons to learn. I was well-trained to create things—plans, events, measures, programs. I invested more than half my life in trying to make the world conform to what I thought was best for it. It's not easy to give up the role of master creator and move into the dance of life. But what is the alternative, for me or you?

To this end, Honoré wants us to develop a "Slow frame of mind" that emphasizes the importance of "making real and meaningful connections—with people, culture, work, food, everything" (pp. 14-15). Someone wise once said, and I wish I could tell you who, that sometimes the best thing to do when you do not know what to do is nothing. One thing I know for sure, even in the face of deeply pressing social problems, is that "wisdom lies in knowing when to sit back and wait for [life] to unfold" (Remen, 2000, p. 76) and knowing when to act. I have found, time and again, that if I put aside my sense of urgency, which is often a desire to control that which I cannot, then I make more room for my students, for me, to change. As a result, I am more effective as a teacher, mentor, activist.

FEELINGS

Two or three things I know for sure, and one of them is this—
we have to feel our way through.

Several years ago, my colleague Kenneth Jones and I were leading a dismantling racism workshop at a rural retreat center in North Carolina. We had spent the first day and a half in the intellectual task of deconstructing racism, its institutional and cultural aspects, as well as the dynamics of white privilege and internalized racial superiority and inferiority. We had explained our definition of racism as a system of advantage based on race, noting the implication that all white people are conditioned as racist. We then broke into caucuses—a People of Color caucus and a white caucus devoted to exploring the dynamics of racism impacting us as a group and individually. Facilitating the white caucus, I started out, as I almost always do, by asking everyone in the circle to share how they were feeling.

In this particular caucus, as happens every once in a while, one young woman was emotionally reeling from what she had heard. She was feeling it in her bones, embodying the sense of shame, despair, guilt that comes with fully understanding what it means to be complicit with oppression. She was taking it in so deeply that, through wrenching tears, she wondered about her right to exist, to take up space on this planet.

Also in the group was a philosophy professor from a neighboring university, a man whose field of study was logic. His response to the definition, and to the woman's distress, was to suggest "if racism is so painful to both white and Black people, then why don't we simply genetically eliminate the Black race?" He posed the question in an attempt to offer what was to him a purely logical solution. He was completely serious, ignorant of the implications of the erasure of a whole group of people and oblivious to the racism in his choice of which group to eliminate.

These two responses to the realities of racism by those in the dominant group represent ends of the spectrum—and I note that one sat in a position of influence at an educational institution. I have the deepest respect for the woman who was feeling her racism to her very core; our culture does not generally support this level of feeling. As Schaef notes, "we live in a culture that demands dysfunction. The purpose of dysfunction is to keep us out of touch with our own living process" (1998, p. 183). In fact, I would say our culture is terrified of people who feel so deeply, particularly if that feeling occurs in people and in ways that transgress the predictable.

Audre Lorde points out that our culture "does not want women, particularly white women, responding to racism. It wants racism to be accepted as an immutable given in the fabric of your existence, like eveningtime or the common cold" (1984, p. 128). She makes the case for anger, particularly the anger of Women of Color in response to "being silenced, ... being unchosen, ... in a world that takes for granted our lack of humanness, and which hates our very existence outside of its service" (p. 129). She argues "when we turn from anger we turn from insight, saying we will accept only the designs already known, deadly and safely familiar" (p. 131).

While not wishing to appropriate the specificity of her argument about the right of Women of Color to anger, I would suggest that we *can* generalize in the sense that when we turn from our feelings we turn from insight, all of us. As I argue in a previous chapter, our feelings have everything to do with the perpetuation of racism or the dismantling of it. As Lorde so aptly notes, one of the ways that oppression operates is to cut us off from our feelings, numbing us to our exploitation or to the costs of benefiting at the expense of others. Once numb, we easily succumb, collude. Oppression also teaches us to turn our unexamined feelings inward, paralyzing us in paroxysms of self-hatred and self-doubt—another way we succumb, collude.

The other alternative, culturally supported when enacted by those in power, is to direct unexamined feelings of fear and hatred, often violently, toward others. Those with immense power start wars; those with less direct their violence in predictably racist ways. One contemporary example is the right-wing "tea parties" where white men and women are gathering to express their deep-seated fears about cultural change with signs declaring "The zoo has an African; the White House has a lyin' African" next to one saying "We came unarmed [this time]" (Lewison, 2009). The media portrays these impassioned and hate-filled claims as the entitlements of engaged citizenry; if the same rage is to be enacted by those on the margins, the framing is very different. We are accused of being threatening, too feeling: "women are just too emotional," "why do Black people have to be so angry all the time?"

The educational system participates in constructing this double standard by equating "educated" as synonymous with unfeeling, "rational" intellect. As a result, "we have made the assumptions that learning must ... be as devoid of feelings as possible" (Schaef, 1998, p. 152). Schaef points out "in many circles, objective thinking is seen as the highest and purest level of thinking. This myth of objectivity is touted as value-free, when in actuality, it is valueless" (p. 162).

So when someone is brave enough to feel in my classroom, I do my best to make space for it, unless the feelings are being used to target or berate another student or me (which has not yet happened). In the case mentioned above, I gave the young woman the room she needed to speak her feelings to the group and then asked for silence so we could contemplate what she had shared with us. I am not a therapist and the caucus or classroom is not a therapy session, so I make no assumptions about my abilities in that regard. Yet what I know for sure, after making some bad mistakes about this, is that feelings, our own or those of our students, are not right or wrong, and as Jung suggests (Jung & Dell, 1933), we do not liberate with condemnation.

Rachel Naomi Remen talks about having to unlearn her medical training, saying "it has taken me years to realize that being a human being is not unprofessional" (2000, p. 148). She recounts a story about one of her patients, a woman with metastic cancer, who came to realize that "there are only two kinds of people in this world—those who are alive and those who are afraid" (2000, p. 168). While I may not agree with this dualistic either/ or, I do believe that a widespread, underlying, and unacknowledged fear is one of the primary barriers to personal and social change. Remen notes that "sooner or later we will come to the edge of all that we can control and find life, waiting there for us" (p. 169). This is why I devote a chapter to the power of privileged resistance, which in essence is fear about loss of control. In a culture that values control, Remen wants us to understand that life is uncontrollable process and, while frightening at times, we cannot "serve life if [we] are unconsciously afraid of life" (p. 169).

Few of us have had good practice at knowing and understanding our feelings; at the same time we tend to believe what we have been taught— that objective reason and intellect are not only possible but also better, more valuable. As a result, part of our job is to help students sit with the feelings they are conditioned to deny. Buddhist Pema Chödrön explains that "when pain presents itself to us in any form whatsoever, we run like crazy to try to become comfortable" (1997, p. 67). She suggests that we learn to bring compassion to our feelings and even to our desire to flee; part of our work, she says, is to "start cultivating our innate ability to simply be there with pain with an open heart and the willingness not to instantly try to get ground under our feet" (p. 81).

Learning to acknowledge our feelings, like developing critical thinking, is best done within a context of compassionate inquiry. In other words, it is not enough to feel, we must also develop the skill of examining our feelings to understand how they influence our thinking and behavior.

In the classroom, I always respond to feelings with affirmation, both of the feelings and the person doing the feeling. In the case of the distressed young woman at the workshop, I communicated, both in the caucus and then one-on-one, my deepest respect for the strength of her feelings and my absolute belief in her right to exist on the planet, her goodness. I gently pointed out that painful feelings are a part of the process of coming to grips with our own racism, our own internalized superiority as white people, and that acknowledgment of those feelings is an intensely important part of the lifetime process of learning to be free. [I should also note that I talked with the professor, who both discounted the young woman for her "irrational" feelings and my suggestions to consider how his logical solution was actually illogical.]

In the classroom, I use a range of methods to help students acknowledge their feelings and then explore why they feel the way they do. For example, after watching a movie about the massacre at My Lai (Sim & Bilton, 1989), a disturbing and moving film raising questions about when and why we obey authority, I usually call for the class to sit in silence to give everyone a chance to feel their response. Then I ask each student to share what they are feeling; we do this as a go-around, so that each student speaks into the circle while the rest of us listen. After everyone has spoken, I might ask the students to journal, reflecting on why they feel the way they do. Sometimes I ask them to choose a person from the film and write a letter to them sharing what they are feeling and thinking. Or I ask them to take the position of a person in the film and have them write to the class from that position. Students then share their letters with each other. In these ways they begin to explore what they are feeling and why; they get an opportunity to see the range of feelings and responses in the room. Once the intensity of the feelings abates, I might use a fishbowl format (where a smaller group of students sit in the middle and has a discussion) to allow students with very different responses to discuss why one supports the soldiers and the other condemns them.

As teachers and facilitators, we might wonder whether feelings will come up that we will not be able to handle. As long as we are not trying to produce feelings artificially, in a kind of manipulative "now it's time to feel" kind of way, then we can trust that any feeling that comes up is "an indicator that [the person doing the feeling] has reached a level of strength, maturity, awareness, and spiritual growth that [they] *are* able to handle" (Schaef, 1998, p. 189). In other words, feelings come because we are, in some meaningful way, prepared for them, because they are necessary for our development. When feelings come that we are not ready for, we tend to push them off, or as Schaef suggests, to "recycle" them until we are ready, until "we have whatever we need to deal with [them]" (p. 184).

We must also remember that moving out of conditioned thinking (or healing) is a process; it does not happen in a single moment but over time. As I noted earlier, we can trust ourselves, and our students, to move through this process at their own speed.

In all my years of community training and teaching, I have yet to encounter a level of feeling that I cannot hold and, in the simple act of receiving it, help a student move through it to a place of deeper reflection. This includes feelings of guilt, shame, anger, rage, bitterness, confusion. I am talking about genuine feeling, not the self-righteous anger where people, often sitting in positions of privilege, challenge the group or me disrespectfully and inappropriately. In those cases, I set limits and I set them firmly. I have often asked to speak to students outside of class; I have once asked a workshop participant to leave. Also, I have had to learn to distinguish between what I would call genuine feeling and the "acting out" of feelings that students and workshop participants use to avoid actually dealing with class content, to remain the focus of attention, to take up space while the rest of us, uncomfortable with someone in distress, spend our collective energies trying to make the emotive person feel "better." When I talk about our responsibility as teachers to become comfortable with feelings, I am referencing those times when students are genuinely struggling with the material and their response to what they are being called upon to learn.

Finally, we have to learn to develop our own sense of comfort around the reality that people will leave our classroom with unresolved feelings.

Again, I do not want to suggest this is easy (this seems to be rather a mantra at this point; perhaps I should simply say that one of the things I know for sure is that doing this work is not easy). As I argue earlier, we have to develop a fearless and compassionate relationship with our own feelings so that we are prepared to hold the feelings of our students without defensiveness.

I end this story by noting that the logic professor, whose commitment to "objectivity" led him to a justification of cultural genocide, has, in my view, little chance of coming to grips with his own racism, his own participation in a racist system, as long as he allows his misuse of logic to shut down any nerve connections he has to his body, his heart, his feelings.

HOLDING CONTRADICTIONS

Two or three things I know for sure and one of them is this—
we have to get good at believing two or more
contradictory things at the same time.

Challenging cultural conditioning requires us to constantly negotiate the fine line between two seemingly contradictory tensions. I first became aware of this when I found myself trying to explain to groups of white people that we are both racist and antiracist at the same time. We are conditioned to be racist from the moment we are born; our best intentions cannot prevent us from this conditioning. While we are bound to act out of that conditioned racism, we can at the very same time act to see it, know it, address it, change it; we can, in essence, operate as committed antiracists. In opposition to traditional western thought, which assumes things are a binary one or the other, I see these tendencies as overlapping and concurrent; both are true at any given moment.

A central tenet of many Eastern philosophies, many have marked this important dynamic of both/and. David Korten notes that "love and fear are both integral to our human nature and necessary for our full development … how we resolve the tension between love and fear has major consequences for the course of our lives" (2006, p. 34). In a similar vein, he writes that "to bring the feminine and masculine principles into balance is a defining challenge of the cultural turning" (p. 105).

The call to love the other, for example, offers an escape from either/or, a challenge to learn to live with the ambiguity such loving demands. David Purpel (class discussion, November 16, 2005) sees our conflicting impulses—we want to help people, we want to help ourselves; we are caring, we are selfish—as a reflection of our collective confusion about how to find meaning. I would like to suggest that meaning is found in the exquisite balance between.

Much like Purpel's (Purpel & McLaurin, 2004) response to the dynamic relationship between fundamental and incremental change, we are called on to say yes and yes and yes as we seek to love those in need (a traditionally acceptable and applauded approach) as well as those who hurt us and/or have power over our lives (an approach with which we are much less familiar). I am not suggesting a "turn the other cheek" love, or as Dr. Martin Luther King (1967) would call it, an "anemic" love; I am talking about the deep love that acknowledges the connectedness among all living things and so seeks to resist oppression with non-violence and regard. American Indian Movement activist Leonard Peltier, unjustly imprisoned for decades and having more reason than most for bitterness, says

> I don't know how to save the world. I don't have the answers or The Answer. I hold no secret knowledge as to how to fix the mistakes of generations past and present. I only know that without compassion and respect for *all* (his italics) of Earth's inhabitants, none of us will survive—nor will we deserve to. (1999, p. 201)

Chicana feminist Gloria Anzaldúa acknowledges the challenge this involves, naming her belief that "by changing ourselves, we change the world" (1981, p. 208) as we travel what she calls the El Mundo Zurdo path that involves "a going deep into the self and an expanding out into the world, a simultaneous recreation of the self and a reconstruction of society." What I love about Anzaldúa is that she does not pretend to have answers for what she does not know, as she struggles how to resolve the realities of the "thousands that go to bed hungry every night, ... that do numbing shitwork eight hours a day, ... that get beaten and killed every day" (p. 208) with her belief that "we create our own world." She acknowledges the tension that exists as she attempts to "make peace between what has happened to me, what the world is, and what it should be" (p. 208)

Anzaldúa suggests that this practice of "hold[ing] opposites long enough without taking sides" leads to a "new identity" that she names nepantla, the "site of transformation" (2002, p. 548). From this "in-between place of nepantla," we are able to "see through the fiction of monoculture, the myth of the superiority of the white races, ... through ... [the] myth of the inferiority of mujeres" (p. 549). She frames this task or stage of nepantla as necessary to what she considers the spiritual task of both personal and collective liberation.

Here, then, is a call to hold the extreme contradictions of oppression and love. As a teacher, I set myself the task of holding contradictions and supporting my students to hold them as well.

One of the contradictions we try to hold is that between liberation and responsibility. Derrick Jensen echoes Freire's stipulation that we must balance liberty with responsibility when he writes:

> If the first quarter [of our life] is about liberation, the second would be about responsibility. Every person needs to learn and experience—incorporate, take into the body—both. And they're inseparable. Either without the other becomes a parody, and leads to inappropriate, destructive, and self-destructive behaviors generally characteristic of unconscious or unintentional parodies. Responsibility without freedom is slavery. As we see. Freedom without responsibility is immaturity. As we also see. (2004, p. 194)

Freire talks about the need to pair liberty with responsibility using the example of "right thinking," emphasizing that an ingredient of right thinking is a "generous heart" (1998, p. 40), an openness to other possibilities, including the possibility that I/we may be wrong. Purpel describes right thinking as "dialogical and not polemical" (2004, p. 43) and understands it as a collective endeavor.

In my classroom, I work with students steeped in the culturally conditioned belief that freedom means the right to do what you want. A popular method for helping students question this assumption is an assignment where they are instructed to count all their clothes, noting where each piece of clothing is made. [Students have a range of assignments to choose from so that students without resources who do not have many clothes and might feel embarrassed or uncomfortable with this particular project can make a different choice.] This project inevitably helps them make connections between their consumer habits, globalization, sweatshop labor, the true "cost" of what they buy, and their connection to people across the globe. In this way, they start to investigate the tension between their "freedom" to buy and their responsibility to others and the earth.

Another dialectic is that identified by Maxine Greene (1988) as the constant tension between freedom (our wish to be free) and what exists (the material, social world in which we are situated). We have to learn to maneuver the space between our vision of what we want the world to be and the world as it is given to us. If we simply accept the world as it is from a position of realistic pragmatism, then we end up constantly negotiating our sense of integrity. If we focus only on the world that we want, we are subject to cynicism and despair.

I am witness to this contradiction every semester, as students struggle with the implications of the class material. Inevitably some of my students attempt to share what they are learning in class with their family or friends and are met with hostility. They must then make decisions about the implications of adopting a broader understanding of the world, one that their community rejects. Hooks talks about the fear her Black women students feel that "a commitment to feminist politics would lead them to be isolated" while understanding at the same time that "an analysis of gender from a feminist standpoint … was necessary for the collective development of black consciousness" (1994, p. 117). This tension is not easily resolved (if resolution is even possible) and yet to ignore the tension would be irresponsible. One of the reasons I spend so much time building relationship in the classroom is so that students who are struggling with this tension can feel "at home" in a three-hour block of time each week. I want them to understand the power of community to help with feelings of isolation; I continually encourage them to think about collaborative possibilities both in our classroom and once they enter into full-time teaching because I believe that a collective consciousness can help them maneuver this tension.

We must also work to move beyond how this culture employs absolutes to limit our choices and bind us. Rather than an either/or approach, where we are often asked to choose between two equally bad options, Anne Wilson Schaef offers the linguistic power of both/and:

> I rarely use "but." I substitute "and." I do this for two reasons. The first and easiest reason is that often everything before the but is either discounted or a lie—for example—"I really like you but …" The second and more important reason is that "but" sets up a dualism of either this or that. Since I am trying to encourage us to move beyond dualisms, I substitute "and." The use

of 'and' in such a sentence throws us into an entirely different mind-set and creates different experiences in our bodies. (1998, p. xv)

In my classroom, I try to help students notice when they are engaging in either/or thinking, encouraging them to regroup and consider new approaches. When we begin to deconstruct racism, I tell them that one of the reasons the topic can be so difficult to talk about is because we are afraid that it is really a conversation about who is good and who bad. I assure them that while racism certainly affects people differently based on racial identity, my assumption is that everyone in the room is both and we are going to fight the culturally conditioned tendency to reduce our analysis to such a useless binary.

We also need to learn to hold the tension between the gifts offered by our strengths and weaknesses. Again, our culture prefers to disdain vulnerability and has never done well admitting mistakes. Parker Palmer encourages us to notice how our "limitations and liabilities are the flip side of our gifts, how a particular weakness is the inevitable trade-off for a particular strength" (2000, p. 52). I do a story-telling exercise in class, asking people to reflect on the strengths and weaknesses of their class and ethnic background; inevitably many in the group note that what they identify as a strength is often the result of having to address a weakness. Rather than encouraging the popular attitude that we must reject what makes us uncomfortable, I want students to see discomfort (weakness, frailty, vulnerability) in terms of the insights and gifts it has to offer.

We also have to look at the balance between learning based in our experience and the need to know beyond our experience in order to grow. Transformative education is that which makes connections between new ideas and lived experience without reifying either. I am reminded of the long-held belief in the organizing community, rooted in the theory and writing of Saul Alinsky (1971), that "real" organizing is that led by those most affected by whatever issue is being addressed. During my early years as an activist, I noticed the gap between this theory and the reality, where organizers were often middle-class college-educated young people who rarely came from the communities in which they were working. This was partly due to issues of class and education privilege and partly due to the fact that people most affected by the issues often do not have access to information or analysis that provide the context of a bigger picture (although many are able to make these connections regardless). In many cases where leaders or organizers (often white, middle-class and college-educated) try to faithfully follow the theoretical model, community people sometimes approach issues with racist, sexist, or homophobic thinking and strategies because they have never been challenged to think beyond their own conditioning (not that the organizers always have either).

I believe we must negotiate a balance between following the lead of those most affected by any issue with both a set of collectively constructed values that embrace concepts of love, justice, and ongoing political education (my shorthand phrase for the teaching and learning processes that bring light to power). This negotiated balance takes into account that our membership in a privileged group does not mean we have answers for other people, an assumption made from the internalization of our superiority. Likewise, our membership in an oppressed group does not guarantee that we have exclusive wisdom about our circumstances, particularly when that wisdom is constrained by the internalization of conditioned toxic thinking.

In the classroom, I balance respect for the lived experience of my students with what I have had the privilege to learn and understand about the larger world. Every semester, I have at least one white student who recounts a story of her or his experience with "reverse" racism, reciting with great passion how she or he did not get into a school or a program or a job because the opportunity was unfairly given to a less qualified person of color. This is always very challenging for me and I have to work at reminding myself to allow the story to unfold without interruption, to allow the feelings attached to this experience full rein. At my best, I use these stories to pose a series of questions about the assumptions we carry. For example, I might ask the class to deconstruct the word "qualified" or to consider why we feel so strongly about unfairness attached to race while ignoring its attachment to class. When students make racist assumptions in their writing, I respond by posing questions or offering alternative ways of looking at the situation, trying very hard to never deny their experience.

As I noted earlier, we cannot change that which we do not at first accept. The moment I become insistent about the student's ability to see the bigger picture is the moment I make the student resistant and defensive. The tension I must negotiate in this situation is to accept where the student is coming from while pushing them to consider their situation differently and letting go of any stake in whether they are able to do so or not.

Another place of delicate balance is that between comfort and dis-ease. Hooks reminds us that whenever we engage in subjects that students care about, "there is always a possibility of confrontation, forceful expression of ideas, or even conflict" (1994, p. 39). She challenges the idea of the classroom as a "safe, harmonious" place given that any level of truly critical pedagogy should make all of us uncomfortable because it is challenging us to change. Change is discomforting, even for those of us who want it.

I used to think that I had to resolve every conflict and counter every remark made out of conditioned ignorance. I am slowly learning to step back, to allow the discomfort engendered by such moments to simmer. When a student says something that reinforces conditioned stereotypes or ignorance, instead of responding directly myself, I turn to the class and ask "does anyone have a different take on this?" or in some other way invite reflection or discussion. I try and promote different points of view, often calling on a student I know might offer a fresh perspective, even if it is one with which I do not agree. I know that if one student is having trouble with the information, then others are as well; these viewpoints need to see the light of day if they are to be addressed. Bringing disparate perspectives into the open raises the trust level in class, helping students to see that their opinions are valued even when they are different from mine. Once the discussion is in full swing, I then feel free to enter into it, offering points or additional questions, sometimes weeks later when students have gained new information or just had the time to sit with the tension for a while.

I have already talked extensively about the role of emotion and feelings in learning. This is another place of tender contradiction, that fine balance between emotion and intellect. Hooks talks about how she learned from Freire to think of transformative education as that which liberates the mind and from Buddhist leader Thich Nhat Hanh as that which "emphasizes wholeness, a union of body, mind, and spirit" (1994, p. 14). As I said, we live in a culture that privileges an idealized "masculine" and objective kind of rational thinking, assuming as it does, that rational (higher) thought is disconnected from body and spirit and therefore more "reliable." I have already mentioned the important role of emotions in learning, a direct contrast to dominant culture beliefs that intellectualism requires its erasure. In the classroom, then, it becomes important to help students acknowledge their emotions, knowing that we have to understand what we are feeling before we can begin to change (see discussion above). At the same time, we want to challenge our students intellectually, helping them to sharpen their critical and compassionate thinking skills.

Finally, perhaps the most profound contradiction we must maneuver is that between what we say and what we do. Freire reveals this contradiction as one of his "major preoccupations," as he struggles "between what I seem to be and what I am actually becoming" (1998, p. 88). Remen explains that she has come to realize "how much stress is caused by the sad fact that many of us believe in one way and live in quite another. Stress may be more a matter of personal integrity ... determined by the distance between our authentic values and how we live our lives" (2000, p. 177). I contend this struggle gives our lives integrity.

I have spent the last 20 years of my life working for groups holding an explicit social justice mission while at the same time many exploit their workforce and perpetuate the same racist, sexist, and homophobic practices their literature says they deplore. I have to go no further than my clothes closet and count my innumerable pairs of shoes to see the gap between what I say my values are around consumerism and my actual practice.

As Purpel (class discussion, November 16, 2005) so eloquently acknowledges, this is not always a matter of ideological naivité; he wants us to realize that we're often put in terrible situations—the need, for example, to act in ways which are inconsistent with our own best interests in order to keep a job and feed our children. He pushes us to understand that we are placed in very challenging moral binds as we try to live our values and suggests that rather than assume we can choose either to be morally righteous or morally corrupt, we have to negotiate, in what I would call an exquisite balance, this desire to live our ideals while understanding that the constraints under which we live may require mercy towards ourselves when we cannot. Hooks describes it this way:

> To have work that promotes one's liberation is such a powerful gift that it does not matter so much if the gift is flawed. Think of the gift as water that contains some dirt. Because you are thirsty, you are not too proud to extract the dirt and be nourished by the water. (1994, p. 50)

Freire points out that it is the very nature of the world to be in tension—that the only reason we can experience joy is because we also experience despair, the only reason we can experience liberation is because we also experience oppression. In fact, he describes human existence as

> a radical and profound tension between good and evil, between dignity and indignity, between decency and indecency, between the beauty and the ugliness of the world. (1998, p. 53)

This tension, this pairing of contradictory opposites, is the very nature of life itself. As Shapiro notes (personal correspondence, August 10, 2009), "living with contradiction is itself a kind of emotional maturity." One of the things I know for sure is we must understand both that these essential contradictions exist and support our students, ourselves, to learn to negotiate the gap between them.

TOGETHER WE CHANGE THE WORLD

Two or three things I know, two or three things I know for sure,
and one of them is that I need you, and you need me, and
together we might change the world.

In the middle of the semester, after a class where we had been talking about racism and its historically pervasive power, I realized that everyone had left except for one student, a young white woman, who looked visibly upset. She was on the verge of tears as she collected her notebook and papers. I asked her if she wanted to talk. We sat and she told me, in a halting voice filled with distress, that she understood the concepts we were discussing in class—the institutional and cultural nature of racism, white privilege, internalized racial superiority—and she understood their application to her own life. But, she said, she could not possibly take this information home, she could not talk about it with her family; essentially, she was feeling in her body the ways in which knowing this information was going to isolate her from the people that she loved.

Korten (2006, p. 84) describes what my student was feeling:

> This awakening [from the trance induced by the prevailing culture] commonly leads to a deep disconnect between the realities of family, work, and community life grounded in the previously unexamined values and the examined, authentic values of a maturing consciousness. This disconnect confronts the individual with the often painful choice between conformity and authenticity.... The individuals undergoing this transition may at times feel like creatures from outer space in the midst of a family gathering or class reunion. With time, however, they find others, ... Together they help one another discover that the craziness is not in themselves, but in what many institutions decree as "normal."

I belong to a writing group that meets every other week; the group was established by women survivors of sexual assault, primarily but not exclusively Women of Color, looking for supportive community after a nationally publicized incident involving an alleged rape by members of the Duke lacrosse team in 2006. What strikes me about this group is not simply the privilege of being part of a gathering of insightful, intelligent, funny, and powerful women. What strikes me is how despite our insight and power, each of us still feels isolated as we navigate our daily lives in a culture largely hostile to our deepest hopes and desires. We meet week after week, using writing as one vehicle to break through our sense of separation.

Remen suggests that our cultural "striving for excessive independence ... makes many of us so vulnerable to isolation, cynicism, and depression" (2000, p. 197). One consequence of living in a culture that reveres individualism is the way in which so many of us feel isolated, thinking that what's happening in our lives is personal, private, and a reflection of our own inadequacy or shortcoming. Audre Lorde, in her essay about the *Transformation of Silence into Language and Action*, talks about how a medical diagnosis left her facing death for a three-week period during which she became aware that what I most regretted were my silences. Of what had I ever been afraid? To question or to speak as I believed could have meant pain, or death. But we all hurt. In so many different ways, all the time, and pain will either change or end. Death, on the other hand, is the final silence. And that might be coming quickly, now, without regard for whether I had ever spoken what needed to be said, or had only betrayed myself into small silences, while I planned someday to speak...." She describes how she the women "who sustained me through that period ... all shared a war against the tyrannies of silence. (1984, p. 41)

To paraphrase Audre Lorde is a kind of travesty, like reading Cliff notes instead of the original Shakespeare. Her point, like the powerful bumpersticker states, is that silence equals death, particularly for people who are discarded by society anyway—those who are Black, lesbian, ... She ends by noting how "we have been socialized to respect fear more than our own needs for language and definition, and while we wait in silence for that final luxury of fearlessness, the weight of the silence will choke us" (1984, p. 44).

One thing I know for sure is that as teachers we must help people break silence and one of the best ways I know to do that is through community. In community, we can see, as June Jordan says, that we are not alone in our challenges; in community, we can see and act out the potential of our collective desires for meaningful change. My teaching is based in the belief, as Wheatley reminds us that

in this participative universe, nothing living lives alone. Everything comes into form because of relationship. We are constantly called to be in relationship—to information, people, events, ideas, life. Even reality is created through our participation in relationships.... Through these chosen relationships, we co-create our world. (2006, p. 145)

Davis, Sumara, and Luce-Kapler, like Wheatley, make the point that "collectives of persons are capable of actions and understandings that transcend the capabilities of individuals on their own" (2000, p. 68). Levine talks about building a "committed community of learners" and describes it as an inevitable process resulting from increased engagement, risk-taking, and the freedom to "expose [our] authentic inner-selves more fully to each other" (2003, p. 56).

Influenced by the U.S. dominant culture emphasis on individualism, one of our challenges is how often our students can only conceive of taking action on their own; they have little experience of the collective as a vehicle for change. As I discuss in chapter 4, students often place themselves at risk when they do act, either by stepping out in ways that make it easy for those in power to target or marginalize them, or by stepping out in ways that put those they are trying to help at risk. Therefore, another important goal in my classroom is to help students understand the power of collective and collaborative action, both historically and in their own lives.

I believe that teaching must be oriented toward praxis—the purpose of the analysis is to lead people towards thoughtful action, to "peel away the layers of meaning that give shape to our everyday lives, ... to serve as a guide to action designed to alter those life forces that embody the power of an oppressive reality" (Giroux, 1999, p. 11). The ultimate hope is that we will make the "transition from critical thought to reflective intervention in the world" (p. 11)

The final thing I know for sure is that the practice of social justice is a collective endeavor. Given our cultural conditioning into individualism, one of our roles as teachers is to expose students to the potential of the collective, both historically and in the here and now.

IN CONCLUSION ...

Alexis Pauline Gumbs, a friend, scholar, and poet, writes that "the poetic is necessary in a relationship between a theoretic that makes the unimaginable imaginable and practices that are practically impossible" (personal communication, September 15, 2008). She references scholar and writer, Sylvia Wynter, who believes that "poetry is the way we make a transformed relationship to our environments and each other by seeking to describe things that we cannot describe in the languages we have produced so far." Alexis understands "teaching ... to be a poetic act, where a(n im)possible relationship to the world is made possible through a classroom relation."

And so, once again with much reverence for and credit to Dorothy Allison (1995, whose words are in italic), here are two or three things I know for sure about teaching for the cultural turning.

Two or three things I know for sure, and one of them how long it takes to learn to love yourself, how long it took me, how much love I need now.

Two or three things I know for sure and one of them is just how important love is, how important love is in the classroom.

Two or three things I know for sure, and one is that I would rather go naked than wear the coat the world has made for me.

Two or three things I know for sure and one of them is that we have to question everything with a critical eye and a compassionate heart.

Two or three things I know for sure, and one of them is that change when it comes cracks everything open.

Two or three things I know for sure, and one of them is that timing is everything.

Two or three things I know, two or three things I know for sure, and one of them is that you can't push the river.

Two or three things I know for sure, and one of them is this—we have to feel our way through.

Two or three things I know for sure, and one of them is the way you can both hate and love something you are not sure you understand.

Two or three things I know for sure and one of them is this—we have to get good at believing two or more contradictory things at the same time.

Two or three things I know, two or three things I know for sure, and one of them is that to go on living I have to tell stories, that stories are the one sure way I know to touch the heart and change the world.

Two or three things I know, two or three things I know for sure, and one of them is that if we are not beautiful to each other, we cannot know beauty in any form.

Two or three things I know, two or three things I know for sure, and one of them is that I need you, and you in turn need me, and together we might change the world.

I can tell you anything, All you have to believe is the truth.

The Long Road

Alone, you can fight,
you can refuse, you can
take what revenge you can
But they roll over you.

But two people fighting
back to back can cut through
a mob, a snake-dancing file
can break a cordon, an army
can meet an army.

Two people can keep each other
sane, can give support, conviction,
love, massage, hope, sex.
Three people are a delegation,
a committee, a wedge. With four
you can play bridge and start
an organization. With six
you can rent a whole house,
eat a pie for dinner with no
seconds, and hold a fund-raising party.

A dozen can hold a demonstration.
A hundred fill a hall.
A thousand have solidarity and your own newsletter;
ten thousand, power and your own paper;
a hundred thousand, your own media;
ten million, your own country.

It goes one at a time,
it starts when you care

The Emperor Has No Clothes: Teaching About Race and Racism
to People Who Don't Want to Know, pp. 167–168
Copyright © 2010 by Information Age Publishing

to act, it starts when you do
it again after they said no,
it starts when you say We
and know who you mean, and each
day you mean one more.

—Marge Piercy (Life Prayers, p. 142)

AFTER THE PARADE

Epilogue

Hans Christian Andersen ends his parable of the Emperor with the young boy calling out the Emperor's nakedness and, with his cry, giving permission for the townspeople to finally admit that they see it too. I always wonder what happens next in the story. Does the Emperor flee in humiliation? Do the townspeople laugh at the Emperor? Do they throw stones? In our contemporary culture, the young boy would probably be recruited to star in a reality series, the Emperor's court would hold endless and fruitless hearings about the tailors' fraud, the tailors would retire to the Caribbean, and the Emperor would go to war with a neighboring country to insure that no one would laugh at him again.

I like to imagine it differently. The boy, amused by the sight of the naked Emperor, encourages those around him to get naked too. The Emperor sighs with relief that he no longer has to carry on the charade. The tailors come to grips with the cost of their swindle to their own souls and join the naked melée. Everyone, stripped of their clothing, begin to laugh and dance, and the town square vibrates to the rhythm of the men, women, and children jumping, swinging, swaying in joy at their newfound freedom.

As teachers, my hope is that we can be the young boy, crying out the obvious, with love and compassion and deep faith in our collective desire

The Emperor Has No Clothes: Teaching About Race and Racism to People Who Don't Want to Know, pp. 169–170
Copyright © 2010 by Information Age Publishing

to see the world as it is which in turn allows us to make the world we want, one pulsating with joy, justice, love.

REFERENCES

Adams, G., Edkins, V., Lacka, D., Pickett, K. M., & Cheryan, S. (2008). Teaching about racism: Pernicious implications of the standard portrayal. *Basic and Applied Social Psychology, 30*(4), 349-361.

Adelman, L. (Producer), & Smith, L. M. (Writer, Producer, Director). (2003). *Race: The power of an illusion* [Documentary]. United States: California Newsreel.

Alinsky, S. (1971). *Rules for radicals: A pragmatic primer for realistic radicals.* New York, NY: Random House.

Allen, R. (1983). *Reluctant reformers: Racism and social reform movements in the United States.* Washington, DC: Howard University Press.

Allen, T. (1994). *The invention of the white race: Racial oppression and social control* (Vol. 1). New York, NY: Verso.

Allison, D. (1995). *Two or three things I know for sure.* New York, NY: Plume.

Andersen, H.C. (1837). *The emperor's new suit.* Retrieved from http://hca.gilead .org.il/emperor.html

Anzaldúa, G. (1981). La prieta. In C. Moraga & G. Anzaldúa (Eds.), *This bridge called my back: Writings by radical Women of Color* (pp. 198-208). Watertown, MA: Persephone Press.

Anzaldúa, G. (2002). Now let us shift ... the path of conocimiento ... inner work, public acts. In G. Anzaldúa & A. Keating (Eds.), *This bridge we call home: Radical visions for transformation* (pp. 540-578). New York, NY: Routledge.

Applebaum, B. (2007). Engaging student disengagement: resistance or disagreement? *Philosophy of Education Yearbook*, pp. 335-345.

Associated Press. (2006, March 6). *UNC grad in court on alleged hit and run.* Retrieved from http://www.foxnews.com

Au, W. (Ed.). (2009). Introduction. In *Rethinking multicultural education: teaching for racial and cultural justice.* Milwaukee, WI: Rethinking Schools.

Aveling, N. (2002). Student teachers' resistance to exploring racism: reflections on 'doing' border pedagogy [Electronic version]. *Asia-Pacific Journal of Teacher Education, 30*(2), 119-130.

Barndt, J. (1991). *Dismantling racism: the continuing challenge to white America*. Minneapolis, MN: Augsburg Fortress.

Bauman, Z. (1997). *Life in fragments*. Oxford, England: Blackwell.

Bender, L. (Producer), & Guggenheim, D. (Director). (2006). *An inconvenient truth* [Motion picture documentary]. United States: Lawrence Bender Productions.

Bennington, A. (2008). *General writing and grammar help*. Retrieved from http://en.allexperts.com/q/General-Writing-Grammar-680/2008/8/Capitalization-5.htm

Berger, D., Boudin, C., & Farrow, K. (Eds.). (2005). *Letters from young activists; Today's rebels speak out*. New York, NY: Nation Books.

Bigelow, B. (2008). *A people's history for the classroom*. Milwaukee, WI: Rethinking Schools.

Bigelow, B., & Peterson, B. (Eds.). (1998). *Rethinking Columbus: The next 500 years*. Milwaukee, WI: Rethinking Schools.

Billig, S.H., & Eyler, J. (Eds.). (2003). *Deconstructing service learning: Research exploring context, participation, and impacts*. Greenwich, CT: Information Age.

Bonilla-Silva, E. (2006). *Racism without racists: Color-blind racism and the persistence of racial inequality in the United States*. New York, NY: Rowman & Littlefield.

Books, S. (2007). *Invisible children in the society and its schools* (3rd ed.). Mahwah, NJ: Erlbam.

Brodkin, K. (2000). *How Jews became white folks: and what that says about race in America*. New Brunswick, NJ: Rutgers University Press.

Brooks, J. G., & Thompson, E. G. (2006). Social justice in the classroom. In H.S. Shapiro, S. B. Harden, & A. Pennell (Eds.), *The institution of education* (4th ed., pp. 449-454). Boston, MA: Pearson.

Browne, J., Franco, M., Negrón-Gonzales, J., & Williams, S. (2005). *Towards land, work, & power*. San Francisco, CA: Unite to Fight Press.

Burns, E. M. (1941). *Western civilizations: Their history and their culture*. New York, NY: Norton.

Chödrön, P. (1997). *When things fall apart: Heart advice for difficult times*. Boston, MA: Shambala Classics.

Cohen, C. J. (1997). Punks, bulldaggers, and welfare queens: The radical potential of queer politics. *GLQ: A Journal of Lesbian & Gay Studies, 3*, 437-465.

Concise Rules of APA Style. (2005). Washington, DC: American Psychological Association.

Cooper, A. (2004, September). Twenty-eight words that could change the world: Robert Hinkley's plan to tame corporate power. *The Sun, 345*, 4-11.

Cooperrider, D. L., & Whitney, D. (n.d.). *A positive revolution in change: Appreciative inquiry* [Draft]. Retrieved from http://appreciativeinquiry.case.edu/uploads/whatisai.pdf

Copp, D. & Kinsella, S. (Producers), & Sington, D. & Riley, C. (Directors). (2007). *In the shadow of the moon* [Motion picture documentary]. United States: THINKFilm.

Cowhey, M. (2006). *Black ants and Buddhists: Thinking critically and teaching differently in the primary grades*. Portland, ME: Stenhouse.

Davis, B., Sumara, D., & Luce-Kapler, R. (2000). *Engaging minds: learning and teaching in a complex world*. Mahwah, NJ: Erlbaum.

Davis, J. H. (2009, May 28). GOP senator doesn't expect a filibuster. *The News & Observer*, p. 3A.

Davis, K. (Director). (2006). *A girl like me* [Video documentary]. United States: Media That Matters, Reel Works Teen Filmmaking.

DeGraaf, J., Wann, D., & Naylor, T. H. (2005). *Affluenza: The all-consuming epidemic* (2nd ed.). San Francisco, CA: Berrett-Koehler.

Dewey, E., Costello, K., & Garcia, J. T. (2009, June). *Survival through liberation: Trans and gender nonconformity.* Workshop handout at the Pedagogy of Privilege Conference, Denver, CO.

Diamond, J. (2005). *Collapse: How societies choose to fail or succeed.* New York, NY: Penguin Books.

Durham, W. (2001). *Oral history interview with Walter Durham, January 19 and 26, 2001*; interview K-0540, from Southern Oral History Program Collection (#4007) [Electronic ed.]. Chapel Hill, NC: University Library-UNC.

Durán, L. (2002). *The politics of philanthropy and social change funding: a popular review of the literature.* Denver, CO: Grassroots Institute for Fundraising Training.

The Earth Charter Initiative. (2000). *The Earth charter.* Retrieved from http://www.earthcharterinaction.org/content/pages/Read-the-Charter.html

Eisner, E. (2002). *The educational imagination: on the design and evaluation of school programs.* Upper Saddle River, NJ: Merrill/Prentice Hall.

Ericsson, S., & Talreja, S. (Producers), & Jhally, S. (Director), & Katz, J. (Writer). (2002). *Tough guise: violence, media, and the crisis in masculinity* [Videorecording]. Northampton, MA: Media Education Foundation.

Feagin, J.R. (2000). *Racist America: Roots, current realities, and future reparations.* New York, NY: Routledge.

Frankl, V. (1963). *Man's search for meaning: an introduction to logotherapy.* New York, NY: Pocket Books.

Freire, P. (1995). *Pedagogy of the oppressed.* New York, NY: Gardners Books.

Freire, P. (1998). *Pedagogy of freedom: Ethics, democracy, and civic courage.* New York, NY: Rowman & Littlefield.

Gardner, H. (2004). *A Multiplicity of intelligences: In tribute to professor Luigi Vignolo.* Retrieved from http://www.howardgardner.com/Papers/documents/T-101%20A%20Multiplicity%20REVISED.pdf

Gause, C. P. (2008). *Integration matters: Navigating identity, culture, and resistance.* New York, NY: Peter Lang.

Gazel, J. (2007). Walking the talk: multiracial discourses, realities, and pedagogy. *American Behavioral Scientist, 51*(4), 532-550. Retrieved from http://abs.sagepub.com/cgi/content/abstract/51/4/532

Giroux, H. (2001). *Theory and resistance in education: Towards a pedagogy of opposition.* Westport, CT: Bergin & Garvey.

Giroux, H. A. (1999). Dialectics and the development of curriculum theory. In W. P. Pinar, (Ed.), *Contemporary curriculum discourses* (pp. 7-23). New York, NY: Peter Lang.

Gladwell, M. (2002). *The tipping point: How little things can make a big difference.* New York, NY: Little, Brown, and Company.

Goodman, D. (2007). Dealing with student resistance: sources and strategies. *Diversity Digest, 10.* Retrieved from http://www.diversityweb.org/digest/vol10no2/goodman.cfm

Greene, M. (1981). The humanities and emancipatory possibility. *Journal of Education, 163*(4), 287-305.

Greene, M. (1988). *The dialectic of freedom.* New York, NY: Teachers College Press.

Griffin, P. (1997). Facilitating social justice education courses. In M. Adams, L. A. Bell, & P. Griffin (Eds.), *Teaching for diversity and social justice* (pp. 279-298). New York, NY: Routledge.

Guglielmo, J. (2003). *Are Italians white? How race is made in America.* New York, NY: Routledge.

Hall, D. E. (2003). *Queer theories.* New York, NY: Palgrave Macmillan.

Hardiman, R. (1994). White racial identity development in the United States. In E. P. Salett & D. R. Koslow (Eds.), *Race, ethnicity, and self: Identity in multicultural perspectives.* Washington, DC: National Multicultural Institute.

Harman, W. (1998). *Global mind change: The promise of the 21st century* (2nd ed.). San Francisco, CA: Berrett-Koehler.

Helms, J. E. (Ed.) (1990). *Black and White racial identity: Theory, research, and practice.* Westport, CT: Greenwood.

Higginbotham, E. (1996, November-December). Getting all students to listen: analyzing and coping with student resistance [Electronic version]. *Multiculturalism and Diversity in Higher Education, 40*(2). Retrieved from http://find.galegroup.com/itx/infomark.do?&contentSet=IAC-Documents&type=retrieve&tabID=T002&prodId=ITOF&docId=A19016839&source=gale&srcprod=ITOF&userGroupName=gree35277&version=1.0

Honoré, C. (2004). *In praise of slowness: Challenging the cult of speed.* New York, NY: HarperCollins.

hooks, b. (1994). *Teaching to transgress: Education as the practice of freedom.* New York, NY: Routledge.

hooks, b. (2000). *All about love: new visions.* New York, NY: HarperCollins.

Horowitz, R. (2009, July 16). How it looks to Jefferson Beauregard Sessions III. *The News and Observer*, p. 11A.

The Hoot Editorial Board. (2009, October 2). *Editorial: Sustaining student activism.* Retrieved from The Brandeis Hoot Website: http://thehoot.net/articles/6677

Huber, C. (2000). *How to get from where you are to where you want to be.* Carlsbad, CA: Hay House.

Hughes, L. (1924/1994). Lament for dark peoples. In A. Rampersad & D. Roessel (Eds.), *The collected poems of Langston Hughes* (p. 39). New York, NY: Vintage Books.

Ignatiev, N. (1995). *How the Irish became white.* New York, NY: Routledge.

Inglehart, R. (1997). *Modernization and postmodernization: cultural, economic, and political change in 43 societies.* Priceton, NJ: Princeton University Press.

Inglehart, R., & Welzel, C. (2005). *Modernization, cultural change, and democracy: The human development sequence.* New York, NY: Cambridge University Press.

Institute of Education Sciences, National Center for Education Statistics. (2009). Indicator 20: status dropout rates. In *The condition of education 2009.* Retrieved from http://nces.ed.gov/programs/coe/2009/pdf/20_2009.pdf

The James Logan Courier. (2008, November 18). *"Don't ask yourself what the world needs. Ask yourself what makes you come alive and then go do that." Howard Thurman.* Retrieved from http://www.jameslogancourier.org/index.php?itemid =4493

Jensen, D. (2000). *A language older than words.* New York, NY: Context Books.

Jensen, D. (2002). *The culture of make believe.* New York, NY: Context Books.

Jensen, D. (2004). *Walking on water: Reading, writing, and revolution.* White River Junction, VT: Chelsea Green.

Johnson, A. (2006, April 27). *Dealing with defensiveness and denial.* Presentation and workshop at the 2006 WPC7: Seventh Annual White Privilege Conference, St. Louis, MO.

Jordan, J. (2002). *Some of us did not die: new and selected essays.* New York, NY: Basic Books.

Jost, M., Whitfield, E.L., & Jost, M. (2005). When the rules are fair, but the game isn't. *Multicultural Education, 13*(1), 14-21.

Jung, C. G., & Dell, W. S. (1933). *Modern man in search of a soul.* Orlando, FL: Harcourt.

Kahne, J., & Westheimer, J. (1996, May). In service of what? the politics of service learning. *Phi Delta Kappan, 77*(9), 592-600.

Kandaswamy, P. (2007). Beyond colorblindness and multiculturalism: Rethinking anti-racist pedagogy in the university classroom. *Radical Teacher, 80,* 6-11.

Keup, J. R., Walker, A. A., Astin, H. S., & Lindholm, J. A. (2001). *Organizational culture and institutional transformation.* ERIC Digest 464521, Retrieved from http://www.ericdigests.org/2003-1/culture.htm

Kilbourne, J. (Creator), & Jhally, S. [Producer]. (2001). *Killing us softly 3: Advertising's images of women* [DVD]. Northampton, MA: Media Education Foundation.

Kincheloe, J. L., & Steinberg, S. R. (1993). A tentative description of post-formal thinking: The critical confrontation with cognitive theory. *Harvard Educational Review, 63*(3), 296-320.

King, M. L. (1967). Where do we go from here, SCLC presidential address. In J. M. Washington (1986), *A testament of hope* (pp. 245-252). San Francisco, CA: Harper.

King, T. L., & Osayande, E. (2007). The filth on philanthropy: progressive philanthropy's agenda to misdirect social justice movements. In Incite! Women of Color Against Violence (Eds.), *The revolution will not be funded: Beyond the nonprofit industrial complex* (pp. 79-90). Cambridge, MA: South End Press.

Kivel, P. (2002). *Uprooting racism: How white people can work for racial justice.* Gabriola Island, CA: New Society.

Korten, D. (2001) *When corporations rule the world* (2nd ed.). San Francisco, CA: Berrett-Koehler.

Korten, D. (2006). *The great turning: from empire to earth community.* San Francisco, CA: Berrett-Koehler.

Krysan, M., & Faison, N. (2008). Racial attitudes in America: A brief summary of the data (University of Illinois Institute of Government and Public Affairs *Data update to racial attitudes in America*). Report retrieved from http://igpa.uillinois.edu/programs/racial-attitudes/brief

Ladson-Billings, G. (1994). *The dreamkeepers: Successful teachers of African American children*. San Francisco, CA: Jossey-Bass.

Ladson-Billings, G. (2007, October). *Education research in the public interest*. Paper presented at the annual meeting of the University Continuing Education Association, Alexandria, VA.

Laing, R. D. (1967). Persons and experience. In *The politics of experience* (chap. 1). Retrieved from http://www.marxists.org/reference/subject/philosophy/works/en/laing.htm

Lee, E. (1992, Autumn). The crisis in education: Forging an anti-racist response. In S. Martinas (Ed.), *Challenging White Supremecy Workshops: Creating anti-racist organizing strategies*. Retrieved from http://www.cwsworkshop.org/about/5Creating_AR_Org_Strat.PDF

Lee, E., Menkart, D., & Okazawa-Rey, M. (2006). *Beyond heroes and holidays: A practical guide to K-12 anti-racist, multicultural education and staff development*. Washington, DC: Training for Change.

Leondar-Wright, B. (1999, September 30). The racial wealth gap: Left out of the boom. Retrieved from http://www.faireconomy.org/press_room/1999/the_racial_wealth_gap_left_out_of_the_boom

Leondar-Wright, B. (2006, May 31). *Widening the racial wealth gap*. Retrieved from http://www.commondreams.org/views06/0531-20.htm

Levine, J. (2003). Impassioned teaching and critical thinking: or, "It don't mean a thing if it ain't got that zing." In H. S. Shapiro, S. B. Harden, & A. Pennell (Eds.), *The institution of education* (4th ed., pp. 11-20). Boston, MA: Pearson Custom.

Lewison, J. (2009, September 14). *912 teabaggers in their own words*. KosMedia, LLC. Retrieved from http://www.dailykos.com/storyonly/2009/9/14/779699/-912-Teabaggers-in-their-own-words

Library of Congress. (2004). *Brown v. Board of Education* in Topeka, KS. In *With an even hand: Brown v. Board at fifty*. Exhibition pages. Retrieved from http://www.loc.gov/exhibits/brown/brown-brown.html

Lienhard, J. H. (2000). *The engines of our ingenuity: an engineer looks at technology and culture*. Oxford, England: Oxford University Press.

Linturi, R. (2000). The role of technology in shaping human society. *Foresight, 2*(2), 183-188.

Lipsitz, G. (1998). *The possessive investment in whiteness: how white people profit from identity politics*. Philadelphia, PA: Temple University Press.

Loewen, J. W. (2007). *Lies my teacher told me: Everything your American history textbook got wrong* (2nd ed.). New York, NY: Simon & Schuster.

López, I. F. H. (1996). *White by law: The legal construction of race*. New York, NY: New York University Press.

López, N. (2008, Winter). Anti-racist pedagogy and empowerment in a bi-lingual classroom in the U.S., circa 2006. *Theory Intro Practice, 47*(1), 43-50.

Lorde, A. (1984). *Sister outsider: Essays and speeches*. Berkeley, CA: The Crossing Press.

Low, S. (2004). Behind the gates: Social splitting and the "other." In M. Fine, L. Weis, L. P. Pruitt, & A. Burns (Eds.), *Off white: Readings on power, privilege, and resistance* (2nd ed., pp. 35-51). New York, NY: Routledge.

Lubrano, A. (2004, March-April). Blue-collar roots, white-collar dreams: The divided soul of a Brooklyn boy who straddles the class line. *Utne Reader*, 76-80.

Lukes, S. (1971). The meanings of "individualism," *Journal of the History of Ideas*, *32*(1), 45-66. Retrieved from http://www.jstor.org/stable/2708324

Maalouf, A. (2000). *In the name of identity*. New York, NY: Penguin Books.

Macedo, D. (1998). Foreword. In P. Freire (Author), *Pedagogy of freedom: Ethics, democracy, and civic courage* (pp. xi-xxxii). New York, NY: Rowman & Littlefield.

Martínez, E. (2004). Race: The U.S. creation myth and its premise keepers. In S. Martinas (Ed.), *An introduction to grassroots anti-racist organizing: A reader for spring 2004*, 1-6. San Francisco, CA, CWS Workshop, 240 16th St., PMB 275, San Francisco, CA 94103.

McCarthy, S. (2006). Why Johnny can't disobey. In H. S. Shapiro, K. Lathan, S. N. Ross (Eds.), *The institution of education* (5th ed., pp. 43-49). Boston, MA: Pearson Custom.

McIntosh, P. (2003). White privilege: Unpacking the invisible knapsack. In S. Shapiro, S. B. Harden, & A. Pennell (Eds.), *The institution of education* (4th ed., pp. 165-169). Boston, MA: Pearson. (Original work published 1989)

Mel-o-Toons (Producer). (1996). *Christopher Columbus* [Animated cartoon]. Vintage Tooncast: Young People's Records. Retrieved from http://www.youtube.com/watch?v=QQzBJDoRDsc

Milburn, M. A., & Conrad, S. D. (1996). *The politics of denial*. Cambridge, MA: The MIT Press.

Montada, L. (2001). Denial of responsibility. In A. E. Auhagen & H. W. Bierhoff (Eds.), *Responsibility: The many faces of a social phenomenon* (pp. 79-92). London, England: Routledge.

Morgan, G. (1997). *Images of organization* (2nd ed.). Thousand Oaks, CA: Sage Publications.

Morrison, T. (1993, December 2). On the backs of blacks. *Time Magazine*. Retrieved from http://www.time.com/time/community/morrisonessay.html

Morton, A. (2004). *On evil*. New York, NY: Routledge.

Nye, N. S. (2002). *19 varieties of gazelle: Poems of the Middle East*. New York, NY: HarperTempest.

Okun, T. (2000). White supremacy culture. In *Anti-Racism Reader*. Greensboro, NC: Leadership and Empowerment Institute.

Okun, T. (2006). *From white racist to white anti-racist: the life-long journey*. Retrieved from http://www.dismantlingracism.org/resources.html

Okun, T., & Jones, K. (2000). *Dismantling racism: A workbook for social change groups*. Atlanta, GA: dRworks.

olsson, j. (1997) *Detour spotting for white anti-racists: A tool for change*. (Available from Cultural Bridges, HC81 Box 7015, Questa NM 87556).

Palmer, P. (1993). *To know as we are known: education as a spiritual journey*. New York, NY: HarperCollins.

Palmer, P. (2000). *Let your life speak: Listening for the voice of vocation*. San Francisco, CA: Jossey-Bass.

Palmer, P. (2004). *A hidden wholeness: The journey toward an undivided life*. San Francisco, CA: Jossey-Bass.

Peltier, L. (1999). *Prison writings: My life is my sun dance*. New York, NY: St. Martin's Press.

Pitts, L. (n.d.). *Though well-intentioned, white guilt keeps nation from moving forward*. Miami, FL: Knight-Ridder.

Public Broadcasting System. (nd). *History of affluenza*. Retrieved September 17, 2007 from http://www.pbs.org/kcts/affluenza/diag/hist1.html

Piercy, M. (1996). The long road. In E. Roberts & E. Amidon (Eds.), *Life prayers from around the world: 365 prayers, blessings, and affirmations to celebrate the human journey*. New York, NY: HarperCollins.

Purpel, D. E., & McLaurin, W. M., Jr. (2004). *Reflections on the moral and spiritual crisis in education*. New York, NY: Peter Lang.

Remen, R. N. (2000). *My grandfather's blessings: Stories of strength, refuge, and belonging*. New York, NY: Riverhead Books.

Revilla, A. T., Wells, A. S., & Holme, J. J. (2004). "We didn't see color": The salience of color blindness in desegregated schools. In M. Fine, L. Weis, L. P. Pruit, & A. Burns (Eds.). *Off-white: Readings on power, privilege, and resistance* (2nd ed., pp. 284-301). New York, NY: Routledge.

Richardson, T., & Villenas, S. (2000, Spring). "Other" encounters: Dances with whiteness in multicultural education. *Educational Theory, 50*(2), 255-273.

Risner, D. (2006). What Matthew Shepard would tell us: Gay and lesbian issues in education. In H. S. Shapiro, K. Lathan, & S. N. Ross (Eds.), *The institution of education* (5th ed., pp. 287-296). Boston, MA: Pearson.

Roediger, D. R. (2005). *Working toward whiteness: How American's immigrants became white*. New York, NY: Basic Books.

Scaring Americans into justifying torture. (2008, March 11). Retrieved from *The New York Times Website* at http://www.nytimes.com/2008/03/11/opinion/11iht-edradio.1.10925730.html

Schaef, A. W. (1998). *Living in process: basic truths for living the path of the soul*. New York, NY: Ballantine Wellspring.

Schorr, D. (2008, January 28). *A new, 'post-racial' political era in America*. Retrieved from National Public Radio Website: http://www.npr.org/templates/story/story.php?storyId=18489466

Segrest, M. (1994). *Memoir of a race traitor*. Boston, MA: South End Press.

Senge, P., Smith, B., Kruschwitz, N., Laur, J., & Schley, S. (2008). *The necessary revolution: how individuals and organizations are working together to create a sustainable world*. New York, NY: Doubleday.

Shapiro, S. (2006). Banality of evil. In H. S. Shapiro, K. Latham, & S. N. Ross (Eds.) *The institution of education* (5th ed., pp. 51-60). Boston, MA: Pearson.

Sim, K., & Bilton, M. (Producers), & Sim, K. (Director). (1989). *Remember my lai* [Videorecording]. Alexandria, VA: PBS Video.

Smith, D. G. (1999) Identity, self, and other in the conduct of pedagogical action: An East/West inquiry. In W. F. Pinar (Ed.), *Contemporary curriculum discourses: twenty years of JCT* (pp. 458-473). New York, NY: Peter Lang.

Smith, L. (1949). *Killers of the dream*. New York, NY: W.W. Norton and Company.

Sotomayor, S. (2009, May 14). Lecture: 'A Latina judge's voice' [Electronic version]. *New York Times*. Retrieved July 22, 2009 from http://www.nytimes.com/2009/05/15/us/politics/15judge.text.html?_r=3&pagewanted=1

Spring, J. (2005). *The American school: 1642-2004* (6th ed.). New York, NY: McGraw Hill.

Stout, L. (1996). *Bridging the class divide and other lessons for grassroots organizing*. Boston, MA: Beacon Press.

Sullivan, N. (2006). *A critical introduction to queer theory*. New York, NY: New York University Press.

Tatum, B. D. (1992, Spring). Talking about race, learning about racism: The application of racial identity development theory in the classroom. *Harvard Educational Review, 62*(1), 1-24.

Tatum, B. D. (1997). *Why are all the black kids sitting together in the cafeteria? and other conversations about race*. New York, NY: BasicBooks.

Thompson, B. (2009, June). *Teaching liberation, countering trauma*. Paper presented at The Pedagogy of Privilege Conference, Denver, CO.

United for a Fair Economy. (2006). *Closing the racial wealth divide: Training manual*. Retrieved from http://www.faireconomy.org/resources/workshops/the_growing_divide_workshop

Walker, D. F., & Soltis, J. F. (1997). *Curriculum and aims*. New York, NY: Teachers College Press.

Walker, M. (2009). [Interview notes transcribed February 4].

Washington, H. (2006). *Medical apartheid: the dark history of medical experimentation on Black Americans from colonial times to the present*. New York, NY: Broadway Books.

Webster's new universal unabridged dictionary (2nd ed.). (1983). New York, NY: Simon & Schuster.

Wheatley, M. J. (2001, March). *Restoring hope to the future through critical education of leaders*. Retrieved from http://www.margaretwheatley.com/articles/restoringhope.html

Wheatley, M. J. (2006). *Leadership and the new science: discovering order in a chaotic world* (3rd ed.). San Francisco, CA: Berrett-Koehler.

Wilson, W. I. (1999). A black girl talks of the United States. In L. O. Okutoro (Ed.), *Quiet storm: Voices of young Black poets*. New York, NY: Hyperion Books for Children.

Wright, S., & Stamm, R. (2006, May). *DNA and the social psychology of skin tone*. Workshop at the White Privilege Conference, St. Louis, MO.

Yoshino, K. (2000, January 1). The epistemic contract of bisexual erasure. [Electronic version]. *Stanford Law Review*. Retrieved from http://www.kenjiyoshino.com/articles/epistemiccontract.pdf

Zandy, J. (2006). Decloaking class: Why class identity and consciousness count. In H. S. Shapiro, K. Lathan, and S. N. Ross (Eds.), *The institution of education* (5th ed., pp. 175-185). Boston, MA: Pearson.

Zinn, H. (1980). *A people's history of the United States*. New York, NY: HarperCollins.

ABOUT THE AUTHOR

Tema Okun, PhD, teaches in the Department of Educational Leadership at National Louis University in Chicago. Tema came to the academy after many years collaboratively developing and implementing long-term anti-racism liberatory curriculum with and for organizations and communities nationwide. She continues to work with social justice and community-based organizations, offering facilitation, consulting, and training as a member of the DRworks training collaborative. She holds a BA from Oberlin College, a masters in adult education from North Carolina State University, and a doctorate in curriculum and teaching with a specialization in cultural studies from University of North Carolina-Greensboro. She is also active in Middle East peace and justice work with the Israeli Committee Against House Demolitions-USA.

CPSIA information can be obtained at www.ICGtesting.com
Printed in the USA
BVOW04s1150280713

326991BV00004B/18/P